Baroque Painters

THE LIVES OF THE PAINTERS
by John Canaday

Baroque Painters

JOHN CANADAY

The Norton Library

W · W · NORTON & COMPANY · INC ·

NEW YORK

Books That Live
The Norton imprint on a book means that in the publisher's
estimation it is a book not for a single season but for the years.
W. W. Norton & Company, Inc.

ISBN 0 393 00665 4

PRINTED IN THE UNITED STATES OF AMERICA

1 2 3 4 5 6 7 8 9 0

Contents

Preface to *The Lives of the Painters*

Contents

Preface to
The Lives of the Painters

This book is a history of painting from the end of the Middle Ages to the eve of the twentieth century—from Giotto's revolution to Cézanne's—told in the form of several hundred biographies strung together on a historical cord. By way of its index it can also double as a reference encyclopedia, since each biography is self-contained, whether within a brief paragraph or a long essay.

If the book is an acceptable history, I am glad. If it is a helpful encyclopedia, so much to the good. But what I most hope is that these biographies will enlarge the reader's enjoyment of painting, and I like to think that this is a book that can be picked up and opened anywhere for a bit of pleasurable reading from time to time. It was written in somewhat that way: the biographies were composed not in chronological sequence, but according to my interest from day to day and were collated en route.

The question may be asked why a history of painting should be told in the form of linked biographies. There are good arguments to support the contention that knowledge of a painter's life and personality should not be allowed to intrude upon our response to his paintings, since paintings are objects with independent existences. This is a principle upon which I used to insist and with which I still agree in the cases of living artists. We have our own firsthand experience of our times as a basis for putting the work of our contemporaries in context. But even the greatest art of the past can be fully understood only if we can see it in the context of the society in which it was conceived as well as in its timelessness.

Preface

If we accept the truism that art is not produced in a vacuum (and we must), it follows that artists' lives tell us about the air they breathed, how it differed from one part of the world to another, and how it changed from one century to another —all of which explains the changing forms that in their succession make up the history of art.

Some of these biographies may seem too long or too short as measures of the painters' worth. No such proportion has been observed. A minor painter may have had an interesting life or a life that, as in the case of one very dull Spaniard, Francisco Pacheco, affords the best opportunity for describing the climate in which painters better than he were working. In an instance or two I have included artists not because they were important but simply because I like them. This personal indulgence accounts for the presence of, for one, the minor Florentine mannerist Bernardo Buontalenti. I hope there are no omissions except those explicable by the truth that a book can't go on forever.

Cézanne's birth year, which was 1839, has been adopted, with a few self-explanatory exceptions, as the boundary date for artists included in this story. The story ends with the triumph of impressionism—shared by Cézanne—and the rift between nineteenth- and twentieth-century painting, which Cézanne initiated. Cézanne's fellow post-impressionists, as they have come to be called (Vincent van Gogh, Seurat, and Gauguin) were all younger than he and thus are ruled out by date. In any case their biographies would have had to begin yet another volume in this already very long book, and we would have had to go on to a shift in fundamental premises corresponding to the radical change in the concept of creative art represented by Cézanne's descendants, Picasso among them.

The list of acknowledgements that usually concludes an author's preface would in this book have to include the hundreds of museums and private collections in Europe and America that have given me for many years the opportunity to see paintings, and then the hundreds of historians whose work over the centuries has supplied the factual material that has been given yet another winnowing here. Some special debts to other winnowers, and researchers, are acknowledged in the course of the text. The general debt, shared by every art historian who has followed him, goes back to Giorgio Vasari, the father of us all, whose biography appears on pages 284-86. But I should mention that Rudolf and Margot Wittkower's book on the character and conduct of artists, "Born Under Saturn," was particularly helpful not only as a guide through Vasari but as a summary of references to other early histories.

Inevitably, a major source was the work of that great and delightful man, the late Erwin Panofsky, and I want to say here that I treasure our friendship of more than twenty-five years. He was wonderfully generous and patient with me as a writer who could not aspire to his kind of scholarship; on my part, as a writer, I once complained to him that he was a difficult scholar to crib from because he expressed everything so perfectly that to rephrase anything he had written was to butcher it.

Essays on several of the artists have appeared in somewhat different form in *Horizon* magazine. Permission for the use of this material is gratefully acknowledged.

I cannot conclude without thanking Robert E. Farlow, who wanted this book written and gave me the chance to write it.

JOHN CANADAY

New York

10

CARAVAGGIO AND A
REVOLUTION

The seventeenth century produced such a staggering quantity of painting in such a bewildering variety of expressions—elegant to homely, grandiose to intimate, stormy to serene, hopelessly pedantic to brilliantly inventive—that it cannot be presented as a whole but must be chopped up into parts, as if all these manifestations did not interlock. The very word "baroque," the only single one that can be applied to the century as a label, has been given so many definitions, and has taken on so many shades of meaning within each definition, that it has become almost useless.

Neither can the century be presented sequentially. Too many kinds of things were happening at once all over Europe, and the art historian must find some kind of organizational subterfuge. The conventional first resort is geographical. But artists moved around so much (and when they didn't, their paintings did, which amounted to much the same thing) that national boundaries lose a great deal of their meaning in art-historical context. What we will try to do here is divide the artists into several groups, presenting each group chronologically within itself, and then dropping back to the beginning of the century with another group, and so on, taking advantage of geography wherever possible, asking the reader to keep in mind that when Rubens, for instance, turns up two chapters later than Caravaggio, this does not mean he painted later: the two men were born at almost the same time—Rubens four years after Caravaggio.

Caravaggio and his tradition as it ran through (and changed during) the century have been decided upon as a starting point, partly for reasons of chronology, but largely because of the enormous influence exerted by Caravaggio's revolutionary art. From Caravaggio in Rome to Rembrandt in Amsterdam and La Tour in provincial France, all the artists in this chapter are part of a tradition of realism and strong light, although the variety of the ends to which they put this general interpretative means is, of course, extreme.

In 1573 a master mason-architect named Fermo Merisi had a son whom he named Michelangelo, not for the great artist inevitably evoked by the name, but for the hardly more distinguished personage for whom the artist himself was named, the archangel Michael. The birth occurred in the town of Caravaggio near Milan. With "from Caravaggio" attached, Michelangelo Merisi da Caravaggio, always called Caravaggio, went south to Rome as a youth, later fled to Naples and Malta, and within a short lifetime managed to fulfill his genius as a painter while establishing a record of lawlessness unequaled in the history of art and surpassed only in the history of brigandage.

Caravaggio's stormy personal history has always colored

too strongly our way of seeing his art, to our loss. We tend to deform the dramatic force of his painting, which is perfectly controlled, by misreading it as the expression of a violent temperament. It is hard to rid ourselves of the notion that the intellectual, emotional, and moral character of an artist flows straight through his brush to lie exposed for us on the canvas. Perhaps the best thing to do in the case of Caravaggio is to tell about his life and then to tell about his art as if they were fenced off from one another, with only one common denominator: in his life and in his art, Caravaggio was a rebel.

Not a great deal is known about Caravaggio's life until it began to be documented in the criminal courts. According to most accounts, he was in Rome by the time he was sixteen; according to some, he stayed in Milan through his teens and then had to leave town in a hurry. In either case there were some years of abject poverty until, in his middle twenties, he became well known as a painter and notorious as a roust-about. In 1600, at the age of twenty-seven, he had all professional doors opened to him through the favor of Cardinal del Monte and was the Cardinal's guest in the residence known today as the Villa Madama, which sounds elegant enough. During that same year he was hauled to court twice (twice on record). Over the next four years his name appears every few months on the police blotter.

He brawled in the streets, picked quarrels at swordpoint with acquaintances and strangers, once threw a platter of artichokes at a waiter he thought insolent, cutting his face, and threatened him with his sword; he was arrested for carrying sword and dagger without permission, "gave offense," unnamed, to one Laura and her daughter Isabella, was sued for rent and damages by his landlady and retaliated by stoning the windows. He precipitated a quarrel in the Corso over "a girl called Lena who is to be found at the Piazza Navona," an indication of another aspect of his activities. He assaulted a notary, insulted a constable. He was sued for libel. At least once he very nearly got his throat cut: found in bed with wounds on his neck and left ear, he was interrogated but avoided arrest with the tale that by accident he had fallen on his own sword in the street, although just which street it had been he said he could not remember.

On this occasion he was forbidden to leave his rooms under penalty of a large fine; on another he was jailed in his own house for a month, forbidden to leave it without written permit from the governor of Rome. But nothing could keep Caravaggio out of trouble. And trouble arrived in earnest one May night in 1606—a Sunday—when he killed a man who had won ten scudi from him in a ball game that afternoon.

After some of his misdemeanors, Caravaggio had been excused with a scolding from the court; after others, he had been bailed out by friends ranging from the French ambassador to a shoemaker. On one occasion the court had pardoned him at the request of a soldier he had wounded. But this time there was nothing to be done.

The ball game was a form of tennis with four players on each side. One member of Caravaggio's team was the minor artist Onorio Longhi, whose reputation as a troublemaker was about on a par with his own, and in a way worse: where Caravaggio was short-tempered and impulsive, Onorio was scurrilous and vindictive. The combination was too much, and when the players' rackets were exchanged for swords, Caravaggio mortally wounded the leader of the opposing team, Ranuccio Tommassoni.

Badly wounded himself, Caravaggio fled Rome, going first to the villa of a patron in the hills beyond the city, and then to Naples. He seems to have behaved himself there, but if he was chastened, he had one last relapse that, indirectly, was fatal.

We may remember, parenthetically, that all this time Caravaggio was hard at work and increasingly famous as a painter. In 1608—he was now thirty-five—he went from Naples to Malta, where the Grand Master made him, to their mutual gratification, a *cavaliere* of the order. The citation referred to Caravaggio as an adopted citizen whose glory redounded to the island of Malta as the glory of the ancient Apelles redounded to the island of Cos.

This happy situation lasted not quite three months. The nature of Caravaggio's quarrel with another *cavaliere* is not recorded, but it was serious enough so that he was imprisoned. He escaped. The Grand Master and the General Assembly in special session drummed him out of the order. In the meanwhile, the late Apelles of Malta had found his way to Sicily, where he worked busily, leaving no criminal records, before returning to Naples in the fall of 1609.

All this time, Caravaggio had not given up hope of returning to Rome, where his friends made efforts to clear him in the courts by arguing that he was not guilty of homicide, his own wounds having proved that he had had to defend himself against his victim. He was far from forgotten. The story went around Rome that he was still his old self in Naples, so much so that he had been attacked and very nearly killed by enemies there. Apparently his enemy in Malta had traced him, and he was assaulted at the entrance of a tavern and beaten nearly to death. But a few months later he was on the move again, on the way back toward Rome by a circuitous route. Perhaps he had received further threats; perhaps he hoped to be able to see his Roman friends outside the perimeter of the city and speed his pardon. At any rate he boarded a ship in Naples but avoided debarking in territory under Roman authority. He left the ship about eighty miles from Rome at Port'Ercole, a Spanish protectorate, and there, for the first time in his long experience with the law, he

suffered false arrest. Put ashore not at the town but on a
desolate spot some miles away, he was imprisoned by a patrol
and held for several days before it was discovered that he had
been mistaken for someone else.

The ship had left, carrying everything he owned with it.
Abandoned, friendless, unknown, helpless and desperate,
wild with frustration, he set out along the swampy shore for
Port'Ercole, where he might send word to friends. But during
his imprisonment or during the last frightful miles of his
trek, he had contracted malaria, and he died of the fever in
Port'Ercole, two months short of his thirty-seventh birthday.
The year was 1610. He had been allowed hardly more than a
decade of maturity as an artist, but he had established for
himself in history a position among the handful of painters
whose originality is the originality of genius.

So much for Caravaggio's life. We have already said that
at least one characteristic was common to his life and to his
art: in both, Caravaggio was a rebel.

Yet his definition of what an artist should be hardly
seems revolutionary: "In my use of the word, a good artist
means a man who knows how to paint well and to imitate
natural things well." The definition sounds like that of an
archconservative, unless we see it within the context of Caravaggio's generation in Italy.

He improvised this definition in 1603 in answer to a
question when he was testifying as a defendant along with
three other artists (Onorio Longhi, Orazio Gentileschi, and
Filippo Trisegni) in a suit for libel brought by the painter
and art historian Baglione, whose reputation had been be-
smirched in a pamphlet circulated around Rome. Giovanni
Baglione (1571-1644) was certainly not a good artist by Caravaggio's definition, but on the other hand neither was any
other living Italian except Caravaggio himself. Baglione was
a leader of the *Maniera*, the late-mannerist group in Rome

whose decorative affectations were based on the principle that art was entirely an affair of artificial concoctions and that "to imitate natural things" either well or ill was to violate all acceptable aesthetic principles. "Beauty" and "nature" were opposite terms.

As a painter to Pope Sixtus V, Baglione represented the triumphant position held by an enfeebled style. Artifice was the standard of excellence. Even the Carracci, who were already established as opponents of mannerism when Caravaggio appeared, made their reforms by going back to the study of earlier masters rather than to the study of nature.

Caravaggio drew everything directly from living models, and insisted that everything that existed, in the state in which it existed, was legitimate subject matter for painting—not only human beings with their imperfections intact, but also flowers and such inanimate objects as the commonest tables and pitchers. In defining a good artist as he did, he was defending an approach that had been introduced by Giotto three hundred years earlier, developed by the artists of the Renaissance, and abandoned as exhausted by the mannerists. His only teacher had been a provincial mannerist in Milan named Simone Peterzano (*c.* 1540-1600), who claimed to have studied under Titian but whose work shows little sign of it. Caravaggio's return to nature was self-generated. Even his earliest works, although in the elegant mood of mannerism, deny every principle of mannerist distortion. His compositions are elegant and his subjects are elegant, and he drew from elegantly handsome models, but he presented them as elegant natural objects.

In this style, Caravaggio was easy enough to take, and by the time he was twenty he had a considerable reputation. It was at about this time (1593—although some scholars put the date as late as 1600) that he ran into difficulties as a revolutionary realist. He received an important commission for a series of panels on the life of St. Matthew for a chapel in the Church of San Luigi de' Francesi, and represented the saint, in the first painting of the series, as what he had been —a laborer. He not only painted a stocky, muscular laborer's body and a rough, common man's face, but pictured the Evangelist as a man who had a bit of trouble putting his thoughts into writing. An angel at his side served less as an inspirational vision than as a school teacher, patiently reaching forward to show him how to hold the pen. Worst of all— and this detail became the crux of the objections—St. Matthew's bare feet were dirty. The painting was rejected, and Caravaggio substituted for it a more conventional one showing Matthew in the usual saintly robe instead of a laborer's tunic, with the angel in the air above him in an acceptable swirl of drapery. The incident has become a standard illustration of the realistic, or naturalistic, approach in painting and of the popular objections to it as either ugly or irreverent.

Caravaggio never compromised again to such an extent. He did not have to, for he attracted an influential group of supporters. But they were not quite the audience he wanted. He intended his art for the man in the street—precisely the man who was most offended by it: conditioned to accept prettification as the imperative form of reverence, the man in the street did not want saints with dirty feet. Caravaggio's patrons were cultivated men of the world who recognized him as a superb technician, were interested by his originality, and probably enjoyed taking an avant-garde position in an aesthetic battle.

And these connoisseurs were offered, by Caravaggio, much more than the mere imitation of nature. Caravaggio always overstated, or only partially stated, his credo of naturalism. He claimed he had "no teacher but nature," but he had others. His life and his own statements have produced a myth, the myth of the direct, uneducated, almost primitive genius. In point of fact, he was a complicated and analytical artist, whose teachers included, by their example, Michelangelo and the Venetians. True, he set another of the St. Matthew series, *The Calling of St. Matthew,* in a common tavern and was scrupulously realistic in details of furnishing and costume, but he transfigured the scene by dramatic and celestial light emanating from an unseen source above the head of Christ that obliterates such daylight as might come in through the tavern's window, and plunges whole areas into dense shadow from which the realistic figures emerge no longer as a part of life but as part of a miracle.

Like any truly great painter, Caravaggio is legitimately subject to multiple interpretations because his art is a harmonization of complex and sometimes contradictory factors. It is true that he was a phenomenal realist, even naturalist. It is also true that he was a painter of miracle. Historically, he forecast the principles of two major art movements. In showing that the supernatural could be conceived in rational terms and given at the same time a dramatic tangibility, he established a principle that was to be followed by the baroque artists of the Counter Reformation. And in his direct reference to nature, in his conviction that every detail of nature is worth attention, especially the commonest details, he anticipated ideas found revolutionary and greeted with catcalls two hundred and fifty years later when Courbet proposed them in France.

Ten years or so after his death, Caravaggio's reputation began to decline, and for three hundred years his art was subjected to distortions in the oddly bent mirror of his life. The full realization of his genius did not come until after the triumph of nineteenth-century realism and the re-evaluation of the baroque drama in the twentieth century. He was not so much rediscovered as discovered for the first time in his essential nature, and he stands firmly now within the most select company of masters.

Agostino Tassi deserves a note just here, not because he was the best of painters but because his escapades illuminate an aspect of Roman mores during the seventeenth century and supply, at the same time, an opportunity for mentioning two other artists of greater merit than he—Orazio Gentileschi and his daughter Artemisia. The three were involved in an unsavory—or savory, as you wish—lawsuit in which Gentileschi accused Tassi of deflowering Artemisia by force.

Orazio Gentileschi (1563-1638), a Tuscan by birth, went to Rome in 1576 or 1578. He was a friend, probably a fellow carouser, and an excellent follower of Caravaggio's, and his reputation as an artist has, deservedly, risen lately in the wake of enthusiasm for that master. His work included fresco murals as well as ·easel painting, and he was of sufficient prominence to be called to London, where he worked for Charles I and the Duke of Buckingham. He became a naturalized Englishman in 1629, at the age of sixty-six, and died in London at the age of seventy-five. As a painter of decorations for noble houses he was in great demand, but most of these decorations have disappeared.

His daughter Artemisia (1597-*after* 1651) was an extremely talented painter of portraits and religious subjects who also has an increasing public today. She worked in Rome, Florence, and Naples as well as in London for Charles I and his circle during a visit to her father.

Agostino Tassi (*c.* 1580-1644) would be only a name attached to numerous proficiently executed decorative paintings except for the sensational episode of his trial for the rape of Artemisia, which Rome enjoyed as the best show in years. He was one of dozens of artists skilled in their craft; his battle scenes, architectural perspectives, and land- and seascapes are still effective enough in numerous Roman palaces. It was in Tassi's capacity as a decorator that the innocent Claude Lorrain assisted him, some dozen years after the trial.

Tassi and Gentileschi were not only professional colleagues but close friends, and Gentileschi too trustingly put
the fifteen-year-old Artemisia under Tassi's instruction. Tassi's offense against the girl, which occurred in Gentileschi's
house during his absence, and in which Tassi was assisted by
one Cosimo Quorli, was aggravated in the father's eyes by
Tassi's having induced her to turn over to him several of
Gentileschi's paintings, "especially a Judith of considerable
size," as Gentileschi complained in hurt tones when he
petitioned the Pope to bring the rapist to justice.

During the ensuing trial another artist, G. B. Stiattesi,
testified that to his certain knowledge Tassi had employed
thugs to murder his (Tassi's) wife after she had run away
with one of her lovers. As a piquant complication, Stiattesi
and Tassi themselves were identified as lovers with the introduction of an exchange of love poems.

Tassi was indignant over being brought to court and
said that not he, but Stiattesi, had committed the rape. Indeed he presented himself as an upright angel of vengeance,
maintaining that he had assisted in beating up another man
who had consorted with Artemisia. Artemisia, however, stuck
to her story even under cross-examination by torture. When
the thumbscrews were applied, she complained that they
were very poor substitutes for the wedding ring Tassi had
promised her.

Tassi, who had a reputation as a wit, put on a good
performance in the box. Admitting that he had served several
terms in prison, he called his condemnation to the galleys an
adventure in "seeing the world on the galleys of the Grand
Duke [of Tuscany], by his orders." He spent eight months in
prison pending judgment, but then the case was dismissed.

There was never any question as to Tassi's misdemeanors (if a list including incest can be called a list of misdemeanors), and he was notorious for his loose living in general.

But the Romans seem to have found all this rather endearing, so long as it did not interfere with his delivering a good job of painting. He continued to deliver until 1644, when he died at the age of about sixty-four. After the trial he lived not only long but elegantly in the manner of a Roman gentleman, receiving large commissions from the nobility and even from the Pope.

Tassi and Gentileschi (who had brought the suit not as a point of honor but because Tassi had refused to marry Artemisia) renewed their friendship after the brief unpleasantness. They probably enjoyed one another's company as fellow rogues. Gentileschi was a grasping man with a wicked tongue, and although his reputation was not quite as spectacular as Tassi's, it had its bright spots. He had served as codefendant with Caravaggio in a libel suit. His way of life was disorderly enough to give him a reputation for undependability, and his belligerence earned him countless enemies. It was probably because he was losing commissions at home that he worked first in France (for Marie de Médicis) and then in England. While he was in England his two sons, Francesco and Giuliano, served as his agents in acquiring Italian paintings to be sold to the gentry. The boys' manner of business is hinted at by the fact that on one occasion they were imprisoned for fraud in Portugal.

As for Artemisia: whether or not because of the nature of her introductory experience with Tassi, assuming that this experience was really introductory, she demonstrated until her death, which occurred sometime after 1651, when she was in her mid-fifties, an enduring enthusiasm for the art of love that paralleled her very great talent as a painter.

One is reminded, somehow, of a more recent drama of Roman mores, Federico Fellini's film "La Dolce Vita."

At one stage, Bartolomeo Manfredi (*c.* 1580-1620/21) was threatened with extinction because so many of his paintings were attributed to Caravaggio. Like Caravaggio, he was a Lombard, but went early to Rome. Less than a decade younger than the great innovator, he became a very close follower, so expert that he could easily have forged a few Caravaggios after the master's death, as he is rumored to have done. All of this means that Manfredi was an excellent painter. He was especially fond of depicting locales or characters of the disreputable kind Caravaggio used as realistic accessories in the representation of religious subjects. Manfredi painted them for themselves. He was highly successful —one of the earliest Italian artists to achieve success through private commissions only. He is allocated a special niche in the history of art because it was his pictures, rather than Caravaggio's, that inspired the adoption and vigorous growth of raffish genre subjects in Northern painting.

José de Ribera, an ardent Caravaggist who set the style for the entire school of Neapolitan painting, was born in 1591 near Valencia, the son of a shoemaker. He left Spain early for Italy, where José became Giuseppe (or, in the Spanish version, Jusepe) and acquired the nickname Lo Spagnoletto, "The Little Spaniard." Young Ribera went first to Parma and Lombardy, was in Rome before 1615, and then, about 1616, when he was twenty-five, settled in Naples, where he died thirty-six years later at the age, arithmetic shows, of sixty-one.

By that time, Ribera had gone through a career as the favorite of a series of Spanish viceroys (Naples having been part of the Spanish kingdom) and was considered passé. But during most of his life he was thought of as the dean of Neapolitan painters, a title that he has regained. He was a

hybridizer whose native Spanish realism was perfectly adaptable to crossbreeding with Caravaggio's tenebrism—his practice, widely propagated by his followers, of intense partial
illumination of a scene otherwise plunged in gloom—and his
use of common people as the protagonists in holy dramas. In
Ribera, the tenebristic contrasts are violently exaggerated
and so is the commonness of the actors, who become very
nearly brutish. There is a brutality, too, in Ribera's realistic
treatment of tortures and saintly agonies—which can be
linked to the fascination with pain that runs through Spanish
creative arts, entertainments, and sports. Ribera made the
most of this fascination not by exaggerating tortures but by
presenting them as real events happening—or about to happen, an aesthetic refinement—to real people. This was true,
at any rate, of his early work. He was possibly a student of
Francisco Ribalta (1565-1628), one of the earliest seventeenth-
century realists of the Valencian school. Ribalta made a
happy change from early efforts as a mannerist, and like his
more famous pupil was greatly affected by Caravaggesque
illumination, but he could not have passed it on to Ribera,
since he learned it after Ribera had left for Italy. We have
almost no trace of Ribera's earliest years.

Ribera's sometimes brutal realism has fostered legends
that he led the jealous Neapolitan artists in the baiting that
drove Guido Reni from the city and reduced poor Domenichino to hysteria when he had the audacity to come and execute commissions the Neapolitans wanted for themselves. But
there is no reason to think that Ribera's style as a painter was
a reflection of his character. Actually, he was turning out a
product that appealed mightily to his best patrons. The
Spanish viceroys apparently liked it for itself, and the Church,
especially in Spain, found it a harmonious tool in fulfilling
the Inquisitional program of adapting art to religious-educa-
tional-propagandistic purposes. When a subject demanded it,

Ribera did not hesitate to adopt some of the graces of the Carracci and Guercino. And during a period in mid-career he softened his gloomy, violent manner to accommodate a new interest in the opulent, luminous manner of Veronese; the alteration may also have come about under the inspiration of Velázquez, who visited Naples in 1630.

Beginning about 1640, however (when he was nearly fifty), Ribera reverted to his early manner, and continued in it until his death in 1652, with certain modifications. He seems to have responded to a changed mood in Naples and to have been affected as an artist by unhappy circumstances in his personal life. The city-state was in a desperate economic depression; there were street riots and other disorders. Ribera's health was failing, and, most harrowing, one of his daughters (he had at least seven children by his Italian wife) was seduced by Don Juan of Austria, who was in Naples in 1647 to cope with an uprising. Don Juan (so well named) was the natural son of Philip IV, but the seducer's royal connections were of little comfort during the ensuing scandal. This was five years before Ribera's death. His last works, including numbers of penitential saints, are more sober versions of his Caravaggesque beginnings and, being less dramatic, were less in demand. A new generation of painters taunted him as a has-been, but posterity has rejected the jibe.

Gerard van Honthorst (1590-1656) was the most successful and probably the most influential member of the Utrecht school, which in the early seventeenth century brought Caravaggesque tenebrism to the North. But Honthorst's importance does not make him very interesting. He went to Rome when he was about twenty, just after Caravaggio's death, and stayed there for ten years, absorbing the new realism directly from Caravaggio's example and perhaps from contact with Manfredi, whom he could have known. He found important patrons and was so successful with his night scenes, where the participants are illuminated by the light of a candle that is concealed by a member of the group, that he acquired the nickname Gherardo delle Notti. Equally successful after his return to Holland, he settled in Utrecht, where he had been born and had first studied under Abraham Bloemaert (1565-1651), whose fate it has been to be remembered more for the painters he taught than for his own respectable Italianate product.

In Utrecht, Honthorst married, joined the guild, served several times as its dean, and became conspicuous enough to receive an invitation from Charles I to come to England, where he spent most of the year 1628 executing such allegories as *Charles I and Henrietta Maria with the Liberal Arts* for the decoration of Hampton Court. For work of this kind he used his Italianate manner; in portraits—malleable artist that he was—he modified his treatment in accordance with the English preference for the elegant style of Van Dyck.

After returning home he was invited to another court, at The Hague, where his brother Willem (1594-1666) assisted him. He returned to home base—Utrecht—in 1652, a very wealthy man. Four years later he died there at the age of sixty-six. Both Hals and Rembrandt were influenced by his light effects. But Honthorst has something besides the influence he exercised on his betters to recommend him. It is possible—by trying hard enough—to find a genuine poetic charm in the best of his work.

With Gerard van Honthorst, Hendrik Terbrugghen (1588-1629) was the most important member of the Utrecht school in the transmission of Caravaggesque realism to the Low Countries—this in spite of the fact that Caravaggio's influence on him was rather superficial. He grafted the strong Caravaggesque light and shade onto a less dramatic concept of realism than Caravaggio's and, toward the end, shifted to a lighter palette that anticipated Vermeer's more uniform illumination. Originally a student of Abraham Bloemaert, Terbrugghen spent ten years in Italy, from 1604 to 1614. He then returned to Utrecht, where he was settled by 1616, and died at the age of forty-one with his promise for some reason unfulfilled.

Frans Hals was a portraitist of genius who has suffered the misfortune of wide popularity based on the shallowest understanding of his work. He was a master of the kind of fireworks technique in which the artist seems to slash away with his big brush in a spirit of enthusiastic abandon, creating the end of a nose with one blob of paint, making an eye glitter with another, striking in a shadow at the corner of the mouth that turns it up in a smile and bunches the cheek above it—pulling one trick after another like a sleight-of-hand performer who leaves us one jump behind him until, after a matter of minutes, he steps aside and leaves us amazed by an image still wet and sparkling.

In popular appreciation, Hals's work in this manner has the feeling of immediate presence so beloved in the impressionists (and he was a strong influence on Manet) and the theatrical stuntsmanship of fashionable portrait painters (he was also a strong influence on Sargent). These are legitimate responses, as far as they go. But this dazzling, apparently offhand technique was anything but offhand; it was a means of describing form that allied the disciplines of painting to those of sculpture. The brush that seems to have dashed about on the canvas with such abandon was controlled like a sculptor's chisel. With each stroke, Hals defined a plane as uncompromisingly as if he had cut it in stone. Occasionally it is possible to catch him in error—the chisel-brush has slipped and he has let the mistake go—but ordinarily the hundreds of planes into which he divides and subdivides a form are organized into flawless structures—heads, hands, whole figures—that combine sculpturesque solidity with painting's sparkle and fluidity.

Even though Hals painted many portraits, including group portraits, of highly respectable citizens, he is usually associated with pictures of jolly topers, grinning wenches, semiderelicts, and other characters of the roistering low life in the taverns of Haarlem. Their dramatic reality, their vivid presence, their oneness with the hand of the artist—virtually at work before our eyes—establishes a false identity between these characters and the artist himself. It is easy to concoct a Hals who was one of their company, especially as some of the few known facts about his life seem to fall in line with such an intepretation.

Thus Hals has been conventionally thought of and usually written about as a kind of roistering, carefree, and jovial alcoholic. One early biographer, the undependable Houbraken, reported or invented the story that Hals's pupils had to keep watch on the lovable old drunk and carry him home from the tavern every night and put him to bed, to keep him from staggering into the canals and drowning himself. It is on record, and undeniable, that Hals was always being sued by his creditors, among them his shoemaker, his carpenter, his butcher, his canvas merchant, and even the guild, where his dues were in arrears. At least twice he failed to pay the periodic allotment for the support of his two children by his first marriage. On several occasions he had to apply for help from public funds, and during the last years of his life was himself a public charge.

Hals probably did suffer from a fundamental instability of temperament. He had an imbecile son whom he could not afford to care for and who finally had to be put in solitary confinement as a dangerous person, as well as one daughter who nowadays would be described as a juvenile delinquent and who was brought to court by her parents in an effort to correct her spectacularly lax morals.

But there is the other Hals, a respected citizen and the recipient of important commissions, hardly a candidate for the role of town eccentric tolerated for his talent in spite of his aberrations. There was the Hals who in 1664 when he was about eighty (his birth date is uncertain) painted with a firm hand, a clear eye, and a profound perception of human character his masterpiece, *The Women Regents of the Old Men's Home at Haarlem* (Haarlem, Frans Hals Museum), a quintuple portrait more than 8 feet long and close to 7 feet high, that can stand with some of Rembrandt's work in its emotional and philosophical exploration of character. Its profound perceptiveness is matched by the brilliance, harmoniously subdued and perfectly controlled, of the artist's representation of the textures of stuffs and of flesh, and their integration in light and space. This is the austere final expression of the superb Hals whose style even at its most vivacious was never the spontaneous legerdemain that it seemed to be. The fussy Sir Joshua Reynolds, later, regarded some of Hals's completed paintings as unfinished lay-ins; he did not recognize the calculation in a way of painting that was as careful as it seemed instinctive.

Hals was born between 1580 and 1585, probably in Antwerp, but moved with his parents to Haarlem as a child. Aside from one visit to Antwerp he never left Holland again, and died in Haarlem in 1666. By 1610 he was a guild member. In 1615, when he was between thirty and thirty-five years old, his first wife died, leaving him with two children. Two years later he remarried, and by his second wife had at least eight children, perhaps ten or even more. Such responsibilities, including the care of his imbecile son and problem daughter, help explain why even a busy painter was always in financial difficulties. His commissions included group portraits as well as individual portraits of members of leading families and of professional men and intellectuals (Descartes among them), but his reputation was a local one.

Nothing is known about Hals's youth. Not much, really, is known about him as a mature personality. He was apparently considered a dependable craftsman rather than an important artist, and the histories written after his death have very little to say about him until the nineteenth century. The French realists—Courbet and then Manet—rediscovered him as a technical master, and even a revolutionary one, in his brushwork and his subtle adjustments of tonalities for their own sake in what seemed direct representations of the immediate visual world.

Hals cannot be fully understood unless it is realized that the visual world was something more for him than a surface that could be dramatized. He was a painter not of faces merely, but of character, and he was frequently a painter of the spirit.

A romantic legend that will not down tells of the brilliant young painter Rembrandt van Rijn who at the height of his early success flew in the face of convention with a picture called *The Night Watch* and, as a result, fell overnight from riches to rags and ended his life as that stock figure, the neglected genius—ill, poverty-stricken, forgotten, spending his last days in the squalor of the Amsterdam ghetto as a combination of acknowledged social pariah and unrecognized aesthetic messiah. The tale has been refuted time and again, but it persists. It can, in truth, be hung on a skeleton of the facts of Rembrandt's life, but it bears to that life the relationship of a caricature to a true portrait.

Rembrandt was born in Leiden on July 15, 1606, the son of a miller and a baker's daughter—an attractive, sturdy-sounding combination that produced a son with the honest, rather lumpy, and altogether undistinguished features of a loaf of bread. When he was fourteen his parents enrolled him in the faculty of letters of the University of Leiden, an indication that they had ambitions for him to rise in life, but he was less interested in the prospect than they were. In the same year, he left his studies to enter the studio of Jacob van Swanenburgh (*c.* 1571-1638), a painter of unrelieved mediocrity. In 1623 or perhaps 1624 he went to Amsterdam for six months and studied with Pieter Lastman (1583-1633), who had more to offer. Shortly thereafter, the boy was back in Leiden, where at only eighteen he set himself up as an independent painter.

His success was sound if not spectacular. But the Amsterdam that Rembrandt had briefly known must have put Leiden in the shade. The big commercial city offered a more varied life and sources of more important commissions than his home city of professors and weavers. Rembrandt returned to Amsterdam when he was twenty-five, and never left it again.

He was immediately successful, and for ten years was Amsterdam's ranking portrait painter. He was not thought of as a genius, and if nothing existed but the work from this period, he would hardly have become known as one of the greatest painters of all time, although he would certainly be considered a fine one. Some of the good Amsterdamers who were his clients may have recognized his increasing power as something more than increasing technical skill; they may have seen that in his paintings on biblical and other subjects he went beyond the superficially appealing theatricality of baroque illumination to explore the deeper meanings of his themes. They may have been aware, too, of the subtlety of his perception as a portraitist. But his great popularity with the solid, wealthy citizenry came from their delight in the amazing veracity with which he delineated their faces (it is apparent from these portraits that they did not demand flattery) and the relish they took in the detailed perfection of his rendering of their fine clothes.

Rembrandt earned a great deal of money during these years, so much that even his exceptional indifference to the profitable management of his affairs could not keep him from becoming wealthy. When he was twenty-eight, after three years in Amsterdam, he married a young Frisian girl, Saskia van Uylenburgh. It was a love match on both sides, but Saskia happened also to be an heiress. The couple established themselves in a fine house that before long was filled with Rembrandt's collection. As a collector he disregarded the usual standards of quality and simply bought anything that struck his fancy. He must have been the delight of the Amsterdam auctioneers: he never allowed anyone to outbid him, and just about everything seemed to interest him. He bought not only paintings but art objects of all kinds, as well as armor and weapons, both ancient and modern. He could never resist fine stuffs, even when they were offered in the form of old clothes, and he would buy any bit of Near Eastern paraphernalia—partly with the excuse that these oddments served him as studio props in his paintings of Old Testament subjects.

His and Saskia's only sorrow was that the several children she bore died in infancy. But in 1641 a son, Titus, was born and lived. At almost the same time, Rembrandt was engaged on his most important commission for a group portrait, *The Company of Captain Frans Banning Cocq,* which is the more accurate title of the painting generally called *The Night Watch* (Amsterdam, Rijksmuseum), a huge affair 12 feet high and 14½ feet long even though it has been trimmed around the sides. Nominally an organization of the civil guard, the company was more social than military, and the commission was connected with celebrations accorded Marie de Médicis during a visit to Amsterdam.

Rembrandt at this time—only in his middle thirties, rich, vigorous, in love with his wife, with a beautiful son, esteemed by his fellow citizens, famous within the world of his choice, and (we may certainly presume) conscious of his own powers and absorbed in his development as an artist— Rembrandt at this moment offers such a picture of fulfillment, as well as promise, that it is no wonder the rest of his life is pictured as a kind of vengeance visited upon him by jealous gods. The rest of his life was indeed a decline in worldly fortune, but there were multiple compensations, including love and the greatest satisfaction beyond love that a man can have, the consummation of a creative passion.

On June 14, 1642, just a month before Rembrandt's thirty-sixth birthday, Saskia died. In the same year he completed *The Night Watch,* and legend has made it a professional disaster. It was an extraordinary and unconventional painting, in which Rembrandt dramatized a completely imaginary moment when the company was called to arms. He introduced figures having nothing to do with the incident for the sake of compositional convenience, and threw various members of the group into shadow while vividly illuminating others—a violation of the primary requisite of a group portrait, which is that each member must be given his own clear spot in order to avoid wounded feelings. The evidence as to the picture's reception is contradictory, but none of it supports the story that it was a total disaster, which, coinciding with the death of Saskia, shattered Rembrandt's world. If Rembrandt's fortunes began to decline, they did not toboggan.

His personal life shifted in a direction that has embarrassed idealistic biographers, but then settled into a new balance that in its way was as happy as his marriage. To begin with, there was a somewhat unsavory interlude when a woman named Geertghe Dircx, the widow of a trumpeter, moved into the house as Titus's nurse, according to tactful accounts, but actually as Rembrandt's mistress. She was a strange, irascible, apparently thoroughly unpleasant woman who later sued Rembrandt for breach of promise and after prolonged litigation was finally committed, in 1650, to an insane asylum.

Her place had been taken—more accurately, Saskia's place had been taken—by a young woman named Hendrickje Stoffels, who came to the house as a servant girl but in short order became Rembrandt's mistress, which she remained until her death. She was faithful, patient, loving, and sensible. To say that she took Saskia's place actually does both women an injustice. Hendrickje occupied a place of her own in Rembrandt's life, not quite comparable to Saskia's. Rembrandt never married her (in spite of pressure from both the Catholic and Protestant Churches) because under the terms of Saskia's will the income from her estate came to him only so long as he remained single. A daughter, Cornelia, was born in 1656, the only child of the several born to Rembrandt who survived him.

In the same year as the child's birth (Rembrandt was fifty), he was declared bankrupt. His collection, which had cost him around 17,000 florins, was auctioned and brought only 5,000. During the next three years his furniture and then his house also went on the block, again at a loss. He moved into a poor neighborhood and rented a warehouse as a studio, where he supplemented his income by teaching.

However wretched the situation was, it was not really desperate. Rembrandt had never known how to take care of his money, but his financial troubles at this time were common to other painters who had been more prudent. The maritime war between England and Holland had reduced the prosperity of Amsterdam, and there was a general decline in commissions. But Rembrandt retained the respect of the city and the loyalty of his friends. He continued to receive at least his share of such commissions as were offered during the 1650's and 1660's, including some of the most lucrative ones.

Hendrickje and the growing Titus did what they could to hold things together. They opened a small business as art dealers and also served as Rembrandt's agents, taking over all rights to his work and putting him on an allowance. The ménage was not unhappy. Rembrandt's portraits of Hendrickje show a comfortable, plump woman who would be the balm of any man's late middle age, and those of Titus show a handsome boy with sensitive features. He was his father's delight.

In 1662 Hendrickje died. For another six years Rembrandt, at the full tide of his powers as an artist, was cherished and solaced by Titus, until Titus died in 1668 at the age of twenty-seven. Rembrandt died a year later, on October 4, 1669, at sixty-three. He was buried in the Westerkirk, to the disruption of the legend that should have given him a pauper's grave. It is true that in his last years he had been reduced to poverty, but he was still Rembrandt van Rijn, the respected painter and citizen of Amsterdam.

In outline, Rembrandt's life is a sad one, since its dates so often mark the deaths of people he loved and the stages in his reduction to poverty. But the reverse of that coin is that to have lost so much a man must have had a life rich in good things. We think first of Saskia's death, and forget to count the bliss of that marriage. Because Titus died young, we forget that he was his father's pride and joy (no other phrase does quite as well as this cliché) until the last year of Rembrandt's own life. And the wonderful Hendrickje was with Rembrandt for a full seventeen years in what amounted to a perfect marriage.

The richness, warmth, and calm of Rembrandt's union with Hendrickje from early to late middle age replaced the youthful exuberance and excitement of the years with Saskia. Rembrandt celebrated his first marriage with a painting (now in Dresden) of himself as a grinning young buck raising a glass of wine toward the spectator beyond the frame as if toasting his own vitality and good fortune while displaying the pretty young bride seated on his knee. In her ladylike way she seems to submit to the whole business with a combination of amusement and embarrassment. Rembrandt drew Saskia many times with exquisite tenderness. He liked best to paint her decked out in her richest clothes, a beloved object decorated to the limit with fine stuffs and flowers like votive offerings. The portraits reflect both his adoration and his pride of possession—a perfectly healthy response in a young male.

Rembrandt's drawings and paintings of Hendrickje, on the other hand, are revelations of the profundity of mature experience, of the peacefulness of deep affection and mutual dependence that must succeed passionate love and, if a man is lucky in his choice, may more than reconcile him to the loss of youth. Saskia, Titus, and Hendrickje make an enviable trio of blessings, without mentioning the excitement of early success and the satisfaction of continued high reputation over a lifetime. Rembrandt was constantly at work, day by day and year after year after year, as an artist who never stopped growing from the time he began drawing as a child until he died an old man. His art was not something that sustained him in adversity (even if, secondarily, it did so) but the central fact of his life, and it never failed him.

Rembrandt was as original an artist as ever lived. Like any genius, he appeared from nowhere inexplicably. It is easy to tie him, historically, to the realistic tradition of Caravaggio as imported from Italy through his Dutch teachers, and to baroque dramatics in general. But this is a mechanical liaison. Like other great original artists, he was a plant of a new kind produced from the same seed that, all around him, yielded an expectable crop. It is significant that he never had any interest in going to Italy, although he could have made the trip in princely style as the reigning young artist of Amsterdam. His colleagues could not understand this. An Italian trip with firsthand study of Raphael and the other Renaissance masters was thought of as a painter's baccalaureate, providing not only a professional cachet but the necessary acquaintance with Renaissance theories of anatomy, proportion, and design that was the standard of aesthetic literacy.

Rembrandt was content to remain illiterate in this respect (as well as in another one: he spoke no foreign language and wrote his native language poorly and with difficulty) and was regarded as provincial by his contemporaries. To us, however, it is apparent that Italianism has always been an uneasy bedfellow with the native Dutch tradition. Elegance, graceful proportions, and harmonious artificialities are foreign to the sturdy Dutch ambience, whether we think of the landscape, the physical type of the Hollanders, or their practical and forthright way of life. Nature was Rembrandt's professed model, and nature as it existed within his native country sufficed him. He never drew an ideal figure, and by the standards of ideal classical form he never drew a beautiful one.

Nor had he any use for the interpretative conventions considered intellectual and elevated. From the first, even in his earliest paintings, when he was a youth in Leiden still finding his own style within a semi-Italianate baroque formula, his interpretations were his own. He was fascinated by the stories of the Old Testament, which he saw not in the conventional way, as prophecies of the events recorded in the New Testament, but as themselves, accounts of man's relationship to a God who might be violent in His wrath and was stern even in His love. He saw the dramas taking place in an Eastern world both barbaric and splendid, cruel and opulent. He staged the episodes with full use of baroque theatrical effects, but elevated them from theatricality to drama in the same way that Shakespeare (for instance) translated familiar blood-and-thunder plays into tragedy—by his perception of character and motivation. Stories treated by other artists as allegories, historical anecdotes, or pegs for decorative schemes became again, with Rembrandt, revelations of the psychological forces of good and evil, of strength and weakness, that determine man's relationship to his fellows and his God.

As Rembrandt grew older his dramas grew more and more simple as their meanings grew more profound and less translatable into narrative, until at last the drama was altogether spiritual, enacted without gesture by a single character, an old man or an old woman revealed in golden light as the weathered vessel of the spirit. His model as often as not was himself; his plain and even ugly face, coarse-featured and sagging, bore the record of his pondering. There is not much that can be said about these paintings without reducing them to platitudes about life, experience, and death. They withstand utterly a last test of the greatness of a painting: their meaning is relayed in terms so totally pictorial that words cannot be substituted for the paint.

The current conception of Rembrandt as we understand him now is hardly a hundred years old. The romantic revolution with its insistence that the inner world of the spirit is at once too mysterious for explanation and too powerful for suppression, and that its revelations must be accepted as the core of any meaning that life may have, transformed Rembrandt from the dramatic realist that he seemed to his contemporaries into a philosopher. He is a philosopher without a system who begins with the unexceptional premise that man lives and dies, and who concludes that the experience is beyond calculating on a balance sheet of joys and sorrows.

Georges de La Tour was born in 1593, but he might be included just as appropriately in a chapter on modern art as in the history of his century, the seventeenth. Almost everything that is known about him has been discovered since 1914, with most of the research concentrated in and since the 1930's. The appreciation of his art, which is fervent, has been reached in terms of twentieth-century movements. La Tour is not so much an old master rediscovered as a modern painter who has been detected under an old master's disguise. And La Tour the modern is a much clearer figure than La Tour the old master.

As an old master, La Tour is still the subject of research and speculation devoted to separating his work from works wrongly attributed to him, to dating such paintings as are known to be his, to unraveling the various influences (Italian, Dutch, and French) that formed his style, and to gathering factual information about his life.

Even during his lifetime La Tour seems to have been an exceptional and isolated figure if not the mysterious one he has become. We know this much:

He was born in Vic, the small capital of the bishopric of Metz in the duchy of Lorraine. In about 1615, when he would have been twenty-two, he probably made a trip to Italy. Two years later he married, and then moved to Lunéville, which, with some interruptions, remained his home until his death in 1652 at the age of fifty-nine.

While still a young man he visited Holland. In 1633,

then forty years old, he presented a painting of St. Sebastian, now lost but known through eight replicas, to Louis XIII of France, which indicates the French sympathies that took him to Nancy and probably to Paris during the disorders of 1638 when Lunéville was burned and sacked in the struggle between the French and the local partisans. La Tour may have visited the Low Countries again at this time. We know that he returned to Lunéville in 1641 as a Frenchman, wealthy and in favor with the court. The people of Lunéville abominated him, and must have been galled in the extreme when they were forced to raise money to purchase some of La Tour's paintings as a gift to the royal governor in Nancy, by the governor's order.

In Italy La Tour could have become acquainted with Caravaggesque realism, and in both Italy and Holland he would have encountered work by the tenebrists, with their exaggerated drama of brilliant artificial light played against dense shadow. At any rate, upon his return to Lunéville he was working in the variation of this style that is specifically his own, where the picture space is in darkness except for light radiating from a candle flame shielded by a raised hand, or from a night light, a torch, or a firebrand. The participants in his dramas—St. Sebastian mourned by St. Irene, the Magdalen alone in her room, her hand resting upon a skull, two women holding a newborn child—exist in an enchanted stillness, absolutely and eternally motionless, utterly silent, their eyes as unwavering as the eyes of sculpture. As they contemplate an object within the picture, unaware of us as observers beyond the limits of the small space they occupy, they take on the quality of visionary beings unrelated to the world. No figure is ever fantastic: in the tradition of seventeenth-century realism the scenes are performed in the costumes of ordinary people of the day. Yet the air is bewitched, and the light that comes from such ordinary sources is supernatural.

Every pictorial element contributes to a magical quality by the process of reduction to essentials by which consummate statement is achieved by consummate economy. Every form or detail of form that can be eliminated as extraneous has been distilled away. Thus disciplined, reduced to their simplest geometrical equivalents, La Tour's forms are remindful of Piero della Francesca's, although there is hardly a chance that for La Tour, Piero was even so much as a vague historical name. The resemblance is surely coincidental and, also, it is merely formal. The two artists share a quality of sobriety, but Piero's reflects an intellectualism that is in complete contrast with La Tour's mystical intensity. Sobriety and mystical intensity might seem incompatible if La Tour had not shown that spiritual ecstasy and suffering can be expressed in calm and sober terms as well as in the warped forms of visionary excitement that served, for instance, El Greco.

La Tour arrived at the near abstraction of his final style by degrees. His early work includes not only scenes in full daylight, and genre subjects, but experiments in a free, cursive technique. And for all the connections that can be made between him and Italian and Dutch masters, La Tour found his way alone. Summarized, the known data of his life make him sound like a traveler, a man familiar with the great centers, but if the data are examined they show that his trips over a lifetime were few and brief, and that he developed in the isolation of the provinces. This isolation was so great that he was forgotten soon after his death, and for more than two centuries was hardly thought of, even in France, except as a minor provincial painter in a minor tradition.

La Tour's rediscovery in this century is easily understood. The geometrical basis of art insisted upon by Cézanne and then by the cubists (the "Cubist-Classical Renaissance," as R. H. Wilenski calls it) transformed our way of seeing

La Tour's formal structure just as it brought an increased appreciation of Piero della Francesca's. But La Tour, in addition, combined this structure with an emotive power—the supernatural evoked by the tangible—that modern geometrical abstraction has been forced to sacrifice in the achievement of its formal goals. His genius was that he fused two apparently incompatible expressions—one serene and implacably defined, the other intense and beyond the limits of definition —into a single identity.

Modern painters have never quite been able to marry the intellect and the passions; we have come to a bifurcation with half our artists insisting that the emotions must receive spontaneous expression in whatever form, usually a violent one that seems to have erupted under the stress of a welter of impelling forces that demanded release, and the other half insisting that analytical control in the service of intellectual perception must be exercised to produce painting with the chilly clarity of an engineering blueprint. La Tour is never impulsive, but he is always concerned with a release of the spirit. He is never cold, but his paintings are models of logical organization. And in combining these two ideals of expression he compromises neither. It is no wonder that he has become a supreme figure in twentieth-century art.

An indication of the importance attached to La Tour since his rehabilitation as one of the great names of French painting came when the Metropolitan Museum acquired *The Fortune Teller,* painted by La Tour before 1633. Although at this date La Tour had not yet reached his full powers, *The Fortune Teller* is a beautiful painting and a fine example of La Tour's style of that period. Its discovery was one of those extremely rare instances when an important work of art of undisputable authenticity in good condition is identified after remaining unnoticed—but in full view—in an obscure spot. The painting came to the Metropolitan through channels that have never been fully explained—at least not officially. It had been in the possession of a French family in the provinces and through them came to the attention of a monk in a Benedictine monastery, who suspected that it might be something more than just another of the fairly good but not very valuable paintings that exist by the thousands on the walls, or in the storerooms, of old families and antique dealers in Europe.

An astute scholar-dealer recognized the picture as an exceptional one and kept it quietly in his own collection over a period of years, researching it thoroughly. The painting came to the Metropolitan through this dealer, but not directly: negotiations for its purchase and export were carried on at ambassadorial levels. When the announcement of the Metropolitan's acquisition was made (an announcement withheld until the painting was safely out of France and in the Metropolitan's hands), the French press raised an uproar, charging that officials of the Louvre and the Ministry of Fine Arts had collaborated in permitting a national treasure to leave the country.

The point of the story is that twenty-five years earlier the export would have caused no excitement, and twenty-five years before that the owners might even have found difficulty in selling the picture at anything better than the price that hundreds of minor paintings bring every year through minor dealers.

11

THE CARRACCI
AND THE RETURN
TO TRADITION

Caravaggio's revolution, which we have been following, occurred simultaneously and even competitively with another, which was also a revolt against sixteenth-century mannerism but went about reforming art in a different way. Where Caravaggio voyaged forth in a new direction, the Carracci family returned to tradition as a point of departure for new growth, on the well-known principle *"Il faut reculer pour mieux sauter."* The Carracci's school (and, if not the school, then its guiding ideas) formed a group of painters who became the supreme decorators of the baroque tradition, and also, as we will see later, the first academicians—in the sense of artists who adhere to principles they believe to have been followed by revered predecessors. The rules formulated by the academicians overlook the *"sauter"* part of the aphorism and reduce it to, simply, *"Il faut reculer."*

However, the men under discussion in this chapter are

those who continued and developed traditional Italian art, and not those who calcified it.

After they completed their series of frescoes in the Palazzo Magnani in Bologna, the Carracci were asked which of them had done which portions. They replied (and can be imagined replying in unison), "It is by the Carracci—we all have done it."

In their subsequent relationships the two brothers Annibale and Agostino and their cousin Ludovico—all born within a period of five years between 1555 and 1560—were somewhat less harmonious. Annibale complained in a letter to Ludovico that Agostino was leaving all the work to him while he, Agostino, spent his time cultivating famous poets, writers, and courtiers, bringing them up on the scaffolding to watch. From our point of view this was all to the good, since Annibale of all the Carracci has worn best as an artist. But his irritation is understandable.

Whatever their disagreements, the Carracci present a firmly consolidated family partnership, and present as well a consolidation of influences absorbed from everywhere that makes their name synonymous with eclecticism. The term has disparaging associations today: it is supposed that the eclectic artist, selecting what he wants from various sources, has no creative power of his own and seldom gets beneath the surface attractions of his borrowed material. But for the Carracci, eclecticism was a new principle and a kind of reform.

The Carracci held no revolutionary ideas. They were simply out of patience with the artificial theatricality of late mannerism, and rejected it to dig back into the sources of art. For the Carracci, "sources" meant Michelangelo, Raphael, Correggio, and the Venetians. They re-examined these masters and applied their principles anew. With our horror of returning to the past—or, let us say, with the horror of returning to the past that is felt by most modern artists—we may feel, first, that the Carracci were merely reactionaries in the history of art, which until then had, quite naturally, built continuously upon the past rather than returning to it. But the Carracci thought of their eclecticism as a return to nature —which it was, in comparison with the effete distortions designed in mannerist studios, where nature was regarded as something rather vulgar.

Annibale (1560-1609), by far the finest artist of the family, is increasingly respected today after a period when he was relegated to an anomalous position in the art-history books, which recognized his importance while dodging any enthusiastic commitment to his art. Not that he is considered an exciting artist even today, although his frescoes in the Farnese Gallery in Rome's Palazzo Farnese, as decorative schemes only, are admissible to third place in the company of two other triumphant decorative series (not primarily thought of in that category)—the Sistine Ceiling and Raphael's Stanze. Contemporary Romans admitted the frescoes to the same august company of masterworks, but as something more than a consummately planned decorative ensemble: they also placed the highest value on the individual scenes—eclectic treatments of mythological subjects—within that ensemble.

The decorations were commissioned by Cardinal Odoardo Farnese, who holds a rather curious spot in art history as the man who so underpaid Annibale after ten years of service that the artist was thrown into a state of melancholia that lasted until his death. A year after his rupture with the Cardinal, at the age of forty-five, Annibale, who had been notable for his vigor and productiveness, became listless, depressed, and unable to work. His memory failed, his speech became halting. It was the scandal of Rome that the Cardinal had reduced a great artist to impotence.

Before Annibale died, barely forty-nine years old, he had made a partial recovery. His friends and students had managed to get him back to working about two hours a day over the last year or so. The historian-biographer Joachim von Sandrart* laid Annibale's trouble to "amorous disorders," a more reasonable explanation than financial disappointment. In retrospective diagnosis, Annibale's symptoms do suggest paresis.

Ludovico (1555-1619), the cousin, was also a prolific painter, but Agostino (1557-1602), Annibale's brother, seems to have spent most of his time on the administration of the school that the three set up in Bologna in 1585-86. This family-operated academy was extremely influential. Its eclectic program, a counterbalance to mannerism, made it a center for progressive young painters, although, for us, a program that is eclectic and progressive at the same time may seem to be the ultimate paradox. By pulling together the ideals of the High Renaissance, which had become scattered and confused by mannerism, the Carracci brought painting back onto course and supplied a base for the further growth of a faltering tradition.

In the Carracci's immediate circle of influence were the young artists who initiated the baroque style in its classical aspect (stemming from Raphael) and in its operatics (from Michelangelo, Correggio, and others). But their influence went far beyond their studio or even their peninsula. The Frenchman Poussin, the greatest master of seventeenth-

---

* Joachim von Sandrart (1606-1688) is the German Vasari. A prosperous and successful artist, his patrons included such personages as the emperors Ferdinand III and Leopold I, whose portraits he painted. He was a great traveler in northern Europe and especially in Italy, where he was from 1628 to 1635, and he knew most of the prominent artists on both sides of the Alps. As their biographer he is an important figure in the history of art: his "Teutsche Academie" is a valuable source book. As a painter, he had technical skill without individuality, intelligence without imagination, and is quite properly forgotten.

century classicism, found his way at least in part through Annibale's revival of Raphaelesque forms, and the young Rubens, who became the summation of the opposite aspect of baroque art, was influenced by Annibale's sensuous realism.

For the record, there was a fourth Carracci, in the next generation. Agostino had an illegitimate son, Antonio, who was born in Venice about 1583-89 and died in Rome in 1618. A painter of sorts and a proficient engraver, he never quite lived up to the family name.

Guido Reni was born in Bologna in 1575 and by the time he died in 1642 he had been well established for many years as the city's leading painter. But from 1600 to 1613 or 1614, as a young man, he was mostly in Rome. In this adventurous city he was attracted for a while to the new Caravaggesque manner, but he was temperamentally uninclined to naturalism and soon found that Raphael was more to his taste. If it is true that Caravaggio threatened to kill him, the circumstance could have had a cooling effect on Guido's interest in the realistic style of the hotheaded master, but the incident may be legendary. There is not much sign that Guido Reni would have made an acceptable second-string Caravaggio, but he was resoundingly successful in a Raphaelesque manner, modified by Parmigianinesque preciosities, that owed its immediate inspiration to the mythological scenes in Annibale Carracci's decorations in the Farnese Gallery.

His first teacher was the Flemish mannerist painter Denis (or Dionisio) Calvaert (*c.* 1545-1619), who had set up a successful shop in Bologna. It was through Calvaert that Reni acquired a taste for the rather affected grace of Parmigianino. But when the Carracci set up a shop in competition to Calvaert's, Reni (along with Calvaert's two other best pupils, Albani and Domenichino) shifted masters. In the Carracci shop, Reni was given a wide view of the opportunities available to a gifted hand and an eclectic spirit, and his dedication to Raphael was assured even before he went to Rome and suffered the temporary dislocation caused by Caravaggio's impact.

A rather bloodless painter, Reni was an eccentric personality. His contemporaries have left numerous anecdotes concerning him, but these refuse to jell into a consistent whole. He was a successful artist who charged high prices for his product, dressed like a prince, and was notable for the propriety of his demeanor. But he was subject to a form of terror comparable to a morbid wariness of bacteria today: he was in constant fear of subjection to witchcraft or death by poisoning. He was fanatically suspicious of his servants and of any gifts offered him. Perhaps a psychiatrist could find a connection between these fears and his remaining, according to the impressed and bepuzzled reports of his colleagues, a virgin to the end of his life. In seventeenth-century Italy, this was a feat.

A friend (Albani) reported that Guido, in his early days in Rome, was so stingy that he blew matches out as quickly as possible and saved the burnt stub. But when prosperity came to him he turned into a gambler. Rebuked for this bad habit, he said that he didn't need to worry about money. "I have an inexhaustible gold mine in my brushes." (Several artists, over the centuries, are reported to have said the same thing.) But he could not earn money quite as fast as he could lose it, and in his late years his social and professional reputation began to suffer. He became less choosy as to the company he kept, painted more hastily, and consented to traffic in weak copies of his work.

His work itself has seemed weak enough to the twentieth century—polished and graceful in a studied way, but too often cloying and affected. Currently he is being revived as part of the tail of the baroque kite, but it seems unlikely that he will ever again achieve the eminence he attained in the seventeenth and eighteenth centuries. During his own century and the next, he was thought of as Raphael's peer and became a god of the academies. He continued to ride high as a popular favorite through the nineteenth century, even though he began to be rejected by critics before the century was half done. And a generation born in the first decade of this century can remember a time when Guido Reni's *Aurora* (a ceiling fresco in the Casino Rospigliosi in Rome, painted in 1613) was the ubiquitous symbol of beauty. Reproduced everywhere, on candy-box covers and with pseudo-baroque frames for living rooms, *Aurora* vied with such other (if contrasting) favorites as Millet's *The Angelus* and Gainsborough's *Blue Boy* as a kind of license tag identifying its possessor as a person of bona fide culture.

Guercino, born Giovanni Francesco Barbieri, received his nickname because of his squint. He was blind in one eye. But unless he minded the nickname, the disfigurement was no disadvantage. During a lifetime of seventy-five years that began in the little town of Cento near Ferrara in 1591, Guercino was so successful that he turned down bids for his services from the sovereigns of England and France. Trained under obscure painters in his birthplace, where he was working as a full-fledged artist by his early twenties, he had found his models in the paintings of the Carracci brothers.

A document records Guercino's completion of frescoes in Bologna in 1617, when he was twenty-six. Perhaps by that time he had also completed his transformation, described by an early biographer (Passeri), from an uncouth and tactless yokel into a man of the world with an aptitude for elegant living. He was extremely industrious and worked all over Italy as the most serious younger rival of Guido Reni.

When he was thirty, Guercino took Reni's famous ceiling decoration, the graceful *Aurora* of the Casino Rospigliosi, and, as it were, flung the entire thing—chariot, horses, gods, and all—into the air and painted it in perspective, as if seen from below, on a ceiling in another Roman palace, the Villa Ludovisi. Guercino's *Aurora,* a wonderful airy scene taking place in the open sky and filled with exuberant motion, combined Correggio's lightness with Titian's richness. It became the source of a plethora of illusionistic paintings covering acres of Roman ceilings thereafter.

Guercino's first patron in Rome had been the Bolognese pope Gregory XV Ludovisi. When he died in 1623, Guercino returned to Cento and maintained headquarters there while ranging afield where commissions were offered. There were plenty of these, as is shown by the account book kept by his brother, Paolo Antonio (himself a still-life painter). But when Guido Reni died in 1642, Guercino moved to Bologna as if succeeding to an earldom. Unfortunately he also changed his light, ebullient style, as if it were unworthy of a truly important painter, and cultivated a disappointingly tame classicism along Reni's lines. He died in Bologna in 1666.

Guercino's reputation declined badly during the nineteenth century, but was restored in the twentieth along with that of baroque art in general. His increasing popularity, however, is based less on his paintings than on his drawings. These exist by the hundreds, and some of the most appealing are the ones that he dashed off most quickly. They are happy, fluent, assured, and often marvelously economical in their means.

Domenico Zampieri, always called Domenichino—"Little Dominic"—painted religious subjects of tender sobriety and ideal landscapes of lyrical serenity. Poussin is among the artists who, admiring his style and learning from it, have established Domenichino in his historical position as a link in the classical tradition. Domenichino was unyieldingly loyal to the grace and sobriety of the Raphaelesque tradition even while this aspect of Italian baroque art was being rejected for a more theatrical one. He was also the pivotal figure of a real-life story that might be called "Little Dominic and the Killers," which is a standard reference in the history of artists as personalities.

Domenichino was born in Bologna in 1581, and was first a pupil of Denis Calvaert, that unhappy Fleming who set up a school in Bologna only to have his best pupils desert him when the Carracci followed his example. Domenichino's father put the boy under Agostino Carracci's wing for a good reason: Calvaert had found him copying a Carracci drawing and had given him such a beating that he inflicted a head wound.

When Domenichino was about nineteen—a shy, withdrawn, and meditative youth—he followed Agostino to Rome and lived for a while with Guido Reni and Francesco Albani, other Calvaert-Carracci alumni from Bologna who were a few years older and much more given to enjoying themselves. At first they took a big-brotherly interest in the new arrival and the three shared a single room, but when Domenichino complained that they kept him awake all night with their cardplaying, thus hampering him in the conscientious performance of his work the next day, the friendship withered. But he found a patron and friend in a literary-minded monsignor, G. B. Agucchi, who brought commissions his way, and he was also recognized as a loyal follower by Annibale Carracci. Annibale, with his sober, restrained Roman manner, was Domenichino's true teacher.

The years up to 1617 in Rome must have been the closest to serene ones in Domenichino's life. He seems to have gone back to Bologna for a spell then, returning to Rome in 1621 with an appointment as papal architect from his fellow Bolognese, Gregory XV. He was now forty years old.

Three years later he received a very important commission—or at least half of it—for decorations in Sant'Andrea della Valle. Between 1624 and 1628 he completed frescoes in the choir and on the pendentives, but another artist, Giovanni Lanfranco (1582-1647), won the competition for the frescoes in the dome. A pupil of Agostino Carracci, Lanfranco was born in Parma, and he introduced into his dome the illusionism of Correggio in a dynamic, somewhat theatrical, eminently painterly style that made him a powerful champion of the high baroque in its triumph over the more restrained classical manner. From the first, Domenichino resented his victory, and the story went about Rome that he had even tampered with Lanfranco's scaffolding in an effort to make it collapse under his rival's weight. The story sounds invented, since Domenichino was not a villain, even though he had become pathologically jealous and suspicious.

At this crucial point in his professional and emotional life, Domenichino was offered a commission in Naples that any non-Neapolitan artist would have hesitated to accept, and the story of Little Dominic and the Killers begins. Over a period of fifteen years, the holiest shrine in Naples, the Chapel of San Gennaro in the Cathedral, had been in an on-again off-again process of decoration. After a series of false starts, the commission had been given to a Roman painter, Giuseppe Cesari (1568-1640), called the Cavaliere d'Arpino. A great favorite with popes—Clement VIII and Paul V were his patrons, and he even managed to hold his own under Urban VIII—he was an easy-going, old-fashioned mannerist with little interest in the revolutionary examples of Caravaggio, the Carracci, and their young followers. No doubt he found the atmosphere in Naples sinister, and very shortly he quit on the job. Guido Reni was then approached. He accepted, but no sooner had he arrived, with a pupil and a servant, than the servant was attacked and very nearly murdered (or actually murdered, according to the most dramatic version of the incident). Guido fled.

After another false start (with a Neapolitan artist, Santafede), the job was turned over to Belisario Corenzio (c. 1560- c. 1640), whose greatest distinction up to then had been his murderous assault on Guido Reni's servant, for which he had been brought to trial but released for lack of evidence. He proved to be less satisfactory as a painter than as a fighter, and his efforts were erased. The commissioners went to Rome again, this time approaching Domenichino.

Even a bolder man than Domenichino would have thought twice before entering the lists against the Neapolitan painters. Great believers in direct action, their idea of arbitration was a warning threat, and they sent one to Domenichino as soon as they learned that he was a candidate for the much-kicked-about commission in San Gennaro. But Domenichino was unhappy in Rome. He signed, and went to Naples in 1631. He was fifty years old, and when he died in Naples at sixty in 1641, he had spent the last decade of his life in a state of siege.

On his second morning in Naples he awoke to find a note stuffed in the keyhole of his room, threatening his life if he remained in the city. He took this welcome to the Viceroy, who gave him cheerful assurances but no formal protection. For a year, while he finished the first section of the frescoes, Domenichino barricaded himself in his room and in the chapel, hardly leaving either except to dart to the other. The frescoes were accepted, and he went on with the contract under the same strain for another two years—and then broke and ran for Rome, leaving his family behind. Traveling night and day, he managed to get as far as Frascati, where, in a state of collapse, he took refuge with Cardinal Belvedere.

It took him a year to recover, but then he returned to

Naples to finish the job, which now included six altarpieces. The Neapolitan painters continued their persecution so energetically (by then, perhaps, the baiting had become a sport rather than a serious effort to dislodge him) that he was afraid to eat food he had not prepared. And when he died, his wife was convinced that he had, indeed, been poisoned.

And so he had, but not in the way she suspected. It must have been the bitterest and most poisonous twist of all that the same Lanfranco whose dome had been so successful in Rome had come to Naples and during the last years of Domenichino's life had been accepted by the Neapolitans, and not only accepted but admired and imitated.

Bernardo Strozzi was born in Genoa in 1581, trained there under a Sienese mannerist (Sorri), took orders as a Capuchin monk at the age of seventeen (whence his nickname Il Capuccino), left the monastery at the age of twenty-nine in order to support his mother, became a prelate (whence his nickname Il Prete Genovese), and then, when his mother died after twenty years, was imprisoned for his refusal to re-enter the monastery. To date, he has escaped post-mortem psychiatric analysis connecting his religious and Oedipal lives. Upon his release from prison he went to Venice, where he became a monsignor at the age of fifty-four. He died nine years later, in 1644.

As a painter, Strozzi–Capuccino–Prete Genovese was subject to multiple influences: Rubens, Van Dyck, Cambiaso, mannerists of every Italian school, and, after his move to Venice, the golden luminosity of that city's traditional masters. Yet he developed an appealing individual style that— elegant, a bit shallow, but extremely assured in its affectations—was of great influence in the development of seventeenth-century Genoese and Venetian painting.

Although Pietro da Cortona was the grand master of the high-baroque style in painting, he refuses to emerge as an individual. As a supreme decorator, he fulfilled the first demand of either ecclesiastical or secular patrons: he proclaimed by inference (with his effulgent virtuosity, his impressive illusionism, his generally triumphant air) the infallibility of the Church and, equally, the power of the state. In the Church, his patrons were a succession of popes. His great patrons among princes were the Barberini (Pope Urban VIII was of the family), and in their Roman palace, now the Galleria Nazionale, he created his masterpiece, a huge allegorical fresco on the vault of the main hall, *Divine Providence and Barberini Power*. Exuberant, vitally animated, flickering with light, and surging and floating with heroic personages, the ceiling has every dramatic virtue except one: by identifying nobility of spirit with sheer power, it precludes any revelation of the complexity of the soul. But that, for the purpose at hand, was all to the good.

Born Pietro Berrettini in 1596, Pietro took his name from his birthplace, Cortona. He died in Rome at the age of seventy-three in 1669, after a career that had made him one of the most influential painters of his generation. He came of a family of stonemasons. His teachers were obscure artists. He made his way by the multiplicity of his natural talents: he was a born virtuoso who drew like an angel, a practical man of affairs who always delivered the required product. And he was a courtier of sorts—in many ways a Raphael born too late to benefit from the perfect moment that made Raphael a demigod.

Pietro da Cortona's status as something more than an important figure historically has risen and fallen with the rise and fall of appreciation for the operatic baroque style that he did so much to bring to fulfillment. Currently his star is again on the rise. And yet one seldom thinks of him as an artist or as a man: he remains a name. No personality filters through the grandiosity of his pictorial schemes, although his drawings—fresh, fluent, relaxed, and sensuous—can bring him to life for us.

It is impossible, also, to pay much attention to the subjects of his large decorations. Pietro was a classical scholar; at least he was a devoted student of the forms of classical antiquity, and with the help of literati he filled his paintings with well-organized classical references. But just as one accepts the perfection of his vast, faultlessly interwoven pictorial schemes without analyzing them (this is a tribute to his skill), so one is content to savor the theatrical performances in his baroque inventions without investigating their literary skeleton.

Pietro da Cortona was also an important architect. His eminence was such that in 1664 he was invited by Louis XIV, along with Bernini and Rainaldi, to submit plans for the completion of the Louvre. Three of his drawings for the project are still in the Louvre's Cabinet des Dessins.

Giovanni Battista Gaulli (1639-1709) was gifted with the flair, the dash, and the instinct for bravura performance that could have made him one of the most seductive painters of easel pictures of his century. But—a thoroughgoing professional—he directed his talents, instead, to the decoration of churches. In doing so he supplied the history of art with the finest and most daring example, in fact the standard example, of the illusionistic baroque ceiling—his *Triumph of the Name of Jesus* in the Gesù in Rome, where a huge operatic troupe enacts the drama while spinning back into deep space and, in the foreground, spilling out in theatricalized confusion over the borders of the grandiose architecture—some of it real, some of it a painted continuation of the real.

The examples of Rubens and Van Dyck made Gaulli a colorist. The example of the supreme baroque sculptor, Bernini, whose sinuous line and wonderfully expansive, gesturing forms he adapted, made him a pictorial dramatist. His great ceiling is one of the sights of Rome, and his sketches for such works, brilliantly slashed in, are the delights of a modern audience wherever they can be found. Gaulli was also a portraitist of great reputation, but his few known portraits are of no great interest today.

Born in Genoa, this brilliant fellow left the city in his teens and went to Rome, his natural habitat, where Bernini adopted him as a protégé. He began painting *The Triumph of the Name of Jesus* in 1676 when he was thirty-seven and completed it three years later. In his mid-forties he began to temper his almost orgiastic baroque style with classical restraints, to the distress of critics of his own day—with whom, in this case, critics of our day agree. He died at the age of seventy.

12

RUBENS
AND THE GLORY
OF POWER

The seventeenth century's invention of huge ensembles of architecture, painting, and sculpture, set in gardened landscapes or planned cityscapes, was a reflection and usually a deliberate declaration of power, whether these ensembles were built for great states engaged in bolstering their prestige, or whether they were built for the Church, engaged in bolstering its spiritual position against the upstart Protestants. What "baroque" usually suggests is a synthesis of elaborated, flamboyant, surging, often overblown forms in an ecclesiastical style that became the artistic tool of the Counter Reformation. Painters of church decorations like Gaulli, whom we have just seen, tend, for all their talent, to disappear as individuals within the schemes they serve, as indeed the perfect decorator should.

The painter who holds his own above this turbulent complex of activities, in the service of the Church and several states, is a Fleming, Rubens, equaled in this respect only by his Italian contemporary, the architect and sculptor Gianlorenzo Bernini (1598-1680). Other painters before Rubens had enjoyed the company of monarchs, but Rubens established a tradition of the princely artist who supplies a princely product, a tradition that lasted, in diminished and finally in debased form, for nearly three centuries until princes disappeared.

By all subsequent evidence, a congress of the gods was in session when Peter Paul Rubens was born on June 28, 1577, and, being in a state of euphoria one and all, they decided to give to a single human being every good fortune, in his physical self and in the progress of his life from start to finish. They even allowed him, except corporeally, immortality, and if they could not give this to his body, they saw to it that during his lifetime he was aware that immortality was his through his second being, art. They included in the schedule some griefs, since without them no life can be complete, but they doubled, tripled, and quadrupled the joys and formed Rubens in such a way that he could accommodate the lot, griefs and joys together, in full awareness of the richness of his experience.

By all the laws of dramatic irony, and for the comfort of the rest of us, the conclusion of Rubens's life story should have been that he looked back, as he neared the end, and yearned to live his life over again as an average man freed from the strains imposed upon him by a phenomenal career. Nothing of the sort happened. The gods' experiment was a total success.

Rubens was born out of his own country, in Siegen, Westphalia, where his father, an Antwerp lawyer and official who had been born a Catholic, was in exile because he had been suspected of Calvinist sympathies. The exile involved no great hardship. Shortly after the father died in 1587 the family was free to return to the home city, where Peter Paul grew up as a Catholic, which was fortunate in a practical way, since otherwise Rubens could never have become the international painter and diplomat at the Catholic courts of Europe that he did.

By social position, by education, by natural aptitude, and by the attraction of his person (he was the ideal Flemish type of ruddy, blond, full-bodied male) Rubens seemed from the first to be cut out for a diplomatic career. When he was not quite fifteen he became page to a lady, Margaret of Ligne. But after about a year of this he turned to the less respectable profession of painting, and studied under three artists who have little claim to eminence except that they taught him: Tobias Verhaecht, Adam van Noort, and Otto van Veen. Rubens became a member of the Antwerp guild in 1598, at the age of twenty-one.

Two years later he went to Italy for travel and study. In Mantua he attracted the attention of Vincenzo Gonzaga, and spent eight years as a member of his court. He went all up and down the peninsula, developing his own style as he studied Michelangelo, Caravaggio, Annibale Carracci, and a dozen others, sometimes copying them. (His copy of Leonardo's lost cartoon for the projected mural, *Battle of Anghiari*, preserves that great drawing for us at close second hand.) On one of his assignments for the Duke, he was sent in 1603— now a godlike figure at the age of twenty-six—as one of several envoys bearing gifts to the Spanish court. The Spanish interlude, which lasted into the following year, was a further education in courtliness. All the while Rubens was painting. He seemed to be able to do everything at once, and everything well, as indeed was necessary for a man who accomplished the work of several successful lives in the course of his supranormal one.

A famous report on Rubens's capacity for simultaneous activity was made by a young Danish physician named Otto Sperling who had the good luck, probably through good connections, to visit Rubens in his studio. Without stopping work on his canvas, Rubens carried on a conversation with Sperling, asked him questions and answered his, listened to a member of his staff who was reading to him from Tacitus (Rubens himself sometimes wrote essays in Latin), and dictated letters. Rubens's existing business correspondence is a considerable archive in itself.

Sperling's visit took place in Antwerp in 1621. Rubens was forty-four. In the thirteen years since his return from Italy he had amassed a fortune from paintings that went by cartloads to every court in Europe. He had built a mansion so splendid that it was one of the sights of the city for tourists. He had not intended to return to Antwerp; his Italian reputation had been so secure, and he so popular, that he could have made his career there. But when he was called back to Antwerp by his mother's illness he was offered an extraordinarily profitable spot as court painter to the Spanish regents, Albert and Isabella, and accepted it. The next year he married Isabella Brandt, who was celebrated as a beauty then and, from his portraits of her, still is. They had three children.

From his mansion Rubens operated what is always called his "factory," with a company of assistants who worked with him on his paintings. He kept strict records of exactly how much of each painting was from his own hand, and his letters to prospective purchasers are explicit on the point. The composition was always his, and he always put the final touches even on paintings that were largely executed by assistants—and the assistants were no mere hacks, but included such painters as Van Dyck, Velvet Brueghel, and Snyders, all masters in the craft themselves.

In 1623 Rubens and Isabella lost their eldest child, Clara Serena, and three years later Isabella died. Rubens was not quite fifty. Three years earlier (with no letup in his painting) he had begun to serve the other Isabella, ruler of the Spanish Netherlands after her husband's death in 1621, in a diplomatic capacity. He now became the Infanta's special agent in peace negotiations between the Netherlands, Spain, England, and France; at all these courts he executed commissions, often of staggering magnitude in their sheer physical dimensions, but never slipshod. If we think of Rubens first as a painter, his contemporaries thought of him equally or even first as a diplomat. He was not a painter-courtier like Raphael, but a man who performed international negotiations at the highest level and was entrusted with state secrets. He was knighted by both Charles I of England and Philip IV of Spain. As no more than a painter, he might not have received these honors. Painters in the North had never attained the princely status accorded to men like Leonardo, Raphael, and Michelangelo in Italy. Even Velázquez, whom Rubens met at the court of Philip IV, was granted honors in Spain as a great exception, and the Spaniards admired him as an exception, a painter who enjoyed the King's friendship. Rubens's friends at court certainly admired him as a painter, but it was as a statesman that he moved in the great world.

Any account of the grandeur of Rubens's accomplishments begins to sound a little oppressive, because it is difficult for us to remember that a man whose career almost depersonalizes him by removing him from experiences in common with our own could, at the same time, be a man for whom the ordinary tendernesses of life were as important as they are to anyone else. But if Rubens is somewhat dehumanized in this way, he is rehumanized by the story of his second marriage.

His marriage with Isabella Brandt had been a love

match, and his drawings of her and their children testify sufficiently to their happiness. It is conceivable that during the four years between her death and Rubens's second marriage he remained celibate in the full sense of the word; there are no stories to the contrary, and he was a man in whom vigorous sensual appetites were combined with the staunchest moral rectitude. But at fifty-three the appetites were still there, and, as he wrote his friend Nicolas Claude Fabri de Peiresc, "we may enjoy licit pleasures with thankfulness" (he wrote it in Latin: *"fruimur licita voluptate cum gratiarum actione"*). He decided to remarry.

His friends tried to argue him into making a marriage at court, but, as he told Peiresc, he feared pride, the "inherent vice of the nobility," particularly the female nobility—the kind of pride we would call snobbism, which would make a highborn wife look down on a painter. Rubens was already thinking of abandoning everything else for "my beloved profession." And he admitted further to Peiresc that it would have been hard for him to "exchange the priceless treasure of liberty for the embraces of an old woman."

So, in 1630, at fifty-three, he married the sixteen-year-old daughter of an honest middle-class family, Hélène Fourment. He painted her again and again, a luscious, plump, dewy-fleshed creature, sometimes as Aphrodite, sometimes as the mother of their first child, and once, multiplied many times over, as each of the women strolling with their suitors in *The Garden of Love* (Prado). In these last paintings there is nothing of a foolish old man's doting; they are poetic but still full-blooded tributes to the pleasures—the licit pleasures —of the flesh and to its beauty.

Two years after his marriage Rubens went into semi-retirement. The paintings continued to pour out, although the inexhaustible animal vitality that had swirled and exploded through his grandiose paintings for the court was now brought into accord with the intimate scale of his new life and was tempered (or so we can imagine) by an aging man's sensible recognition that time must run out. He purchased the Château de Steen, a small castle surrounded by woodland, orchards, and farmland, as a retreat from his Antwerp mansion, and spent as much time there as he could. As he approached sixty he began to be plagued by ill-health. The ailment was diagnosed as gout, but the term at that time was a catchall for a wide variety of infirmities. By 1639 Rubens was very ill, and he died the next year, at sixty-three. Hélène bore him their second child posthumously, as if in proof that nothing could entirely quench his vitality.

And nothing ever has. Briefly, Rubens's reputation diminished during the late eighteenth century with the vogue for icy classicism, but the romantic revolt soon took care of that. In his huge paintings for churches and palaces his opulence is too rich for some people's blood, with the tons of moist, sumptuous flesh, the vast flying curtains of gold and crimson fabrics, the cascades of gleaming hair, the triumphant naked men-like-gods and gods-like-men, the chariots and the surging clouds, the panoramic rhetoric and the theatrical exuberance. This is the Rubens whose work for the Catholic courts is the ultimate visual expression of the Jesuit Counter Reformation, and, in the Jesuit spirit, his expression is always logically controlled. Rubens may often seem immoderate, but he is never undisciplined; his apparent excesses are perfectly calculated. And there is always the other Rubens of the late paintings, not chastened by age and illness but savoring life so intimately that his art could father in the next century the gentlest poet of them all, another Fleming, turned Frenchman—Antoine Watteau.

"To Fortune I owe great obligation," Rubens wrote to Peiresc. But it was an obligation that he fully repaid. Even so, the gods never repeated their experiment. Baroque art, in its aspect as a supremely confident fusion of physical and intellectual vitality into a single harmonious force, had received in Rubens its fulfillment, and there was no need, thereafter, for another painter of exactly his sort.

Just as Rubens was the prince of painters, so was Antoon (later Sir Anthony) Van Dyck the princeling. He was born in Antwerp in 1599, took his first painting lessons at the age of ten, was a professional with his own studio and pupils at the age of sixteen, and was enrolled as a master in the artists' guild of St. Luke in Antwerp at nineteen.

One week after his twenty-first birthday, Van Dyck was signed on as chief assistant to Rubens in a contract to decorate the Church of St. Charles Borromée. Rubens always referred to him in the most enthusiastically appreciative terms. The boy was as handsome as he was precocious, and the young man was as vigorous intellectually as he was charming socially. Thus endowed, he was so happy in Antwerp that the representatives of James I of England, a country that was still importing its artists, had to wage a four-month campaign to convince him that he should pay their island a visit as court artist.

He yielded, stayed for three months during which he made a friend of the shy and dignified Prince of Wales—a year his junior—and then went back to Antwerp for his twenty-second birthday.

The English had let Van Dyck go reluctantly and only on eight months' leave from his royal contract, for the purpose of visiting Italy. He did go to Italy, but he stayed for six years.

They were wonderful years for him—between the ages of twenty-two and twenty-eight. With letters to all the best people, plus a talent and a personal attraction that were better than any introduction, he was both a social lion and a thoroughly respected painter in Genoa, Florence, Mantua, Venice, Rome, and Palermo—where he survived the plague. He did portraits of aristocrats and of others to whom he gave the air of aristocrats, and was sought out by visiting Englishmen who wanted to bring their portraits home. His brief stay at court had left a strong impression.

As a princeling he followed a mode of life that was touched by arrogance. He had an almost defensive attitude toward the position of the artist in the social scheme. His former master—Rubens—had long since established his own position as a prince in everything but title. But Rubens to his contemporaries was not only a superior painter but an important diplomat. Van Dyck was a painter only, and he rejected any notion of the artist as a bohemian, as a supercraftsman, or even as an exceptional person whose gifts made him acceptable in high society. He demanded unquestioning acceptance at the highest social level, and in return he lived up to the ideal not always achieved by the aristocrat-by-title; he was a genuinely cultivated man. The Romans called him "the knightly painter."

He returned to London in 1632 after five rich years in Antwerp. His friend the Prince of Wales had now grown up to become Charles I, exceptional among English kings for his connoisseurship and his taste for high style as an embellishment to the good life as led at court and in the houses of the aristocracy. It was a brilliant society, so brilliant that even Rubens, who had seen the most brilliant courts of Europe, was astonished by it during a visit. Van Dyck was completely a part of this world, as a host as well as in his elevated capacity as creative artist. He was knighted, was given a town house (with six servants, as we learn from an official roster of foreign residents in London), a summer residence, and an annual pension above the payments for whatever work he did for the King (who ordered portraits of himself and his queen eight or nine at a time). Since he accepted a great many other commissions besides the royal ones, it is not surprising that his studio assistants, who sometimes turned out everything except the face in a portrait, rivaled Rubens's in number.

His health was failing (the cause is not known) in 1639. Although he returned to Antwerp, where he was elected dean of the guild in 1640, and purchased a castle at Steen (later sold to Rubens) as if he intended to stay home for good, it was in London that Van Dyck died. He had come back for the wedding of William of Orange to Mary, the daughter of his friend Charles I, in May, 1641. He died in his fine house, in December of the same year, at the age of forty-two.

Although Van Dyck painted religious pictures in the manner of Rubens that are all but indistinguishable from those of his master, it is as a portraitist that he showed himself more than a merely phenomenally brilliant talent. To Rubens's sensuous images of flesh and blood he added a nervousness, an aristocratic tension, that suggests the third or fourth generation of a lineage that in another generation might be stretched too fine. There is not much variety in his portraits. He had the successful portraitist's capacity to capture a vivid likeness that was not necessarily a literally accurate one, and everyone he painted, including himself, seems to belong to a single family that breeds exceptionally true— fine-boned, slender, rosy-lipped, with fine curly hair, the whole package wrapped in the best satin. It was an image that set a portrait tradition in England perfected in the next century by Gainsborough's more personal vision, and debauched today by hacks.

Rubens had no rival among his Flemish colleagues, but if he had had one it would have been Jacob Jordaens. Jordaens was a member of the generation of Antwerp painters who were just enough Rubens's juniors to be affected, even in spite of themselves, by his magnificent example. As a result, he has been judged ever since by Rubens's standard. This is not quite fair. Jordaens has suffered even more than most of the Northern painters of his century for the paradoxical reason that he was an excellent painter who remained his own man in Rubens's usually overpowering presence. He is always thought of as a vulgar Rubens, and in a way he was, but his heartiness, his good humor, his fellowship with common people (a fact of his life that is reflected in his art) are his virtues. And because they are plainer virtues than Rubens's, they are seldom taken as virtues with their own validity, but only as reductions of the great master's.

Jordaens was born in Antwerp in 1593, died there in 1678, and lived there all his eighty-five years, although he made a visit or two to Amsterdam. He was the eldest of eleven children born to a prosperous linen merchant—painted wall hangings were among his stock—and at the age of ten was apprenticed to Adam van Noort, who had also taught Rubens. In 1615, at twenty-two, he was admitted to the guild, and the next year he married Van Noort's daughter Catherine. They had three children. It was a happy family, and Jordaens painted his father-in-law among rollicking companions in many pictures.

Jordaens's patrons—customers in his case would be a better word—were not the princely company that made Rubens rich, but he did nearly as well with the bourgeoisie, who purchased his work in such quantity that before he was fifty he built himself a house almost grand enough to rival Rubens's. Rubens in some early biographies is said to have been jealous of Jordaens. Whether or not this was true, it did not work in the other direction. Jordaens, fine house or not, was unambitious socially, had no interest in fine company or in travel, and was content with an essentially provincial life.

The one exceptional fact in his uneventful history is his conversion to Calvinism in the 1640's at the height of his prosperity in a Catholic country. The Calvinists met secretly in his house, and he was fined for writing Calvinist pamphlets. But he never ran into really serious trouble and continued to paint for the Catholic Church. His Calvinism had no decipherable effect on his painting; only in the sobriety of some late drawings is it at all apparent. Jordaens's chief characteristic as an artist is an un-Calvinistic richness, a gorged sensuousness, a delight in flesh and food more mundane than Rubens's glorification of sensuous experience.

Jordaens intellectualized nothing. In his religious pictures he may seem too mundane; in his mythological subjects he is often open to the standard accusation of second-rate Rubenism, and his gods are heavy-bodied burghers of less than Olympian presence. But in his genre pictures, and in any aspects of his religious and mythological pictures where the genre spirit can be introduced legitimately, Jordaens can be accused of nothing worse than an excess of cheerful animal vitality. He enjoyed life in so natural and outgoing a way that he often offered it to surfeit in his paintings, crowding them with more than they could easily hold, like a bourgeois host filling the plates with rich food until it runs off over the rims.

Rubens's chief assistant and an extremely successful painter in his own studio, Frans Snyders was the son of an Antwerp tavern keeper. If the establishment's fare was at all comparable to a Snyders still life, it was phenomenal. In a single painting of a kitchen pantry, *The Larder* (Brussels), Snyders shows tables and racks massed with dead game—a deer, two hares, and a huge swan (dead swans were frequently the centerpieces of his paintings), as well as a butchered calf, some hams, an enormous lobster (its red shell played against the swan's downy whiteness), platters of fish and oysters, and mountains of fruit and vegetables, with a serving girl in the background holding a tray loaded with pheasants while a live dog slavers at her side.

Snyders also painted live game (and for that matter, figures), and it was in hunting scenes that he best served Rubens. But his live animals are more like animated still life than like living creatures. Rubens was once offended when a visiting Englishman, Toby Matthew, mistook some animals he had painted ("all alive, in act eyther of escape or resistance," as Matthew wrote) for Snyders's. The relationship between Rubens and Snyders was cordial, however; it began about 1613, when Snyders was in his mid thirties, and endured until Rubens's death in 1640. Snyders was executor of Rubens's will.

Snyders was born (1579) and died in Antwerp and lived there all his life except for an Italian trip in 1608-09. His father's tavern, the Groote Bruyloft Kamere, was a popular meeting place for guild artists, and young Frans became a student of Pieter Brueghel the Younger. At twenty-three, in 1602, he was a guild member. Van Dyck was his close friend, and he married the sister of two other artists, Cornelis and Paul de Vos, who were also among Rubens's assistants. By 1620, as he entered his forties, he was able to buy his own house—a mark of caste and financial position in Antwerp— and was uninterruptedly successful until he died in 1657 at the age of seventy-eight.

The succession to Sir Anthony van Dyck's position as England's leading painter fell to another foreigner, Peter Lely. His real name was Van der Faes, and he was born in

Westphalia in 1618 of Dutch parents. Some decades later, as Sir Peter Lely of London, he was crystallizing the pattern of the fashionable English portrait. Less skilled and less original than Van Dyck, he proved that a capable-to-superior artist with a good formula can make a huge success.

After training in Haarlem, where he became a guild master in 1637, Lely came to England at about the age of twenty-four, just at the time Van Dyck died, and within a few years had moved into Van Dyck's place, routing all native competition. After 1647 he abandoned historical and religious subjects for portraits, and in the 1660's, with the Restoration, came fully into his own as a fabricator of the flattering, decorative, aristocratic image. He was not at all a bad painter although he was far from a great one. Knighted, he lived as the social equal of the nobility and accepted portrait commissions more as if granting favors to the sitters than as receiving professional assignments. Even the greatest lady, late for an appointment, missed her turn.

Contemporary accounts describe Lely's mansion, his corps of servants, his systematic method of work (from nine in the morning to four in the afternoon, with a secretary regulating the appointments), and his table, set for twelve every night, with musicians in the adjoining room. Lely formed one of the first great collections in England outside princely circles—if he can be said to have been outside them —and when it was sold after his death (in 1680 at the age of sixty-two) the event initiated the tradition of the sensational art auction that receives so much attention in the press today.

Godfrey (born Gottfried) Kneller continued and concluded the line of foreigners who, beginning with Holbein, had dominated English painting. In an unpleasantly ambitious manner he set about to make himself the heir of Van

Dyck and Lely, and he did even better than they: where they had been merely knighted, he was first knighted and then made a baronet. A German, born in Lübeck in 1646, Kneller was trained in Amsterdam under Bol, Rembrandt's student, but he later made a point of speaking abusively of Rembrandt, who was not at that time to English taste. His house and studio were opulent, his country house baronial, and he drove back and forth between the two in the finest of coaches.

Assembly-line fashion, his numerous German assistants practiced their specialties in the details that made complete portraits of the faces Kneller painted. He was egregiously self-satisfied, flagrantly a climber, but without question a painter who, in spite of a slightly heavy hand, did have a perception of character and exercised it when he could do so without offending his sitters. In a series of forty-two portraits of the members of a Whig club, the Kit Cat (now in the National Portrait Gallery in London), he left a historical document not quite like any other painter's.

Kneller as a careerist personality is constantly remindful of Sir Joshua Reynolds, who continued the tradition set by the foreigners. By appropriate coincidence Kneller died in 1723, the year Reynolds was born. The private academy Kneller had formed in 1711 forecast the formation of the official Royal Academy in 1768—of which Reynolds became the first president.

VERMEER AND
THE QUIETEST
REVOLUTION

Of all the contrasts between schools of art in the seventeenth century, the most extreme was surely the one between the grandiosity of official art in the princely tradition and the intimacy of the first art ever produced for consumption by burghers. The difference in physical dimensions between paintings that covered walls and ceilings of palaces or churches, and a painting that could be tucked under your arm and taken home and hung in your own room, was paralleled by the difference between the dramatic grandeur of an art dealing with gods, heroes, and saints, or the nature and fate of man, and the coziness of a Netherlandish art—usually Dutch—that depicted familiar scenes for their own sake. While Rembrandt pondered deep questions, his contemporaries by the dozen in Holland were content to record the activities, the landscape, and the appurtenances of daily life. The greatest of these painters, Vermeer, treated light, form, color, and texture as interlocked abstractions that could be analyzed by means of everyday objects. He and his colleagues were aware to one degree or another of the difference between the limitation of the visible world and its translation into art. They did not think of themselves as revolutionaries (they were creating salable objects to meet an existing demand), but they were nevertheless the protagonists of a major revolution—the quietest revolution in art history. It was the natural corollary to the equally quiet social revolution in Holland, where the middle class ruled a country just as, eventually, it was to rule the world.

Adriaen Brouwer, born in 1605/6, left home at the age of sixteen and before he died in 1638, at the age of thirty-two or thirty-three, he had painted so many scenes of debauchery in low places, and such convincing ones, that his early death has frequently been attributed to excessive carousing. More probably he died of the plague.

There are fairly dependable accounts of Brouwer as a carouser and spendthrift. There is no question but that he was imprisoned in Antwerp for seven or eight months, no doubt for debts, or that he died a pauper. Tremendously productive, he would sell his paintings in batches by weight, without regard for the quality of those included, in order to get ready cash. One story, almost too good to be true but current among his contemporaries, has it that once upon receiving an unexpected payment of a hundred ducats he threw the silver pieces on his bed and rolled in them ecstatically, then put them in his pocket and disappeared for nine days, to return broke once more but singing and whistling in the best of humor.

It is quite possible, however, to accept such accounts of Brouwer's loose living and low living with only a grain or

two of salt to reconcile them with the more purposeful character that certainly existed beneath the froth of these spectacular demonstrations of a very young man's high spirits.
If Brouwer frequented the country inns that he painted, with
their tipplers and roisterers, their itinerant dentists yanking
out teeth with the finesse of butchers, their loutish musicians,
and their sordid disarray, he was also, during a period of
residence in Haarlem, a member of the Rederijkers, a literary society. But the most forceful rebuttal to the picture of
Brouwer the wastrel is the counterevidence of his paintings.

It is not only that Brouwer was so prolific. During his
few years, his art deepened in mood, grew more reflective and
more subtle. Always an expert craftsman, he was both adventurous and thoughtful in his exploration of techniques.
Rubens, by this time the patriarch and demigod of Northern
art, admired Brouwer and owned seventeen of his paintings
(he knew the young man well enough to bail him out of
prison). And if Brouwer upon his death was first given a
pauper's burial, his body was shortly removed from the cemetery for a proper funeral in a church, which was attended by
distinguished citizens, both clerics and laymen. They contributed a tombstone engraved with a eulogy. When everything is added up, Brouwer is best seen as the prototype of
today's artist-as-bohemian, flouting convention and pleased to
shock the staid citizenry both by his behavior and by his
art, but a serious artist for all that and one who, in the usual
course, settles down in his middle age, which Brouwer never
came within hailing distance of.

The son of a draftsman of tapestry cartoons, Brouwer
was an independent painter in Haarlem by the time he was
twenty. His earliest work reflects Pieter Bruegel's, but Bruegel's sturdy upstanding man of the soil soon gives way in
Brouwer to a gross boor who drinks, spews, and whores in
squalid hovels—an undifferentiated picture that Brouwer

forced to the point of caricature. In this unconventionally antipicturesque and anti-ideal form of genre painting, Brouwer was an innovator, although he no longer looks like one after centuries of repetition of the type. His free, rich, dashing brushwork has much in common with the style of Frans Hals (who in milder ways treated similar subject matter), and there is a chance that Brouwer was Hals's pupil or assistant.

By 1631 Brouwer (then in his mid-twenties) was enrolled in the Antwerp painters' guild. Apparently under the influence of Rubens he began painting landscapes. And when he died in 1638 he was experimenting with atmospheric light and shade, possibly following the example of a young Dutch painter just his own age—Rembrandt.

Adriaen van Ostade, the son of a weaver, was born and lived all his life—seventy-five years, from 1610 to 1685—in Haarlem. Well-to-do in his own right, he married a wealthy woman in 1657 and led a not very eventful life. He must have been too busy turning out pictures to allow time for much of anything else to happen: as many as a thousand paintings have been attributed to him, most of them without question, as well as about fifty etchings and numerous drawings.

As a Haarlemite, Ostade was probably a student of Hals, perhaps at the same time as Adriaen Brouwer, whom he followed, rather than Hals, in the depiction of the peasant scenes he painted all his life. Ostade, however, was a less forceful and more gentlemanly painter than Brouwer—the word "gentlemanly" in this case representing a limitation. During his twenties he painted rather grotesque peasants carousing in picturesquely low quarters, but if their hearts were in it, his was not. He was good-natured and charming rather than rambunctious. During this period he employed a strong Rembrandtesque chiaroscuro, at first not very well integrated but later applied with some feeling for disposing figures within Rembrandtesque space.

In mid-career, Ostade settled upon a quieter mood more appropriate to his own position and sentiments as a typical prosperous, unassuming Dutchman. Although he continued to paint peasant scenes, he also portrayed his fellow citizens in an idyllically comfortable domestic world. It is an appealing if not very exciting world, and he painted it sensitively and expertly. If his elevation by some eighteenth-century collectors to a position alongside Rembrandt represented something of an inflation of his excellences, his dismissal today in a few lines in encyclopedias is an injustice. Perhaps he is too familiar as a stock figure in every museum. Judged on the basis of only his best forty or fifty pictures, he could hold a position as a rare talent.

Isaack van Ostade, Adriaen's highly gifted younger brother and pupil, now enjoys a more secure reputation than he. Born in Haarlem in 1621, Isaack died at the age of only twenty-eight in 1649. His paintings reflect a gentle spirit. At first he followed Adriaen as a painter of peasant scenes, although in a lowered key. But he came into his own as a painter of expansive landscapes crowded with figures. In his views of Holland at all times of year (the winter scenes are most admired), the inhabitants go about their business happily. Combining a pure landscapist's mastery of atmospheric effects with a genre painter's interest in anecdote, Isaack van Ostade might have become another Bruegel if he had lived and had been awakened to the possibility of revealing the grand cosmic pattern ordinarily concealed from us by our absorption in the trivia of daily life.

For about a century after his death, David Teniers the Younger was considered the greatest of the seventeenth-century genre painters, but hardly anyone today would rank him first except as the most prolific. He painted at least two thousand pictures. Most of them had genre subjects, since the demand for barracks, tavern, and village scenes was inexhaustible. Teniers was first of all a moneymaker who painted for the market, and if he had not been, at his best, so excellent a technician, he would have to be called a hack. He was not blessed with much spirit or originality: his religious subjects and portraits are undistinguished, and his genre scenes have little warmth or drollery, although Adriaen Brouwer was his model.

David the Younger, born in 1610, was the pupil of his father, David Teniers the Elder (1582-1649). Both father and son were born and died in Antwerp. The father, although a moneymaking painter and art dealer who married a rich woman to boot, was prosecuted for fraud in connection with real-estate mortgages and had to be rescued by a sale organized by David the Younger, then only nineteen, and other sons. Young Teniers learned early to paint for money. He did many copies for quick sale to ease the family's difficulties.

The father's shady manipulations apparently did not tarnish the family name. David the Younger married a daughter of Jan (Velvet) Brueghel who was a ward of Rubens, and Rubens's second wife stood as a godparent for their first son. He served as dean of the Antwerp guild, was court painter to Archduke Leopold William and curator of his picture gallery in Brussels (painting views of the gallery with the pictures reproduced in accurate minature on the walls, thus creating ideal inventories for future art historians), and worked for and visited with the royalty and nobility of Spain, England, Austria, and Sweden. He would have been given a patent of nobility by Philip IV of Spain if he had been willing to renounce the selling of pictures. Noblemen do not engage in trade.

Like his father, he ran into legal troubles. The Brussels guild, during his stay there as painter to the Archduke, denounced him for irregular practices in the sales of paintings, and there was unpleasantness with the children of his first wife after he remarried. But with a shopful of students, assistants, and copyists, including his brothers Juliaen Teniers the Younger (1616-1679) and Abraham Teniers (1629-1670), he continued to turn out paintings to satisfy a steady demand until he died in 1690 at the age of eighty. When invention failed, an old painting could always be copied. His son, David Teniers III (1638-1685), and his grandfather, Juliaen Teniers the Elder (1572-1615), are other names still met within the endless ramifications of the family.

Gerard Dou, born in 1613, was the son of a glazier and was expected to follow his father's craft. But at the age of fifteen he went to study with Rembrandt (who was then twenty-two). The association lasted three years, and because of it any discussion of Dou's art includes the reservation that he never shared Rembrandt's interest in the soul, a reservation tempered by the concession that he did learn from Rembrandt an exceptional command of light and shadow even though he was content to employ it in reproducing the appearance of things external.

Dou's accurate reproduction of the forms, colors, and textures of common objects, executed with a miniaturist's love of delicate finish, made him tremendously popular. He was one of the highest-paid artists of his day—not because his prices were set according to demand or according to any aesthetic yardstick, but because he was a slow worker who kept a careful record of the time he spent on each painting and then charged a Flemish pound for each hour spent. A perfectionist, he once told a visitor to his studio (Sandrart), who praised the execution of a broom hardly larger than a fingernail, that he would need another three days to finish this one detail.

Dou's subjects were homely, having to do with the running of a household—marketing, cooking, tending children, and, for excitement, such unusual events as the visit of the doctor. He always painted from posed and costumed models, but if he treated them somewhat like household objects, he also painted household objects with a nice perception of the part they play in life. He never left the boundaries of his native Holland, never married, and is reported by Sandrart to have had a passion for orderliness and a fear of dust in the studio that sound obsessive but are understandable in a craftsman of such meticulous purity. The suggestion of old-maidishness is not borne out by Dou's efforts to establish a painters' guild in Leiden: the project succeeded, and gave the city a first-rate school of painting.

Gerard Dou died in 1675 at the age of sixty-two.

Gerard Ter Borch was the most elegant of the Dutch genre painters. An exception in this insular school, he was an international traveler. He saw London when he was eighteen, Rome about five years later, and also visited Spain, where he did a portrait of Philip IV. In 1648, when he was thirty-one, he was in Westphalia, where he painted *The Swearing of the Oath of Ratification of the Treaty of Münster* (London, National Gallery), a rarity in Dutch painting since it commemorates a contemporary historical event. It is also a rarity in that it measures only 18 inches high by 23 inches wide, yet includes portraits of sixty standing men, the negotiators of the treaty between Holland and Spain that gave the Netherlands their independence.

Ter Borch was born in 1617 in Zwolle, and was a child prodigy. Under the tutelage of his father, Gerard Ter Borch the Elder (1584-1662), who is seldom heard of except as a parent, young Gerard was a respectable draftsman by the time he was eight. At seventeen he was in Haarlem, where he painted barracks scenes—but with a sensitive tonality, a delicacy of gradation, a harmoniously subdued palette in grays and muted tints that gave the rough subjects a contradictory refinement.

These exquisite adjustments of visual reality mark Ter Borch from the beginning as a miniature Velázquez by spontaneous inclination. And in Spain he certainly saw paintings by the master, and could even have met him at the Spanish court. Thereafter in his tiny portraits Ter Borch sometimes approximates Velázquez's revelation of character through apparently objective representation of surfaces, yet the word "miniature" persists as a distinction between the two artists in double reference to the comparative dimensions and the comparative expressive power of their pictures.

About 1650, when he was thirty-three, Ter Borch returned to Holland to stay, and not long after his return he settled in the small town of Deventer, where he lived to the age of sixty-four (he died in 1681), painting all the while, without any deterioration of his powers.

Ter Borch's pictures have a way of making you feel that each one is a superior minor effort, that elsewhere he must certainly have pushed his powers to their limits. He was content with a peculiarly conservative and unambitious life considering that he came into contact with art of great strength, invention, and variety during his European travels. But perhaps he recognized his limitations and wisely heeded them. He is always an exquisite painter, a perfect craftsman who values decorum above display, good taste above experiment or exploration. His ladies and gentlemen, dressed in velvets and satins, are disposed gracefully within their well-appointed rooms. No painter has ever reproduced the shimmer of fine stuffs against dim backgrounds more beautifully than Ter Borch, but the suspicion remains that he sacrificed his creative potential to the exercise of charming accessory skills.

Carel Fabritius, at work on a portrait, was killed when the explosion of a gunpowder magazine demolished a section of the city of Delft on October 12, 1654. He was only thirty-two years old. The same catastrophe probably destroyed enough of his work to explain its extreme rarity even considering the brevity of his life. But in spite of its rarity, the work that Carel Fabritius left behind establishes him firmly in a triple position in the history of art: his painting is inherently beautiful, he was the best of Rembrandt's pupils, and at the same time he stimulated the trend in Dutch painting away from Rembrandtesque psychological insight toward objective realism that found its highest expression in Vermeer.

Fabritius was born in 1622 in Midden-Beemster, a village about twenty miles from Amsterdam. His patronym was Pietersz; "Fabritius" refers to his first trade of carpenter, which he followed at least until 1641, when he married at the age of nineteen. Shortly after, he entered Rembrandt's studio. His father, a schoolmaster who is said to have painted on the side, had probably given him his first lessons. In 1650, at the age of twenty-eight, Fabritius moved to Delft and perished there four years later. In the catalogue of might-have-beens, he is one of the tragic names.

Rembrandt was at the height of his career when Fabritius began to work with him—probably in 1642, the year of *The Night Watch*. Carel's slightly younger brother, Barent Fabritius (1624-1673), followed him first as a carpenter and then to Rembrandt's studio, but never became anything more than a Rembrandt imitator. Carel alone among Rembrandt's pupils combined the receptivity to benefit from Rembrandt's instruction and example with a talent vigorous enough to protect him from the seductions of imitation.

Fabritius could not match Rembrandt's dramatic narrative power, nor, although under Rembrandt's influence he painted a number of sensitively perceived portraits of old men, could he plumb the human spirit as deeply as Rembrandt did. But he did not pretend to. He never made the imitator's mistake of believing that a reasonable facsimile of another painter's technical manner carries with it that painter's expressive character. He developed his own technique in modification of Rembrandt's, retaining the breadth and sensuousness of the painted surface but changing from the strong contrast of thin and heavily laden passages to a more uniform layer of rich pigment applied almost mosaic-fashion, as Vermeer was to apply his "pearls" of color.

In his mature manner, if a man cut short at the age of thirty-two can be said to have developed a mature manner, Fabritius shifted Rembrandt's golden tonality into a silvery one—a less drastic change than it sounds if we remember that Rembrandt had not yet fully developed his golden richness at the time Fabritius worked with him. And where Rembrandt was already revealing his figures in artificial illumination, making them emerge vividly into the light from murky backgrounds, Fabritius reversed the scheme and revealed his figures as darks against light, which, generally, is the way we perceive figures in natural illumination.

Natural light was his preoccupation as the reasonable illumination for the everyday subjects that increasingly interested him. One of his most charming pictures, now in London's National Gallery, is a tiny view of Delft that was probably the background for one of the illusionistic peep boxes popular at the time. He revealed here a satisfying order, logic, and clarity in the components of the visual world —and never knew that this assumption of a fundamental harmony was refuted by the violent accident that silenced him.

Biographical notes on Jan Vermeer van Delft always boil down to a frustrating question: Why is so little known about him? The lives of lesser (and less successful) artists who were his contemporaries are much better documented than his, and their personalities are reconstructible from letters and anecdotes. But the documented facts of Vermeer's life are minimal and not very relevant, and not one word that he wrote or one that he is supposed to have said has come down to us.

A part of the explanation is that until this century Vermeer was not thought of as one of the supreme masters in the history of painting. His art, like Piero della Francesca's, has taken on a peculiarly modern look in its reduction of the picture space to geometrical plan. But no further comparison with Piero can be made. Piero, as a fifteenth-century intellectual, dealt with majestic abstractions. Vermeer, as a latter-seventeenth-century Dutchman, lived in a bourgeois world that had settled down to the cozy pleasures of existence during an interval of domestic security and established prosperity, when unquestioned observance of convention guaranteed a comfortable routine of the good, respectable life. Dutch painters served this world by reflecting its everyday aspects rather than extending its boundaries by philosophical reflections.

"Little Dutchmen," a term now seldom used, was a good one for these artists, for it suggests the small size, the small subjects, and the miniature perfections of their art. Like the Little Dutchmen, Vermeer shows us quiet, close-walled, low-ceilinged rooms, inhabited by people whose rich clothes almost make still-life subjects of them, like the jugs and baskets and food on the laden tables, or the velvety rugs that satisfied the bourgeois heart as objects of handsome domestic display. Vermeer's ladies play the virginal while gentlemen listen; a maid hands a letter to her mistress; a woman reads a letter at an open window; a girl works at her lacemaking; another dozes at the table in a comfortable house. We can examine the pictures and read the maps that hang on the walls. The furniture is described in detail. All of this is the Little Dutch world.

Occasionally it is possible to discover in Vermeer a secondary reference. In one picture (Washington, National Gallery) we see a woman standing at a table weighing gold on a tiny scale while the light spreads into the picture from Vermeer's typical source, a window at our left. Behind the woman a picture on the wall frames her head; it is a Last Judgment, and perhaps there is a connection: preoccupied with material things, the gold, the woman forgets that one day she will be weighed in a spiritual balance. Or the young girl asleep at the table, in the painting in the Metropolitan Museum, has been drinking wine, we discover. Are we being warned, in a way so quiet as to be almost inaudible, against the evils of drink in the kind of picture that, traditionally, would have dramatized the subject?

But if Vermeer was making any such concessions to moralistic reference, they are vestigial. His art, for all the literalness of its surface, is essentially an art without topical, explanatory, illustrative, or narrative context. It is an art that offers us serenity, purity, and calm as formal values rather than as concomitants to subject matter. As solutions to an aesthetic problem, his pictures are superb combinations of forms impeccably unified in limited space and revealed by a gentle and logical fall of natural light. The actual physical character of the paint is part of an indissoluble whole. Grain by grain, the paint seems to catch the light even while describing it.

The little that we know of Vermeer's life is neither appropriate nor antithetical to his art: there is simply no connection. But here is what we know.

Vermeer was born in 1632 in Delft. His father, a weaver and innkeeper, possibly did a bit of art dealing on the side. After his father's death, Vermeer continued to operate the tavern and became an art dealer and appraiser. When he was twenty-one, in 1653, he married a Catholic. Whether or not he became converted is unknown. In that same year he entered the guild, and although his wife came from a well-to-do family it took him three years to pay off his entrance fee of five guilders. He was surely respected in his profession, since he was twice dean of the guild—in 1663 and 1670. He died in 1675, aged forty-three.

A few months after his death, his widow filed a petition for bankruptcy. She had eleven children, eight of them under age. But already the questions begin: with three children old enough to work, and with money in the widow's family, why was there a baker's bill of 617 guilders—possibly the all-time record for a baker's bill accumulated by a family. Vermeer had given the baker two paintings as security, which was fair enough since his paintings sold for about three hundred guilders each. The widow petitioned for the return of the pictures, offering to pay the debt over a period of twelve years. There are records of various large and small loans made to Vermeer during his lifetime, including a very large one of a thousand guilders just before his death. His widow explained to the court that during his last years Vermeer had not made much money and that his speculations as an art dealer had miscarried.

Fewer than forty paintings are accepted today as Vermeer's, a very small production unless a great many have been lost. By conjecture he was a slow worker and could not complete enough pictures to support his family in spite of the good prices his pictures brought. His wife died in 1688 (and received an expensive funeral), and in 1696, twenty-one years after his death, twenty-one of his paintings, including the majority of the best ones now accepted as his, were auctioned off by an anonymous collector. Thereafter his name was gradually forgotten. He re-emerged after the middle of the nineteenth century as one of the Little Dutchmen, and in the twentieth century was discovered, for the first time, as one of the greatest masters.

Where did Vermeer come from, as an artist? Carel Fabritius has been called his teacher, and could have been, since he came to Delft when Vermeer was eighteen, dying there four years later. And certainly at this time Fabritius was anticipating in his work the technique that Vermeer perfected. When Vermeer died, his estate included two paintings by Fabritius—but were they pictures he treasured, or only part of his stock, purchased for resale?

Pieter de Hooch alone among seventeenth-century Dutch painters of domestic genre scenes approached the genius of Vermeer, and then only briefly. From 1654, or just possibly a bit earlier, until about 1662, he worked in Delft where, then in his late twenties and early thirties, he produced his masterworks. It seems impossible that during those years in Delft he did not have contact with Vermeer, but like virtually everything in the historical record of that master, this relationship is a blank. A discernible influence on De Hooch as on Vermeer is the work of Carel Fabritius, killed in the Delft explosion of 1654 at about the time Pieter de Hooch came to the city.

De Hooch was born in Rotterdam in 1629. His early

work is not particularly distinguished. He painted scenes in barracks, stables, taverns, and other places where soldiers shared their lives with shady characters. He rendered the scenes fluently enough but with a technical coarseness that contrasts with the refinement he developed in Delft.

In 1654, when he was twenty-five, De Hooch married a girl from Delft and the next year entered the guild there. He was recorded as the servant and personal painter of a burgher named Justus de la Grange, who owned ten of his pictures. The piquantly unprincely combination of servant and artist suggests that De Hooch was a man of modest social position. Combined with his exceptional endowments as an artist, his experience of simple busy lives should partially explain the great tenderness and naturalness of his finest paintings, done during this period. His subjects were housewives or servants going about their housekeeping chores, usually accompanied by children. Totally devoid of sentimentality, these scenes of honest domestic felicity at the simplest level are filled with sunny light, warm and rather strong in comparison with Vermeer's. De Hooch was a true master of spatial construction and enjoyed its complications (where Vermeer dealt in its subtleties). He was fond of revealing successive vistas of rooms seen through open doors, sometimes from the small brick-paved back courtyard of the Dutch house, or its immaculate little garden. The illusionistic recessions from room to room, rendered in sharply geometric perspective, are remindful of the peep boxes that were so popular at the time—a form of gadgetry raised by some of its practitioners, among them Fabritius, to the level of a fine art.

Sometime after 1662, De Hooch moved to Amsterdam, the safe presumption being that he wanted to take advantage of greater opportunities in the capital. Over a period of about twenty years he seems to have been successful enough, but he became again the second-rate artist he had been before he settled in Delft. Or not quite the same. Abandoning scenes of low life, he now devoted himself to the *haut monde,* painting ladies and gentlemen in lavish costumes in formal interiors—reflections of the grandiose French mode that made its own premilitary invasion of Holland. In this world De Hooch was not at home.

His last dated picture, in 1684, shows that he was alive at the age of fifty-five, but the exact year of his death is not known.

In the fifty-odd years of his life that lasted from 1626 to 1679, Jan Steen painted between seven and eight hundred pictures, including some portraits, a few landscapes, sixty or so religious pictures remarkable for their jollity, and a great mass of genre subjects from peasant and middle-class life, most of them humorous. He is dearly beloved in Holland, where his sometimes rather heavy bumptiousness is regarded as an engaging aspect of the Dutch character with its stays loosened.

Steen's father was a brewer, which is appropriate since a rich, beery flavor runs through so much of Jan's painting. In 1654, when he was in his late twenties, Steen himself leased a brewery in Delft, one of the several cities where he lived and worked between returns to his native city, Leiden. A restless and energetic man, he was not much affected by the luminous sobriety of the art of Delft's two great painters, Vermeer and Pieter de Hooch. He was closer in spirit to Hals, although not to Hals at his greatest, and it was in old Hals's Haarlem that Steen became a member of the guild in 1661. He lived there until 1670, when, at forty-four, he returned to Leiden to stay. Two years later he leased a brewery and tavern there, which he operated, all the while painting at full speed, for the remaining seven years of his life until his death at the age of fifty-three.

Steen attended the University of Leiden as a youth but was not an assiduous scholar. He was more interested in the bohemian world of the theater, and was in contact with theatrical people all his life. His pictures are easily translatable into stage scenes, and he enjoyed putting himself on stage in self-portraits, variously assuming the roles of wastrel, solid citizen, innocent bumpkin, and roué. Portraits of members of his family, over three generations, have also been identified among his casts of characters.

As a narrator, Steen was always a cheerful observer of Dutch life, even when adopting a moralizing tone or, like his contemporary Molière, satirizing doctors or lawyers. As a painter, he was wildly uneven. When he cared to, he painted with the nicety of the other Dutch genre masters, but he could also let himself go with work of the sloppiest kind. He had a way of slipping in and out of other men's styles—Brouwer's, Dou's, Adriaen van Ostade's, and, in landscapes, that of his father-in-law, Van Goyen. The lapses were neither those of the plagiarizer nor those of a student; they were natural to Steen's easygoing, adaptable, and generally bubbling nature. For he was completely consistent in his high spirits, almost monotonously so—to the point of treating even his religious subjects as folksy genre. He often found his subjects in proverbs, as did Bruegel, but he never brought his pictures much above the level of humorous illustration. Perhaps it is enough that his art, like good beer, maintained a good head of foam.

Jan van Goyen, a most respectable artist, led the generation of Dutch landscapists who produced sober, realistic, and affectionate portraits of the land (many of the spots still recognizable from the paintings). A generation later, Jacob van Ruisdael transposed the factual records of local topography to a new romantic key, and by contrast the quiet, firm professionalism of painters like Van Goyen seems limited expressively. But his moisture-laden skies, serene above low horizons, are consistently admirable.

Van Goyen, who was born in 1596, settled in The Hague when he was nearing forty, and was apparently prosperous, since a family portrait by his son-in-law, the roistering Jan Steen, shows him rather fashionably set up. He was certainly very productive during the sixty years of his life: twelve hundred paintings are accepted as his. But like other Dutch artists of the time, he seems to have been unable to live as he wished from the money he made by painting, and carried on a business in real estate and tulips. He died in 1656.

Jacob van Ruisdael was the greatest Dutch landscape painter and, by classification within any group, time, or place, an artist of great originality. Ahead of schedule by a century and a half, he saw nature as the nineteenth-century romantics were to see it, as the everyday manifestation of sublime forces. Like most romantics, he was more interestingly stimulated by nature's moods of melancholy, gloom, and violence than by those spells when the sublime manifests itself in more friendly fashion. Other protoromantics were animated by the same feeling; Salvator Rosa, in Italy, was Ruisdael's contemporary. But where Rosa and the other romantic precursors dealt with ideal or imaginary landscapes, Ruisdael dealt with the world at hand, and thus shifted the romantic locale from the fictional world of banditti, exotic places, and weird characters to the world we live in, establishing a precedent for the romantic attitude as a way of life and thought.

Ruisdael's seashores are sometimes gentle enough to accommodate strollers, and he can show a stretch of quiet countryside beneath benign skies, his native Haarlem in the distance. But it was in tumultuous scenes that he came to fullest power—scenes where fitful light plays on dashing waters tumbling through rough terrain, with trees rising from dark undergrowth that threatens or consumes the works of man—the ruined castles, abbeys, and monuments that later became romantic clichés. In true romantic fashion, Ruisdael saw man as transient and nature as eternal. Human beings are never really at home in his pictures, even when nature is resting between storms. The figures in his landscapes look exactly like what, in literal fact, they are—additions made as a concession to demands outside the picture's conception. Pure landscape was not always easy to sell, and Ruisdael employed other painters to add occasional figures, like visitors tolerated but not really at home in his world.

Ruisdael was born in Haarlem about 1629, the son of a framemaker and painter of negligible importance named Isaack van Ruysdael. "Ruysdael" is the spelling used by all members of the family except our great one. This is fortunate since he had a cousin of the same name, whose work is very similar to his. The cousin Jacob van Ruysdael with a *y* died a pauper in Haarlem, a circumstance that until recently was accepted as part of the biography of Jacob van Ruisdael with an *i*. Jacob with a *y* was the son of Salomon van Ruysdael (*c*. 1602-1670), an expert and respected landscapist but primarily a topographical one. This uncle of the great Ruisdael was his teacher after the young man's first lessons under his less distinguished father.

In 1648, still in his precocious teens, Ruisdael was admitted to the Haarlem painters' guild, but about 1655, around the age of twenty-six, he settled in Amsterdam, where eventually he died a bachelor at the age of about fifty-three in 1682. He was tremendously prolific. Something like a thousand of his pictures are scattered around the museums of the world. But he did not sell for high prices, and eked out a living by adopting a second profession. He received a medical degree at Caen, and practiced as a barber-physician, in the combination peculiar to his century made odder still by the association with painting.

Ruisdael's key painting is *The Cemetery,* usually called *The Jewish Cemetery,* which exists in two versions, one in Dresden and one in the Detroit Institute of Arts. The tombs in both pictures are identifiable as those from a Jewish graveyard known to Ruisdael, but the landscape is synthesized; in the Detroit picture a hopeful rainbow, absent in the Dresden version, cheers the sinister gloom. Commenting on man as a feeble creature doomed to oblivion, Ruisdael signed the picture by putting his name on one of the tombs. But he was wrong about our transience, at least in his case, for this painting alone might have secured his immortality.

Ruisdael's trees deserve a special comment. Frequently blasted or misshapen, they are nevertheless always recognizable as trees of a particular genus, rather than as a generalized form, "tree," such as most painters employed at that time. His observation of trees as individuals extends from a study of their characteristic growth to an interest in whatever variations chance has imposed on the pattern. The individuality, the vivid personalities, of his trees may explain the air of redundancy that human beings take on in his pictures.

In contrast with most of his fellow Dutch landscapists, Meindert Hobbema painted relatively few pictures during his lifetime of seventy-one years—two hundred or two hundred and fifty as against the thousand or so of his friend and teacher, Jacob van Ruisdael. Hobbema's early pictures follow

Ruisdael's so closely that in some cases the authorship is in question. But he never shared Ruisdael's romantic spirit, and in his typical work painted the most peaceful of country roads and countrysides dotted with mills and farmhouses.

Born in 1638, Hobbema was signing and dating pictures by the time he was twenty, but his work was not much in demand, and after ten years of producing for a poor market he found a better way to earn a living. In 1668 he married a woman who was cook for a burgomaster of Amsterdam (where Hobbema was born and died), and through a friend of his wife's, a maid in the household, he obtained a post as Sealer of Weights and Measures, his duties consisting of checking the casks of imported wines and translating their measures into local terms. For a period of some years he paid an annual fee of two hundred florins to the woman who had successfully exerted her unexplained backstairs influence.

After this appointment Hobbema painted less and less, but perhaps better and better, since his masterpiece, *Avenue at Middelharnais,* or *Avenue of Trees* (London, National Gallery), showing a tree-lined country road cutting directly back into the deep space of the picture, was painted in 1689, when he was just past fifty. He lived another twenty years, and was listed as a pauper when he died in 1709. The gentle and intimate quality of his landscapes had to wait for full appreciation until it was discovered in England, where in the eighteenth and nineteenth centuries it appealed to the rustic-idyllic inclination of romantic taste in that country. And *Avenue at Middelharnais* remains probably the most widely reproduced single pure landscape in both England and America, even though few people who see it on calendars and in inexpensive frames would recognize the name of the painter.

Considering the range and solidity of his talent, Aelbert Cuyp must have been the quietest, the least ambitious, painter who ever lived. At a time when his fellow artists staked out their claims as specialists in limited fields, Cuyp painted landscape, still life, portraits, religious, mythological, and architectural subjects, and animals, and painted all of them well, or better than well. Yet for all his versatility he was content to pass his life in Dordrecht, the town where he was born in 1620 and where his father, Jacob Gerritsz Cuyp (1594-*after* 1651), a minor painter, taught him his craft. He might almost as well have been painting in Cambodia for all the influence he exerted, but apparently he did not care. He married a woman with a comfortable income of her own, and, from time to time, being a good citizen, he held public office. He finally died in 1691—comfortably, one imagines— at the age of seventy-one.

If this immensely talented man was never quite a great painter, it was because he lacked (or stifled) the artist's exploratory urge. But he was masterly in his painting of the spreading, moisture-softened light of the Low Countries, and he represented it so ideally that he is often compared with Claude Lorrain, who evolved a similar light less from having observed it than from having dreamed it. Cuyp was one of several Dutch landscapists (including Hobbema) who so entranced English collectors in the next century that they helped determine the course of English painting.

A half-mysterious figure among Dutch artists, Hercules Seghers, or Herkeles Segers (b. 1589/90, d. 1638 or earlier), was a painter whose vision ran, eccentrically for the time, to grand and epical invention of vast, rocky landscapes rather than to interpretations of the benign local scene. Did he make a trip to Italy, and thus see the Alps? If so, did he know his poetic fellow landscapist, the German expatriate Adam Elsheimer, there? Rembrandt owned a number of Seghers landscapes, and his own reflect their influence.

Seghers was perhaps born in Haarlem, and worked there and in Amsterdam. He is an important figure in the history of etching. In this medium he was prolific and daringly inventive. There are stories about his dissolute life, about his bitterness over financial troubles that cost him his house in Amsterdam (these troubles attributed to unsuccessful speculations as a picture dealer, and also to the amount of money he spent on presses and materials in his etching experiments), and finally about his dying as the result of a fall down a flight of stairs when drunk. All of this sounds like invention inspired by the wild, romantic mood of his pictures; none of it can be substantiated by plain, factual record.

Although he worked in the first half of the eighteenth century, Jan van Huysum (1682-1749) can be considered at this point because he continued a seventeenth-century tradition. The son of another flower painter, Justus van Huysum (1659-1716), Jan outshone his father in their specialty. During the seventeenth century coveys of Dutch and Flemish specialists were bred who, as we have seen in the case of Snyders, the animal painter, would execute passages for other artists (as Snyders did for Rubens) in addition to producing works entirely their own.

Jan van Huysum's flower pieces were in such demand, not only in his native Holland but internationally (they still are), and his prices were so high, that he had no need to engage in collaborative projects. In painting after painting after painting, he arranged and rearranged bouquets of garden flowers, making each petal, stamen, vein, or tiniest tendril at once a botanical specimen, a superbly decorative bit of shape and color, and a staggering demonstration of his craft. The technical miracle of his paintings is that, in spite of their extreme complexity of detail, they are organized so expertly that they hang together naturally. At first glance each composition is complete, an individual unit, and delightful. But the greatest pleasure these bouquets offer is that of exploration. The artist intended them to be examined at close range and attentively. Studied in this way, a pretty bunch of flowers is like a map that yields inexhaustible new details of a terrain that one had thought familiar. The pleasures offered are almost entirely visual, although a slight frosting of semiphilosophical or moralistic comment may be added in instances where the symbolism of flowers has been observed or, in one instance in the Rijksmuseum, where the vase holding the flowers is inscribed with the biblical exhortation to consider the lilies of the field.

There were so many expert specialists in various branches of still-life painting that the selection of Jan van Huysum to represent them all is somewhat arbitrary. Two other names, among dozens, must be mentioned: Willem Kalf (1619-1693), who painted sumptuous objects with a control of tonalities that rivaled Vermeer's, and Pieter Claesz (1597-1661), whose deceptively casual arrangements of dishes, glassware, and fruit, objects of everyday use, are in a tradition that continued directly through Chardin to Cézanne.

The statement, perfectly true, that Pieter Jansz. Saenredam (1597-1665) devoted his life to depicting with factual accuracy the interiors and exteriors of Dutch churches, makes him sound like what most of his contemporaries in this field actually were—not so much artists as visual recording machines. But he was no machine: there is no more kinship between his paintings and the usual dry architectural study than there is between a fine portrait and a passport photograph.

Saenredam was a systematic craftsman and a veracious reporter, and in both capacities he served his genius as a poet. With Euclidian beauty the vaults, arches, pillars, walls, and floors of his churches are clarified in gradations of pure, blond light. Everything is perfectly logical but nothing is matter-of-fact. Even passages that by definition are uneventful—flat, bare stone or plaster walls—he reveals as fields of perfected textural harmonies.

The knowledge that Saenredam was a hunchback and a recluse adds a poignance to our response to his pure, reserved style. A more valid reason for the great esteem in which this century holds him, however, is that this same purity and reserve, and the geometrical emphasis inherent in his subject matter, ally him to schools of modern painting that strive to attain his special kind of poetry through totally abstract means.

14

CLASSICAL IDEALISM AND DESPOTISM

Philosophers after 1700 won for the eighteenth century the appelation "The Age of Reason." It is a title that might well have been pre-empted by the seventeenth century on the basis of the works of its painters. Even when seventeenth-century painting seems most riotous, as in Rubens and some of the Roman decorators, the flamboyance is a product of calculation, just as the most imaginative and apparently volatile architecture of the century, with forms curling and twisting through exploding space, is as much a mathematical as an aesthetic expression. Thus there is less difference than there appears to be between artists like Rubens and those of the classical school, like Poussin, who seem to be his antithesis. (For decades after the two artists died, the French Academy was divided into warring camps, the Rubenists and the Poussinists.)

The French painters, even when, like Poussin, they

worked in Italy, were given to a classical sobriety paralleled in seventeenth-century French architecture. The century also saw the maturation, in France, of a pernicious idea that grew out of a misunderstanding of classical principles. Classicism assumes that the ideal can be defined and obeys certain rules. The classicists, from believing that laws can be devised for the discipline of the creative spirit (which is true), became hardened in the conviction that they can be made absolutely specific and must not be questioned (which is false). This standard led to the creation of the official academies all over Europe, where such laws were formulated and enforced. The French Academy was the model for them, and Charles Lebrun was the archetype of the academician in France, where the breed was to thrive most vigorously and most viciously.

Artists associated with the classical ideals are grouped in this chapter. Also included are the Le Nain brothers, largely because they were contemporaries who do not quite fit in anywhere else.

Nicolas Poussin was born in 1594 in the hamlet of Villers in Normandy. With parents who were probably farmers, he was one of those children whose interest in drawing, and talent for it, and determination to do something with it, are unexplainable. He perhaps served a brief, abortive apprenticeship in Rouen. Near home, he observed and perhaps assisted an obscure painter named Quentin Varin, who worked for six months on decorations for a church near Villers. The experience must have crystallized a determination to escape his surroundings and to become a painter in earnest. He ran away from home (he was sixteen) and walked to Paris.

He was disappointed there. He apprenticed himself to one painter for a month, left, and apprenticed himself to another for three months. He knew he had not found what he was looking for, although exactly what he was looking for he did not know. He found out what it was through a chance acquaintance, Alexandre Courtois, a custodian of the royal collections, who gave him access to the drawings and engravings. He discovered Raphael and Michelangelo, and from then on, if we do not call Poussin self-taught, Raphael was his teacher by example.

By another chance he was given an opportunity to do some decorations for a château in Poitou. Something went wrong. He was badly treated, escaped, and again walked to Paris. Ill and exhausted, he seems to have appealed to his parents, who took back the prodigal. But after a year he left again, this time for good, and nothing indicates that he ever felt anything but relief at getting away.

Things went better in Paris this time, with commissions for decorations, but for Poussin nothing would be of any account until he reached Rome. Raphael and antiquity were his passion. He made abortive starts on the journey, always running out of money, but finally in 1624, when he was thirty, he got there. He had reached his spiritual home, and he had also reached a city where his classical passion could be understood.

We think of France as a country where the classical tradition is venerated and hence of Poussin as a natural product of its atmosphere, but the straight of it is that it was Poussin who, from Italy, established that tradition. He never returned to France except for a period of two years when, famous, he was called back by Louis XIII. It required a great deal of calling on the part of the King before Poussin, in 1640, reluctantly obeyed. He was given much honor, was paid much money, and was awarded the major plum of decorating the Grande Galerie in the Louvre. He hated every minute of the job. Easel paintings rather than grand projects were his forte; he wrote a friend in Rome that if he stayed in France much longer he would become a hack like the hacks who assisted him. The hacks also set up intrigues. He was miserable. He finally left on some pretext, promising to return; the King's death conveniently relieved him of that promise, and he never left Rome again. Foresightedly, his wife had stayed behind to keep his considerable establishment in order. He had married her in 1630, when he was thirty-six. She was the daughter of a French chef, and with her dowry they had purchased a house on the Pincian hill.

The early years of Poussin's life have some interest as the period of his developing classical passion and his first efforts to satisfy it. The return to France has some interest with its picture of an unusual type, the completely alienated Frenchman. But the Roman years, from his arrival in 1624 until his death forty-one years later in 1665, are the years that count, and their story is a dull one. What happened is known in detail. The story should be foolproof: poverty, struggle, success. The background could hardly be improved on. The protagonist is impressive: the first French artist to achieve international fame, the one who set French art on the course of international dominance that lasted into our century, the greatest classical painter since Raphael and the one who, with Raphael, has stood as the model of classical perfection ever since.

But there is no point in recounting the story of those years, for it reveals none of those interplays between the artist as creator and the artist as a man living in the world that can be so illuminating in the lives of other artists. And this is a tribute to the fullness of Poussin's achievement of the ends he set himself as a painter. It is true that there was a man named Nicolas Poussin who was alive and working during certain years, but this man has little to do with Nicolas Poussin the Immortal, who is an intellect crystallized in an art of supreme detachment and calculated impersonality.

This impersonality extends even to the self-portraits. Turn away from them and you discover that you do not know how the man looked, although he recorded his features without compromise. What you remember is the steadiness of the whole, the analytical intensity of the gaze in eyes whose shape or color you could not describe.

Poussin was an artist who denied any virtue in spontaneity, who believed (and as far as his own art is concerned, proved) that a work of art can be produced by rational plan. He set about to create a world complete within each frame. "Classical," a term of multiple definitions and side definitions, can mean for some artists a reduction of form to harmonious simplicities. For Poussin the ideal was a coherent union of every detail in a transformation of disorderly nature (whether "nature" meant landscape or human passion) into a disciplined harmony where the complexities are not eliminated, but are resolved into a whole by logical, interdependent relationships. A Poussin landscape is not a paean to the natural beauty of hills, clouds, streams, ponds, paths, and bushes, but a declaration of man's intellectual authority that brings meaning out of chaos. He measures the human spirit not by the degree of its sensitivity to a vague thing called beauty, but by its ability to extract a kind of moral energy from a world that is meaningless without it.

A disciplined, analytical art such as Poussin's, an art that proscribes impulse, is readily associated with formulas and rules. Poussin himself was much given to theorizing. His observations and prescriptions, culled from his letters and other sources, form a kind of treatise on painting. Taken separately, many of his statements are lucid enough, but the doctrine as a whole seems to suffer from the very confusions and contradictions that he resolved in his paintings. Nonetheless, his ideas were much admired by the next generation, which mistook him for an advocate of creation by rule, and he joined Raphael as a god in the academies. Two hundred years later, when Cézanne said that he wanted to "do Poussin over again after nature," he was acknowledging Poussin's powers of organization but was probably affected by the chilliness and dryness that seem present in Poussin when he is identified with his academic imitators.

But Poussin is neither chilly nor dry, and he cannot be reduced to a formula. His most quoted single statement about art is that its purpose is "delectation." Delectation as an aesthetic experience may take many forms, none of them altogether intellectual. Poussin certainly did not mean merely the enjoyment of pretty colors and graceful shapes. Nonetheless the key to his art remains "delectation"—the pure delight in a visual creation that has no useful purpose, the enjoyment of its abstract beauties and of the associations it may stir.

Any art so filled with gods, with ancient temples, with references to Arcadia, to legend, to the half-dreamt world of the classical Elysium, cannot be entirely rational. Discipline makes poetry of what otherwise might be mawkish absurdity, and Poussin is as poetic as he is analytical. He is a great artist not because he formulated certain disciplines but because he used them as the painterly equivalent of meter in poetry. His art is often interpreted as proof of the aesthetic value of pure discipline, but as we all know, a sonnet may be metrically perfect and appalling in every other way. Poussin was a poet; his art is the intellectual distillation of a nostalgic dream, and if he proved the importance of meter, he also proved that no art can be of any account if it is not ultimately the projection of a vision born within the artist. And if Poussin presents the dream with calculated impersonality, it becomes for that reason all the more convincing: he shows it to us as a universal and undeniable truth.

Gaspard Poussin, who was born (1615), lived, and died (1675) in Rome, must be mentioned here to be certain that he is not confused with his brother-in-law, Nicolas Poussin. Gaspard adopted the surname; his real name was Dughet. A perfectly respectable painter, he was successful enough during his century, but his reputation reached its high point during the eighteenth, when he and Claude Lorrain and Salvator Rosa were thought of as the best of the Roman landscapists. He maintained this position with the romantics of the nineteenth century, but since then his reputation has declined. He is a pleasant but not very original painter whose work would not be greatly missed if wiped out. The way of contemporary aesthetics that has deified the intellectualism of Nicolas Poussin (an aspect of his art that for two hundred years remained largely invisible to connoisseurs) has correspondingly reduced our interest in Gaspard, perhaps exaggeratedly because the great name he shares immediately suggests comparisons. This may be an injustice, but at the moment does not seem to be one.

Claude Gellée, renamed Lorrain after his birthplace in France, and often referred to simply as Claude, deserves as much as any artist the title of father of European landscape painting. And if the title is in dispute, he can still claim more direct descendants in the field than any other painter. The classical perfections of his contemporary Nicolas Poussin were too rigorous to inspire hosts of followers, and Poussin's landscapes, in any case, were essentially intellectual abstractions rather than paeans to idyllic nature, as Claude's were. Poussin is the epic poet of the classical landscape tradition, and epics do not birth easily. Claude is its lyric poet, and lyrics are easy to write, and paint, whether or not they turn out well.

Claude learned that poetry in landscape can be created from light and atmosphere, and his example not only inspired innumerable followers among his contemporaries (including many downright forgers), but spawned an uninterrupted stream of painters from every land who made the Italian journey during the eighteenth century. The nineteenth-century landscapists from Corot to the impressionists are his lineal descendants. His influence on the impressionists was transmitted along several different paths that eventually converged. One of the transmitters was the Englishman John Constable, who revered Claude and, as a kind of aesthetic grandson to the master, brought Claude's imaginary landscapes down to earth by showing that light and atmosphere could poeticize even the most ordinary scenes.

Claude was a bizarre character, bizarre in reverse because he remained simple and innocent in intimate contact with a corrupt and licentious society. He is probably the only artist whose first training was as a pastry cook. He could hardly read or write either his native language, French, or that of his adopted country, Italy, where he lived for more than fifty years, getting by on a mixture of bad French and worse Italian while growing prosperous and famous. A practical man of affairs in the management of his production, a poet in its creation, a fine technician who was virtually self-trained, he was that paradox, a soul utterly without guile who not only survived but flourished in rapacious company. He never married, and the gossipmongering city in which he was conspicuous has left no tattle about peccadilloes. If he indulged in amorous activities of any kind, the impression is that he must have done so absentmindedly.

Claude Gellée was born in 1600 in the village of Chamagne in Lorraine. During his boyhood he received his negligible bit of schooling, served his apprenticeship as a pastry cook, and picked up some knowledge of drawing, limited to

ornamental motifs. Both his parents died before he was
twelve, and perhaps at the age of thirteen, certainly before
he was twenty, he went to Rome rather meagerly equipped
to cope with the hazards of the world's most outrageously
civilized metropolis. He traveled with a relative, a lace dealer,
who was making the trip on business. There is much uncertainty as to exactly how he spent his first years. A stay in
Naples seems to have interrupted his early activity in Rome.
His first important master was the Roman artist Agostino
Tassi, a jailbird, rapist, sodomite, general rogue and lecher,
and an accused although not convicted murderer.

In his early twenties Claude assisted Tassi in the execution of decorative commissions and is also said to have managed his household, a formidable assignment considering
what must have gone on there. In 1625, when Claude was
twenty-five, he left Tassi's studio and probably returned to
Lorraine via Venice and the Tyrol to work for a while as
assistant on the architectural decorations (now destroyed) of
the Carmelite church in Nancy. But two years later he was
back in Rome, and except for minor absences he remained
there until he died. The Italians, who liked to nickname
their artists, called him Claudio di Lorena or Il Lorenese,
whence his usual appellation Lorrain. Apparently never sure
of his spelling even when it was a question of his own name,
and hesitating between his two nationalities, he signed his
work variously Claud, Claude, Claudio, Gellée, Gelée, or
Gille, singly or in various combinations of his given name
and his surname.

By the time he entered his thirties, Claude had established a secure position in Rome as a good workman in the
field of pictorial and architectural decoration, often in fresco.
But on the side he had begun painting, drawing, and etching
landscapes (also an occasional mythological subject). By the
time he was thirty-five these had become so popular that they

were being enthusiastically forged. In his direct, practical way he countered this inroad on his reputation, and on his income, by beginning his famous "Liber Veritatis," or "Book of Truth," which had nothing to do with the philosophy of good and evil but was a detailed record, in the form of accurate sketches, of all his paintings, plus the names of purchasers. The book, with 195 drawings, is now at Chatsworth.

Claude was famous in Rome for his simple ways and his retiring disposition, but he was approachable by any young artist who wanted advice. As the most famous landscape painter in the art capital of the world, he had constant visitors and numerous acquaintances, but no close friends. He received commissions from the Pope and the King of Spain, among other dignitaries and collectors. His reputation became international during his lifetime, increased further during the eighteenth century, which made a demigod of him, and continued to flourish past the middle of the nineteenth. If it has decreased in the twentieth, it is because appreciation of the informality of impressionism at one pole and the cult of formality at the other—to which Nicolas Poussin owes his current re-emergence as a towering figure—have made his work fall somewhere in between; Claude offers us neither the intimate freshness of Pissarro and Monet nor the ascetic majesty of Poussin. Poussin, however, was Claude's respectful friend and admirer during the many years they shared as expatriates in Rome.

Claude's work is divisible into several periods representing a progressive departure from the definition of form in directed light to the dissolution of landscape in a diaphanous universe where light, atmosphere, and form are indivisible— a statement that would need very little modification to apply to either Turner or Monet. The classical references that tie him to Poussin become in his late work the feeblest of threads. Architecture, conspicuous in his early work, diminishes to an incidental ruin here, an accessory temple there. The nymphs or shepherds or other figures from pastoral mythology who disport themselves in these landscapes of enchanted repose are afterthoughts. As a classicist, Claude is most closely akin to a school of painters whose work he could not possibly have seen, the bucolic idyllists now known in a handful of Hellenistic fragments. The oddity of his character, his apparent lack of significant contact with a society in which he nevertheless succeeded as a kind of natural phenomenon not subject to its rules, finds its parallel in his art, which is more easily thought of in the context of sensibilities peculiar to past and future centuries than it is in the context of his own.

Claude died in 1682 at the age of eighty-two. For forty years he had been able to sell everything he painted, throughout Europe, and he must be, as a result, as widely represented in museums as any painter who ever lived. Among his heirs was an eleven-year-old girl whom the old man had adopted as a daughter.

Charles Lebrun is more easily thought of as an institution than as a painter. Although he was an acceptable artist in most ways and a prodigious one in some, his greatest talent was for intrigue, and if he had genius, it was for organization. In the twentieth century he would have worked his way up from office boy to the presidency of a large corporation. In the seventeenth he attained a comparable position as decorator to Louis XIV (whose palace at Versailles, in its building, its decoration, and its operation, amounted to a national industry) and as head of the Academy, which promoted and enforced a regimen for French art.

Even when we try to think of Lebrun as an artist only, he still remains first of all an organizer. He put pictures together as systematically as if he were designing a machine, and he could put a whole series of them together—like the thirty he painted for the ceiling of the Galerie des Glaces at Versailles—in a way so unified that they ceased to exist as anything but parts of a scheme. Which is just as well, since individually Lebrun's pictures are seldom very rewarding.

Lebrun was born in 1619, one of a family of artists. His father was a sculptor, his older brother Nicolas a painter, and his younger brother, Gabriel, a painter and engraver. By the time he was nineteen, Charles Lebrun had received the title of Painter to the King, which was given to artists whose demonstrated talent promised them a career under patronage. Skipping, as a little tiresome, the stages of Lebrun's rise to power (he was the kind of man who always knows when to make a friend, when to drop one, and just when it is safe to discredit a superior by bypassing him and taking a problem to the man one stage higher in the chain of command), we may meet him first in 1662, at the age of forty-three, when he was put in charge of the King's Gobelins manufactory.

Although we think of this institution first in terms of tapestries, the Gobelins as operated under Louis XIV supplied all furnishings for the palaces. As the Manufacture Royale des Meubles de la Couronne, it produced everything from bric-a-brac and furniture on up. Lebrun had entire control; he made all appointments to its staff—a corps of artists aided by battalions of workmen—and supervised all design when he did not actually do the designs himself. He was a master decorator-designer, and (everyone admits) created virtually singlehandedly the Louis XIV style, probably the most unified, if not always the most attractive, of all historical styles. This uniformity still shows in Versailles in spite of all the losses and modifications that have occurred, and is wonderfully if oppressively a testimony to the rigid protocol that governed French life under Louis XIV.

Painter, interior architect, garden architect, designer of sculpture, fireworks, fetes, and fountains, Lebrun has had few equals in the arts as a versatile performer, and perhaps he has never had a rival in the efficiency with which he applied these talents. As dictator of the Academy he holds an incomparable, if not altogether admirable, position in the history of art.

The Académie Royale de Peinture et de Sculpture (which later ceased to be "Royale" but for two centuries controlled French art) was founded in 1648 for the avowed and admirable purpose of perpetuating the best traditions of art through teaching and patronage. But Louis XIV's minister of finance, Colbert, made no distinction between this ideal and the opportunity to use the Academy as a propaganda machine for the regime. Membership in the Academy became a matter of professional life and death for artists, and their eagerness to win favor by adopting the approved style naturally paralyzed rather than stimulated creative imaginations. Lebrun was a favorite of Colbert's in the welter of intrigue at court, and from the first he and Colbert together ruled the institution. In 1668 Lebrun was appointed life chancellor of the Academy and in 1683 its director, which in effect he had been from the beginning.

Lebrun was sixty-four when he reached this high point of his career. But Colbert died the same year, and his successor, Louvois, was a partisan of Lebrun's only serious competitor, the painter Pierre Mignard. For the first time in his life, Lebrun was out-intrigued. He withdrew—titles intact, but influence gone—in time to save face with the announcement that the times had changed, that a new era of religious faith had been born, and that he was retiring to cultivate his soul. And indeed, with the ascendancy of the pious Mme de Maintenon over the old king, the times had changed at court. But if Lebrun had expected his new religious phase to bring him back into favor, he was disappointed. He painted some feeble pictures on religious subjects, and when he died in 1690, at the age of seventy-one, everyone said that he had died of chagrin.

But the Academy as Lebrun had formed it lived on, reflecting his own belief that art could be taught, and learned, by rule and by rote. Much later, the nineteenth-century nature painter Théodore Rousseau, who like other original artists of his generation was being buffeted by the Academy's pedants, predicted that "the humility of a tuft of grass clearly lit by a ray of sun" would eventually defeat the kind of painting represented by Lebrun's inflated portraits of Louis XIV, and he was right. But for two centuries the Academy had things its own way.

As a painter Lebrun suffered from his fallacious conviction that art could be created by formula. He was always an irreproachable draftsman, and his early paintings often have a degree of freshness. But his history is one of a steady drying out until at last, however we may search for (and occasionally find) admirable qualities in his work, we are left with expert but meaningless exercises, the triumph of dogma over imagination.

Lebrun believed not only that pictures could be constructed by rules for the interrelationship of their parts, which is true to a certain extent, but also that expressive power could be achieved by a similar set of mechanics, which is not true at all. He formulated for the students of the Academy the rules of expression, including facial expressions that "render visible the effects of passion." His rules for these expressions dictate exactly the position of the eyes (up, down, to one side or the other to a stated degree), the eyebrows (knit, raised, in specific geometrical relationships) and the mouth (gaping, tightened, etc.) for a neatly catalogued set of emotions. His lectures, in an English translation of 1791, can make hilarious reading today. In "Simple Love," for instance, we find "the Head inclined towards the Object of the Passion, the Eyes may be moderately open . . . the Eyeball being gently turned towards the Object . . . ," although "the Nose receives no Alteration." "The Mouth must be a little open, the Corners a little turned up," and "the Lips will appear moist, and this moistness may be caused by Vapours arising from the Heart."

From Lebrun's own heart, no vapors ever rose. It is true that Leonardo had also been interested in physiognomy as a reflection of the passions, and that Poussin (whom Lebrun revered) also held to faith in rule, and that Lebrun's interest in the formulation of systems seems in line with the philosophical principles of his century. The difference between Lebrun and Leonardo, or Poussin, or the mathematician-philosopher Descartes, is that he saw method not as a technique of exploration in which intuition also played a part, but only as a kind of recipe by which art could be cooked up.

Pierre Mignard (1612-1695), who succeeded Lebrun as head of the Académie Royale, was seven years older than his hated rival, but lived five years longer (until the age of eighty-three) to enjoy all the honors, titles, and revenues that he had stripped from the former despot. Actually, he had been in the saddle for seven years before Lebrun died, having effectively if not officially become the new despot in 1683, when Lebrun's patron Colbert died and Mignard's patron Louvois succeeded him. These were the seven years that it took Lebrun to expire of chagrin after his retirement from active participation in Academy affairs. As soon as he died, Louis XIV gave Mignard Lebrun's title of First Painter to the King, and then ordered the Academy to assemble and appoint Mignard, in one sweep, to all the offices that, until then, Mignard had haughtily refused in pretended disapproval of the Academy. Thus at the age of seventy-eight Mignard was given the neophyte's honor of election as an associate member, and was then declared full member, rector, chancellor, and director, certainly the most rapid rise in history from novice to dictator, at least on paper.

Although Mignard, as a matter of policy, had opposed the Academy all these years, he was an academician born, and during the twenty years he spent in Rome was quite content to be a power in the Academy of St. Luke there. As a painter, he worked in a style not much different from Lebrun's. They had had the same teacher, Simon Vouet (1590-1649). But he set himself up as the head of the Rubenist faction in opposition to Lebrun, who headed the Poussinists. In theory the Rubenists were colorists in the Venetian tradition and the Poussinists were Raphaelesque formalists, but in effect neither was either to any significant degree. The Academy was not divided aesthetically; the Rubenist-Poussinist split was political, a struggle for power and commissions. If a choice had to be made between Lebrun and Mignard, Mignard would have to be discarded as the lesser painter. He was a good society portraitist, an occasional but not very strong decorator, and the creator (or pasticheur) of Madonnas that so sweetened the already oversweet Italian recipe that the French had to coin a word, *mignardise,* to describe their saccharine quality.

Pierre Mignard had a brother, Nicolas Mignard (1606-1668), who was an etcher and a painter of portraits and decorations of no great distinction. He is often called Mignard d'Avignon, after the city where he did most of his work. Pierre Mignard is sometimes encountered as Mignard le Romain.

Sixteen forty-three was the pivotal year in Philippe de Champaigne's life. He was then forty-one years old and had been an official painter at the French court since the age of twenty-six, when Marie de Médicis had given him the post of Painter to the Queen Mother. Soon he was also working for Louis XIII and Cardinal Richelieu, eventually running a large studio. With a band of assistants he executed a succession of mural commissions, at the same time producing some of the quietest and most dignified paintings in the history of official portraiture. Always a sober man and a sober artist, he was, like Poussin in Rome, but independently from him, modifying the grandiosity of the baroque manner to accord with the French rationalistic temper.

In that crucial year 1643 he was employed by the Jansenist establishment at Port-Royal, near Paris, and suddenly found, in the austerity of this Catholic order, his natural spiritual habitat. Without entering the Church, he modeled his life along Jansenist tenets, and his daughter became a Jansenist nun. His masterpiece is a double portrait in the Louvre showing his daughter and Mother Catherine Agnès of Port-Royal. It was painted in 1662, when he was sixty, in votive tribute to his daughter's miraculous cure from fever and paralysis—a cure that followed upon the prayers of the nuns during a nine-day retreat.

Born in 1602 in Brussels and trained there under the Flemish landscapist Jacques Fouquier (*c*. 1585-1659), Philippe de Champaigne moved to Paris at the age of nineteen and was naturalized there in 1629 when he was twenty-seven. He was one of the original members of the French Academy when it was formed in 1648, and after his Jansenist conversion he continued, for the remaining thirty years of his life— he died in 1674 at seventy-two—to work for the French crown and also for the Jesuits in spite of their opposition to the Jansenists. Politics for him were never a part of religion.

Hyacinthe Rigaud would be a standard name in the history of painting even if he had painted nothing except the portrait of Louis XIV at the age of sixty-two that has become not only the standard pictorial reference on this monarch, but the supertype of the baroque state portrait as well. However, Rigaud (whose full name was a resounding Hyacinthe Honoré Mathias Pierre Martyr André Jean Rigau Y Ros) painted many another portrait—in a good year, as many as one every nine days, according to his records.

He was a great record keeper, soundly methodical in everything he did, from painting to the management of his business and love affairs. Born in Perpignan in 1659, he worked his way via provincial stations to Paris, which he reached by the time he was twenty-two. He entered the Academy, won the Prix de Rome, perceived that his talent lay in portrait painting rather than the academic history picture, made a great success with a portrait of Monsieur (Louis XIV's brother) in 1688—he was now twenty-nine—and settled down to painting court portraits at a rapid clip, and with magnificent competence. He charged more for those in which he did not use one of his standard prefabricated poses and costumes, cranked out as copies by his assistants, to which he added only the face.

Rigaud became a father in his mid-twenties as the result of a liaison with Elizabeth de Gouy Le Juge, the wife of an usher of the King's Grand Council, and married her in 1710 (he was past fifty) in her widowhood. Honor after honor continued to come his way. The culminating one was his appointment as director of the Academy in 1733 when he was seventy-four. He lived another ten years, leaving behind many handsome pictures, some fully baroque, some proto-rococo, and a few reflecting a responsiveness to Rembrandt that jibes with nothing else in his life and work. Rigaud was

an expert painter, but somehow one never pauses for long in
front of his pictures in the museums.

The joint lives of the three Le Nain brothers might
stand as a model of fraternal harmony. At least so one gathers
from the few available facts about them, but one gathers little
else. All that is known of their lives can easily be fitted in a
paragraph or two. Their painting is another matter, although
here, too, there are many gaps and questions.

All three were born in Laon, the sons of a minor civil
official—Antoine in 1588, Louis (the best artist of the three)
five years later in 1593, and Mathieu after a gap of another
fourteen years, in 1607. Thus Antoine, if given a late teen
marriage, was old enough to have been the youngest brother's
father.

Just when the brothers moved to Paris is uncertain, but
they were established there by 1629. In that year Antoine,
who would have been forty-one to Mathieu's twenty-two, is
on record as a master painter, with his brothers mentioned
as painters also. They were settled and at work in Saint-
Germain-des-Prés, at that time a suburb of Paris rather than
its bohemian center. Here they joined a colony of hardworking artists of the second rank, including numbers of Flemings
and Dutchmen. The brothers were always more closely identified with homely Netherlandish realism than with French
finesse and intellectualism, and their first teacher was probably a Netherlandish artist in their native Laon.

In the matter of finances, often a cause of fatal disruption among brothers, the Le Nains seem to have been in
perfect accord. In a document of 1646 they agreed that the
last survivor should receive all the property of the two others.
Antoine was already fifty-eight in this year, and Louis fifty-

three. The will was made pretty much in the nick of time for Mathieu. Two years later, in 1648, the two older brothers died, Antoine at sixty and Louis at fifty-five. The forty-one-year-old Mathieu survived for another twenty-nine years; he died at seventy in 1677.

A pleasant picture—literally—of the brothers' life together in Paris is *The Studio* (London, Marquess of Bute collection), a painting of about 1630, which shows Mathieu painting, Louis posing, Antoine supervising, and all three under the benevolent eye of their father in the form of a portrait hanging on the wall.

The Studio is tentatively attributed to Antoine but might be the work of two or all three of the brothers, as some other pictures undoubtedly are. The idea held during the nineteenth century that brotherly concord extended to combined efforts on all Le Nain paintings has been discarded. Such paintings as are signed are signed without first names, but among them, as among unsigned ones obviously from a Le Nain hand, three styles are recognizable.

Antoine was a rather awkward painter, with a stiffness that today we can find engaging, since we have developed a taste for this quality through such neoprimitives as the Douanier Rousseau. But Antoine was a wretched draftsman. Young Mathieu was a good portraitist and, in genre or religious subjects, a receptive eclectic. It is the middle brother, Louis, who offers us most, and offers it best in scenes of peasant life that have recently been re-evaluated upward and are still rising in critical esteem.

Louis shows peasants at their meals, tending their children or their animals, visiting their relatives, returning from a baptism, listening to the village piper, and often merely sitting in groups either indoors or in the fields. These ordinary subjects were standard with dozens of painters in Saint-Germain-des-Prés, both the Netherlanders who continued their native genre tradition and the French "little masters" who adopted it. But where these painters showed the participants as droll, uncouth, or picturesque, Louis Le Nain employed them as the monumental members of architectural compositions allied, in their repose, reserve, and solidity, to the classical tradition. (Poussin was Louis's contemporary within a year of birth.)

As sociological documents, Louis Le Nain's portrayals of peasants are absurd. French peasants in the seventeenth century were miserable creatures, brutalized by squalid poverty and hard labor. Louis recorded their dress (even to its raggedness) and all the picturesque accouterments of carts, pots, pans, hovels, and pigs, but his skirts and scarves take on folds as simple and as structural as the channeling in columns; his haystacks have the stability of hills; and within such sets, at once realistically observed and highly artificialized, the peasants stand or sit with a dignity beyond that of kings.

This may sound like an anticipation of Jean Jacques Rousseau's romantic ideal of nature's nobleman, but there is little connection. Louis's painting is neither social commentary nor sentimental reinterpretation of peasant life. It is, rather, a hybrid between the formalism of the classical tradition and genre, two extremes in the varied currents of seventeenth-century art. Louis left no statements as to his theories or his expressive goals (and probably never thought of making any, if indeed he ever formulated any theories for himself), but his paintings now seem to pay homage to the virtues that the French call *"simple"*—a word of deeper meaning than the English one, having to do with the integrity of anything honest and firm and enduring, whether it is a human heart or a kitchen pot. It is, or was until recently, the virtue epitomized in French family life, the unit of French civilization. Louis did not idealize or sentimentalize the state of the peasant, but he did use the peasant and his activities as raw material for pictures in which this quality in French life emerges as an abstraction rather than as pictorial record.

Louis Le Nain is ancestor in spirit to Chardin, who in the next century presented this same abstraction in his still lifes of everyday household objects. But Louis was regarded only as a good genre painter until the middle of the nineteenth century, when Courbet and other realists rediscovered him not only as a painter but also as a supposed social commentator. Since then his stock has continued to rise. He exemplifies a constant in French art, the love of order and simplicity that can be traced in changing forms from the Middle Ages to Cézanne.

15

THE SEVENTEENTH CENTURY IN SPAIN

Spanish painting somehow always manages to isolate itself as a special case, and its preference for doing so is respected here. We have seen one Spaniard, Ribera, but he adopted Naples as his base. Another, Zurbarán, could have been included along with those others grouped in association with Caravaggio, yet Zurbarán is so vehemently Spanish that he demands to be set alongside other Spaniards.

Francisco Pacheco, the first of the following group, was already thirty-six years old when the seventeenth century opened. His meeting with El Greco, for anyone who likes to try to maintain a sense of chronology, is a reminder that the boundary lines of centuries are never quite as decisive as they are made to appear in history books as a matter of convenience.

Everything we know about Francisco Pacheco presents a rather appealing picture of a conveniently limited man whose long life—the ninety years between 1564 and 1654—gave him exactly what he wanted. He would surely be surprised if he could know today that his name is unfamiliar even to most museumgoers; nothing in his career hinted that his major reputation would diminish to such minor proportions.

We think of him first as the teacher of Velázquez, and this association with the greatest Spanish master of the day gave Pacheco a pleasure that was increased by an entirely satisfactory relationship as father-in-law to the younger man. He could say with confidence that Velázquez had learned from him "the true imitation of nature," and certainly Velázquez's early work does show the direct impress of Pacheco's teaching.

His connection with the (at the time) less highly considered master of the previous generation, El Greco, also keeps Pacheco's name alive, if a shade less creditably. He visited El Greco in Toledo in 1611 and set down our only eyewitness record of El Greco in old age. Between the lines of his account we see the enfeebled and then neglected but still rebellious master whom Pacheco could see only as an eccentric whose eccentric painting was as eccentric as he. But Pacheco's comments on El Greco are only imperceptive rather than unkind. He was much impressed by the old man's conversation, but deplored the freedom of his brushwork and called his paintings *"crueles borrones"* ("brutal sketches"), adopting a tone of humane tolerance in the presence of affliction, which is the next best thing to perception in a critic of limited insight.

As a critic, theoretician, historian, and teacher of painting, Pacheco summarized his principles in a book published in 1649, the flower of his vigorous old age, called "The Art of Painting: Its Antiquity and Greatness." His writings are an important source today not for any quality of revelation but because they reflect so clearly the accepted points of view of

Pacheco's Spain, give clear instructions for artists that stand as records of the technical processes employed at the time, and are spotted with information about painters that might otherwise have been lost.

Pacheco must have been a happy man to the full extent of his capacity. He was a born academician, so fortunately located in time and place that his routine conservatism was never challenged. He was never forced into those frenetic defenses against innovation that turn the benign pedant into a vicious reactionary made absurd by embarrassing exposure. In 1611, the year of his visit to El Greco, he opened an academy of painting in Madrid, and was also appointed an Inquisitor. But he must not be imagined as carrying a garrote and dancing around executional fires. As the official censor of painting he enforced the Church's rather puritanical position, which was quite in line with his own. Even as a teacher he had rather prim advice for students. When a female nude was unavoidable in a painting, he advised artists to draw the faces and hands "with all the required variety and beauty" from "virtuous women" who could be seen "without danger," and to do the rest from "good paintings, prints, drawings, plaster casts, ancient and modern statues, and the excellent outlines of Albrecht Dürer. And so while choosing the most graceful and perfect parts, I should avoid the danger."

Pacheco tried hard to think in terms of conscientious idealism. The most elevated of his convictions was that a desirable spirituality and an imperative morality could be assured in art by following the didactic conventions he laid down. His conventions now seem a vulgarization of spirituality, and his own art is certainly unimaginative. His heaven and his saints in states of beatitude are perfectly in tune with the widespread formula that still engenders bad holy pictures. But he was a very sound painter technically—a skilled craftsman who could teach these skills, and who today would no doubt be teaching them by correspondence. His god, of course, was Raphael, who has been perverted into the chief source of mawkish religious art. Yet Pacheco, who never left Spain and traveled very little within it, had never seen a Raphael. He knew him through engravings that usually reduced the mellifluous forms to the cold, dry diagrams that Pacheco imitated so successfully.

Pacheco's official attitude as well as his personal conviction was that the function of painting was to inspire the observer to Christian virtue. The inspiration was to come from realistic images rather than from any such aberrations as El Greco's mystical visions. From what Pacheco wrote, it is difficult to tell whether he knew that there was a difference between the Raphaelesque idealism that he thought he cultivated and the realistic representation that he spontaneously admired. Actually, he was a realist *manqué*. He was a good, straightforward portrait painter and, again combining his double profession of artist and writer, left a work of some interest called "Compendium of True Portraits of Illustrious and Memorable Men," not completed but including, even so, one hundred and seventy portraits in black and red crayon accompanied by biographies.

Pacheco's true forte was probably the *bodegones*, or kitchen still lifes, that in Zurbarán and many minor Spanish painters are among the great delights of Spanish art. They delighted Pacheco too, but he was too busy—quite sincerely all the time—being an important and influential artist to bother much with these.

Philip IV of Spain was seventeen years old and had been on the throne for a year when he met a twenty-three-year-old painter named Diego Rodríguez de Silva y Velázquez, whom

Sevillian dilettantes considered promising. The King was so attracted to Velázquez as a person and as an artist that the next year he appointed him court painter. Velázquez was given a studio in the palace (to which Philip kept a key, and where, in a special chair Velázquez kept for him, the King sat day after day watching Velázquez paint) and was also given living quarters in Madrid, a salary, a pension, various benefits such as free medical services, and a series of offices that brought in additional pay: Gentleman Usher—a very humble beginning—and then, over the years, Officer of the Royal Wardrobe, Inspector of Works in the Palace, and, finally, Grand Marshal of the Palace.

The price of these favors, however, came rather high. When he died in 1660, Velázquez was sixty-one years old and had spent virtually all his mature life—thirty-seven years of it—at a court where living was reduced to agonizing boredom by a combination of stifling formality and the physical lassitude of a royal family that barely had the energy to drag around the weight of the royal costumes. Beyond the walls, Spain crumbled away during those years. She was repeatedly humiliated in war and international politics. She lost great territories, her domestic economy was a shambles. But within the palace there seems to have been neither distress nor excitement, nor much response of any kind. Ranged around the great room in the Prado given over to Velázquez's pictures today, Philip and his family stand with a silence, a reserve, an acceptance of ennui as the alternative to action, that in essence must have been the air of the palace while Velázquez painted them there.

It is likely that Velázquez was the man who came closest to being Philip's best friend, and that the affection was reciprocal. But the austerity of the court of Spain demanded a barrier of formality even between members of a family, and precluded anything more than the years of respectful service and respectful patronage that made up the friendship between two men who saw each other constantly from youth until death. When, after Velázquez's death, Philip wrote *"Quedo abbatido"*—"I am crushed"—in the margin of a memorandum concerning the vacancy of the official post Velázquez had held, he was permitting himself an extraordinary demonstration of emotion.

As an official of the court, and perhaps naturally, as a man of a special temperament thought of as typically Spanish, Velázquez reflected this reserve, this deliberate removal from emotion or commitment, in his art. He never permitted himself a single flamboyant stroke of the brush; he avoided any suggestion of the heroics and bombast so popular in his century elsewhere. The vivacious grace and aristocratic flourish of Van Dyck (who was born the same year as Velázquez) would have seemed outrageous indulgences, just as Van Dyck's life of fashionable elegance, which endeared him to his English patrons, would have been an unconscionable offense at the Spanish court. Velázquez never offers so much as an opinion; he is objective to such a degree that he often seems (and is often called) nothing more than a miraculous eye, a lens with the capacity to direct a brush.

But the intelligence that served as transmission between the eye and the brush would not be denied, even when it was restrained from declaring itself vehemently. Velázquez's portraits, even though so frequently tethered to unrewarding subjects (the royal family offered very little surface beauty, and a great deal of inner vacuity), are undeclared revelations of character. Philip IV became the most-painted king in history, with his curiously formed face, his air of unexercised intelligence, and sometimes his air of chronic disappointment, as if he were puzzled that his consistent observance of the royal obligation of reticence should have borne Spain such poor fruit. It is true that with Velázquez in painting, and Tirso de Molina and Calderón continuing a great tradition in the theater, Philip's reign was also a golden age, but it is doubtful that he realized exactly how great a man he had discovered in his favorite painter.

Velázquez, a slow, deliberate craftsman, revolutionized realistic painting, transforming it into a revelation of objects in terms of light. Light became for him not the theatrical weapon that it was for Caravaggio, nor the metaphysical medium that it was for Rembrandt. Light was the agency that made the world visible—an observation that sounds so absurdly obvious that it seems hardly worth setting down. But it is through the recognition of this fact that Velázquez solved the problem of rendering the fantastically complicated manifestations of light in terms of pigment. Shadow became, for the first time, not an absence of light but a change in the color and quality of light. Working without theory—or at least without recording any theories that he held—Velázquez anticipated the discoveries of the nineteenth-century physicists that were given their full painterly expression by the impressionists.

That was his adventure. From a biographical point of view, nothing interesting happened to him. He was born in Seville in 1599 into a good family of Portuguese origin. When he was fourteen he entered the sound, if hardly inspirational, academy of Francisco Pacheco, and four years later emerged as an independent master. The next year, 1618, when he was nineteen, he married Pacheco's daughter Juana. They settled down to respectable family life. The young husband was an excellent painter of *bodegones*—those realistic still-life and genre pictures of servants and other simple people in kitchens, inns, and the like. In these early pictures he shows that he either knew the style of Caravaggio from some indirect contact (he could hardly have known it at first hand) or else arrived independently at a very close variation of the

Italian's strong realism in solid descriptions of sturdy objects and sturdy people emerging into brilliant golden light from deep shadows—the reverse of the style that he evolved in later paintings, where everything is enveloped in a vibrant, silvery atmosphere.

Philip IV's minister, Olivares, was also a Sevillian, and in 1622 he arranged a meeting between the adolescent King and the young painter, in Madrid. The next year Velázquez became court painter. Thereafter, when he accepted private commissions, he was obliged, as an aristocrat by adoption, to refuse payment. The long years were punctuated by only two interruptions of routine, both of them Italian trips. In 1628, Rubens came to Madrid for a year and a half on a diplomatic mission; he urged Velázquez to go to Italy and induced the King to send him. Almost twenty years later, in January, 1649, Velázquez made a second trip, accompanying an embassy that had been arranged to escort the new queen, Mariana of Austria.

On this trip Velázquez bought pictures for the royal collection and gave the one hint during his lifetime that he might have felt a little restricted at Philip's court. He delayed his return to Spain in spite of Philip's pleas (and in spite of letters urging officials to see to it that Velázquez's "lethargic temperament"—an odd idea—did not postpone things). He spent a full year and a half in Italy, during which he painted his only female nude (the so-called *Rokeby Venus* in the National Gallery in London) and the most powerful of all his portraits, an almost audaciously revealing characterization of Pope Innocent X (in the Doria Gallery in Rome).

Then back to Madrid. He was fifty-nine years old when in 1658 Philip knighted him with the Order of St. Jago (or Santiago), given ordinarily only to noblemen.

After Velázquez died in 1660, Philip lived on, after a

fashion, for five years, and Velázquez's place at court was filled, after a very weak fashion, by his son-in-law, Juan Bautista del Mazo (*c.* 1612/16-1667), who is granted the title of a follower of Velázquez for want of a better description. The fact is that Velázquez found no followers. The concentration of his work in Spain hid him from painters who might have learned from him, until the young Goya was admitted to the royal collections more than a hundred years later. And it was as much as two hundred years later—in 1865—that Manet made his Spanish visit and brought the force of Velázquez's genius fully into the current of European painting.

El Greco, Velázquez, and Goya form a trio whose preeminence in Spanish painting has until lately remained unchallenged. And while these painters' claim to first place is not disputed, there is a feeling today that the trio should be enlarged to a quartet including Francisco de Zurbarán. Zurbarán, a fine painter by any standard, has been rediscovered in the light of what must be called post-Cézanne aesthetics.

Zurbarán was born in November, 1598, only a matter of months before Velázquez. Chronologically the two men are all but twins. Zurbarán died four years after his colleague and friend. But while Velázquez was born of an excellent family in the big city of Seville, Zurbarán began life humbly in the village of Fuente de Cantos, near Badajoz. In 1614, while Velázquez was studying in the elite academy of Francisco Pacheco, Zurbarán was apprenticed, in Seville, to a painter named Pedro Díaz Villanueva, none of whose works are known but who seems to have been less an artist than a craftsman who ground out devotional images. It is hardly possible that this almost anonymous artist could have given Zurbarán a stylistic point of departure. Zurbarán, like Velázquez, became an artist of such original genius that he cannot really be said to have had a teacher.

By the time Zurbarán was eighteen, he was signing canvases in a style that, if not yet mature, is recognizable as his great one. But the competition in Seville—the liveliest center of Spanish painting—must have discouraged him. In 1617, the year that his friend Velázquez emerged as an independent master (at eighteen) and the favorite young painter of Seville's cognoscenti, Zurbarán went to Llerena, in southern Spain, where he established himself as a provincial master. Velázquez made a good marriage with Juana Pacheco that was apparently also a love match. In a century when men seldom married women older than themselves, Zurbarán married one sufficiently his elder to inspire some recent biographers to speculations concerning emotional instability, mother images, and the like. (Zurbarán's love life, like his art, has been re-evaluated by our century's yardsticks.) The union produced several children.

Zurbarán specialized in cycle paintings of the lives of the saints, which had become popular through the Jesuit use of painting as a medium of visual religious education. His style, which we admire today for other reasons, filled the bill so well that the city council of Seville invited him to come back and settle there. This was in 1629, six years after Seville had lost Velázquez to Madrid. Zurbarán was quite successful and for ten years very productive, providing cycles or individual paintings for churches and religious houses all over southwestern Spain, and running a shop where similar works were produced for the Spanish colonies in America. He did not get rich. Among other things, as records show, he had trouble collecting his fees for the transatlantic commissions.

Nevertheless, the 1630's were his great decade. In 1634, when he was thirty-six, he was called to Madrid. Philip IV, a bit short on military and political triumphs of his own, was commissioning commemorative paintings of past glories. Velázquez, who was to do the *Surrender of Breda,* asked the King's minister, Olivares, who had brought Velázquez to the King's attention in the first place, to call in Zurbarán to execute a *Siege of Cádiz.* (Both the paintings are now in the Prado.) During his stay in Madrid, Zurbarán made his first significant contact with Italian art. The paintings he saw in the King's collection made his own style fuller and richer.

When Zurbarán and his century entered their forties, he was a superb artist and in steady demand. But during that decade an artist nearly twenty years younger than he, Murillo, captured the public with a sentimental languor just the opposite of his tense asceticism. As commissions dropped off, Zurbarán tried to soften and sweeten his style. The effort was not very successful in attracting patrons, and it was a disastrous compromise for him as a creative artist. He suffered from severe depressions at this time, perhaps as much because he was aware that his modified style was a self-violation as because of other troubles. His wife died, and although he remarried (and bred another family), his good days were past.

In 1658, when he was sixty and in desperate need of commissions, Velázquez asked him to serve as a witness to his knighting into the Order of Santiago. Encouraged by this renewed contact with his friend, now in so astral a position, Zurbarán settled in Madrid. But Velázquez died in 1660, and when Zurbarán died four years later he was still a sadly displaced artist. But these weaker paintings are easily disregarded, for in his others Zurbarán is a magnificent painter. When Sir Charles Holmes wrote, "With Cézanne a mere crumpled tablecloth may take on the majesty of a mountain," he could as well have varied the statement a bit to describe the quality that Zurbarán gave to a fall of drapery, the white wool of a monk's robe for instance, to make it a perfectly constructed arrangement of abstract volumes. Zurbarán (like the early Velázquez) was a tenebrist who by internal evidence should have been in luenced by Caravaggio, but could not have been influenced directly. In Zurbarán's case—with his extreme severity, his almost fanatic reserve, his solemnity, his massive sobriety, and his hard clarity (all of these in the service of a passionate religiosity)—connections are made, tentatively, with the native southern Spanish tradition of hard, literal, straightforward realism.

But nothing fully explains the power of the union Zurbarán effected between realism and mysticism. Until he made his unsuccessful effort to emulate Murillo, he was apparently deliberate in avoiding overdramatization. At any rate, X-rays of his *Vision of Fray Pedro de Salamanca* in the church of San Jerónimo, Guadalupe, Spain, painted in 1638-39 at the height of his career, show that he repainted the faces of the two monks who are witnessing a supernatural event, reducing the theatricality of their expressions. The drama here, as in all of Zurbarán's best work, lies in light and form more than in gesture and facial expression.

Zurbarán also ranks with the greatest painters of still life of any time. His pure still lifes are rare, but the still-life accessories in his other paintings are superb passages that crossbreed the finest Spanish tradition of *bodegones* with a Cézannesque conception of all painterly form as a geometrical transmutation of reality.

And with all this, Zurbarán can also be a ravishing painter in more obvious ways. He painted numerous pictures of female saints in fantastical costumes of rich silks and brocades that are, apparently, not religious pictures at all but portraits of fashionable young women bearing, as accessories, the attributes of their patron saints—an attractive conceit. In these completely delightful pictures Zurbarán offers sensuous seductions of color and texture, as well as of feminine beauty, along with the more intellectual allure of formal mastery.

Never altogether an explicable painter, Zurbarán is least explicable in his deterioration as an imitator of Murillo. No painter of comparable stature has ever voluntarily subjected himself to such diminution.

Bartolomé Esteban Murillo (1617-1682), the Spanish painter of saccharine Madonnas and picturesque ragamuffins, was so overesteemed during his lifetime and for at least another hundred and fifty years thereafter, well into the nineteenth century (and for that matter into the early years of the twentieth, by Sunday-school teachers), that a reaction was inevitable and ever since the 1890's critics have been busy disparaging him. By way of compensation, efforts are now being made to reinstate Murillo as a painter whose virtues have never been properly recognized. His great popularity was the result of a form of bad taste that afflicts all epochs—a fondness for expressions of gooey sweetness that rests on a confusion between cheap sentiment and elevation of the spirit. Known as the Spanish Raphael at the height of his fame, Murillo carried Raphael's dangerous tendencies to a point where even that master's great formal power, which he lacked, could not have saved him.

The current efforts to rehabilitate Murillo are based on a new look at his very fine qualities as a plastic artist, but because these qualities usually cannot be divorced from his abhorrent sentimentalism, the efforts are apt to fall flat. In an occasional portrait or picaresque genre subject—and in some fine drawings—there is hope for Murillo's redemption, but his sins die hard.

Murillo was born and died in Seville. Orphaned as a child, he was taken in by relatives, one of whom was the minor artist Juan del Castillo, his teacher. In his early twenties he was making a living doing religious pictures for export to the Spanish colonies in America, but he rapidly came into demand for important commissions. He was successful in other fields of endeavor, siring nine children and operating his own academy. He died at the age of sixty-five, a few months after a fall from the scaffolding where he was working on a commission in the Capuchin church in Cádiz.

16

THREE
PERSONALITIES:
ELSHEIMER, CALLOT,
AND ROSA

Adam Elsheimer, Jacques Callot, and Salvator Rosa—a German, a Frenchman, and an Italian, born over a period of thirty-seven years—might have been placed in one or another of the preceding seventeenth-century art-historical pigeonholes (just which pigeonholes may be a question), but all three of them are such engaging personalities that surely they may be granted this small terminal enclave of their own. Very different from one another, they are offered neither as a summary of their century nor as a garnish, and not in proof of anything, but simply as themselves.

Adam Elsheimer died at the age of thirty-two, but during that short life he managed to cover a great deal of ground geographically, to develop one of the most appealing styles in the history of idyllic landscape, to win the respect and affection of a large circle that included the great Rubens, and to lead an emotional life of such pathos that it is a wonder he has escaped popularization in a fictionalized biography, for his misadventures are the stuff that best-sellers are made of.

Elsheimer can be claimed with equal legitimacy by the Germans and the Italians. German-born, he adopted Rome as his home, and his work allows the discovery of links with tradition on either side of the Alps.

He was born in 1578 in Frankfurt, the son of a tailor. He studied under a painter named Uffenbach and then at twenty left Germany for Rome by way of Munich and Venice. He spent about two years dawdling on the way. Impractical, introspective, solitary by nature (his biographers report that he walked through the streets of Rome so abstracted that he was blind even to the friends he encountered), he must have been one of those people whose attraction comes in part from the impression they give that they are helpless in life.

Elsheimer's paintings—small and intimate—were the antithesis of those productions in the grand manner that were popular in Rome, and, withdrawn by nature, he had no taste for the dramatic flair cultivated by (or bred into) the most conspicuous artists of the century, such as Caravaggio, Rubens, and Bernini. But Elsheimer was successful both as a painter and as a personality, and he was collected (in both capacities) by Roman cognoscenti, including members of the German and Dutch colonies, many of whom, like himself, were not only Romans by adoption but Roman Catholics by conversion.

Elsheimer, as Rubens said later, might have made a fortune, but he was totally unable to manage his affairs. He was also a poor judge of character, and while he was generally fortunate in the people who sought him out, he was victimized by at least two, the woman he married and a shrewd crank named Hendrick Goudt—who, if not the direct cause of Elsheimer's death, was at least the catalytic agent that hastened the mental breakdown that led to it.

Three Personalities: Elsheimer, Callot, Rosa

Goudt was a wealthy and wellborn Dutchman whose weaknesses at the time he knew Elsheimer were no worse than an excessive vanity and a silly covetousness of any titles he could manage to attach to his name. Athirst for distinctions, he became a Catholic convert in the hope, his enemies said, of adding a papal honor to the list. He lived with Elsheimer after coming to Rome in 1605 and paid him money in advance for work that Elsheimer, already sinking into a melancholy lethargy, failed to deliver. Goudt had the artist put into debtor's prison, and in this hideous place Elsheimer became ill and was released only to die. This was in 1610. Back in Holland, Goudt himself deteriorated mentally but lived another thirty-eight years, dying insane in 1648.

Rubens had met Elsheimer in Rome and had recommended him to friends there. When one of these sent Rubens news of Elsheimer's death, Rubens wrote back from Antwerp, "I do not remember ever having been so cruelly stricken as at the moment when I learned this news, and I will never again have any sympathy for those who brought him to such a miserable end." In Rubens's opinion, Elsheimer "has never had an equal for 'subject' painting and for landscapes." To assist the widow he set about trying to arrange the sale to a Flemish collector of one of Elsheimer's paintings, a Flight into Egypt, although he feared that he could not get the high price that she was demanding.

But there was no real emergency. Elsheimer had married the woman only two months after the death of her first husband, and she doubled her score without delay, acquiring her third husband, another widowhood, and a fourth husband, with hardly a pause for breath.

Elsheimer is one of the originators of a genre whose acknowledged fountainhead is Claude Lorrain—the idyllic landscape that flourished in the seventeenth and eighteenth centuries. The gentleness and serenity of his art hint not at all of his mental disturbance: his lovely painted world can easily be imagined to have served as his refuge from whatever fears and uncertainties finally harassed him to death. The mood of his perfectly assembled landscapes inhabited by elegant, rather placid figures is set by the light that falls on them. The light is an adaptation of Caravaggio's more dramatic illumination and very probably of Savoldo's, since Elsheimer probably saw Savoldo's painting during his pause in Venice en route to Rome. There are also more distant echoes of his countryman Altdorfer. And Elsheimer was greatly admired by Pieter Lastman, who taught Rembrandt. Such ties give Elsheimer a historical spot of some consequence, which, however, has nothing to do with his appeal. This appeal is the appeal of the mood he evokes, a quiet, timeless contentedness that he distilled, somehow, from a brief and disturbed life.

According to undocumented reports, Jacques Callot ran away from home at the age of twelve to beat his way to Rome with a band of beggar gypsies. If the story is not true, it should be: picaresque adventure is perfectly in keeping with the spirit of Callot's art. En route to Rome he is supposed to have stopped awhile in Florence, where he apprenticed himself to a fireworks engineer. This also is too alluring a possibility to reject as fictitious. Callot's style has all the explosive brilliance and planned order of one of those sky-rockets that open up and spread out into a fountain of dazzling blossoms.

If he ran away from home he did it for fun, not to get away from anything. He was born in 1592 in Nancy, where his father, a wealthy man, was herald and master of ceremonies at the court of Lorraine, then an independent duchy. We know for certain that when he was fifteen Jacques was apprenticed to a Nancy silversmith and engraver. This would have been—if we can credit the story—after he had run away, had been located in Rome, had been brought back home, had run away again, and had got as far as Turin before being brought back a second time by his older brother, a monk, to lead the life of a young gentleman connected with the court. "What ever shall we do with the boy?" we can imagine his father saying in a combination of despair and affection.

The apprenticeship lasted a year, and now young Callot got to Rome on the record and without having to beg and steal his way. He went in the company of Count Tornielle de Géberviller, Lorraine's ambassador to the papal court, who turned him loose on arrival.

Callot on the loose in Rome is an awesome subject for contemplation. He did some engraving there, continuing his studies, but his career as an artist did not get under way until 1612, when he was twenty and went to Florence—leaving Rome, according to inevitable legend, after complications following a gallant escapade. Soon he was under the patronage of the Medici, and he stayed in Florence for the nine years that this patronage continued, which was until the death of Grand Duke Cosimo II, whose successors were forced to reduce expenses. Callot returned to Nancy and died there in 1635 from what may be construed as a combination of high living, rough living, and an excitable temperament, taking the form of a perforated ulcer. He was forty-three years old, and in a professional life of hardly more than twenty years he had produced 1,428 etchings and engravings and more than 2,000 drawings. He was always a delightful artist, often a powerful one, and is almost always an underrated one. He was a brilliant technician and a technical innovator, and his expressive range included reportage, theatrical invention, fantastic concoction, and, something that at first seems out of character, social comment of a kind and a force unseen before and not seen again until Goya, nearly two hundred years later.

In Florence Callot had done etchings of the various

Medici fetes and extravaganzas. He could take all the effulgent opulence of a baroque stage set, all the motion of the performers, the whole scheme including not only its organization but its evanescent theatrical air as well, and reduce everything to the dimensions of a small plate without cramping any of it. A major plate done in 1620 just at the end of his Florentine stay, *The Fair at Impruneta,* includes more than 1,300 figures with landscape and all the rickety paraphernalia of a fair, and does so with an aesthetic orderliness that costs not a thing in ebullience and verve. Of all artists, Callot is the great master of diminutive scale with full life.

Callot never painted, and as an etcher he was dealing with a form of art that sold at low prices and had to be produced in quantity, not only as to the number of impressions from a single plate but also as to the number of plates. Back in Nancy, he produced masses of work from sketches he had brought from Italy, including the set of twenty-four plates (the *Balli di Sfessania*) where forty-eight Italian comedians, two inches high against backgrounds of figures about one eighth that size, cavort, leap, fence, grimace, and dance their way through all the characteristic rakishness, ribaldry, acrobatics, grotesquerie, and sheer indescribable wonder of the *commedia dell'arte.* The *Balli di Sfessania* has become the great record not only of the costumes and characters of the purest of theaters but of its spirit as well—its improvisation, its irreverence, its whole outlook, which turns sex into a comic function, intrigue into the best of all possible sports, sorrow and misfortune into temporary inconveniences, and man into the most entertainingly ludicrous creature imaginable. High style in low comedy becomes the ultimate delight and justifies the indignity of staying alive under the absurd conditions that life imposes.

Callot recorded theatricals and tournaments for the dukes of Lorraine, as he had done for the Medici. He was called by the regent of the Spanish Netherlands and by Louis XIII of France to do huge etchings commemorating various sieges and battles—the ones they had won, of course. If any works of Callot's are less than totally alive, these are the ones, with their concessions, here and there, to the convention of representing war as a grandly panoplied spectacle that does honor to the might and the justice of the victors.

But Callot knew better. The Thirty Years' War stretched across all of his adult life, and he knew that war meant rape, pillage, murder, torture, and bestiality. In 1633, two years before his death, he said so in two series of etchings known as *The Little Miseries of War* and *The Great Miseries of War*— the "little" and the "great" referring not to the miseries but to the size of the plates: two by four and a half inches for the six etchings of the first series, three by seven inches for the eighteen plates of the second series.

Callot records the scenes of devastation and violence with the objective eye of a reporter and the stylistic flair of a ballet master. The market square where executions are taking place is detailed building by building; you can count the rungs on an improvised ladder a victim must climb to be hanged on a gibbet. Specialists could recognize the types of swords and firearms. The machinery of torture could be reconstructed with his delineations as working models. But rags flutter and blood spurts with ironic élan. Horses prance and soldiers charge with as much spirit as if they were jousting. The spiritedness is a matter of Callot's hand, just as the reportage is a matter of his eye, and they combine in an accusation where the facts seem the more appalling because of the clarity and bite of the language in which they are presented. For the first time, an artist shows war in its senselessness, its abominably casual and impersonal cruelty, its victimization of the innocent and its brutalization of the guilty.

Callot does not preach or condemn. He makes no comment of any kind. He doesn't need to: he need only say, "Look." To understand how these etchings, offered so unpretentiously, even so drily, could appear at a time when French art was dedicated to the intellectual abstractions of academic classicism, we must remember that Callot was not considered an artist at all, in the sense that the term was applied, for example, to his immediate contemporary, the greatest classicist of them all, Poussin. Etching was not an art but a professional craft, the province of manually skilled hacks who spent their time doing etched versions of other men's paintings, just as reproductions of paintings are now turned out by photoengraving. But in pursuing his craft, Callot invented processes that made etching a more flexible medium worthy of great creative draftsmen like himself. His influence was wide and profound. Rembrandt learned what an etching could be by studying Callot's.

Callot's last great print, made in 1634, stands as a summary of his art. *The Temptation of St. Anthony* shows us a cataclysm that could be a war or the end of the world, set on a stage that is the summary of baroque theatricalism, and filled with hordes of grotesque demons and monstrous creatures so wittily conceived that they could appropriately have been added to the cast of the *commedia dell'arte*—the whole thing served up in breathtaking style.

Callot was a great artist, and he must have been a delightful companion.

Salvator Rosa, a poor boy who made good in high society, is one of the most attractively flamboyant personalities in the history of painting. Near the end of a life that had given him spectacular successes in half a dozen of the arts, he could refer melodramatically to his "shattered hopes and consistent dis-

appointments." Before trying to explain the apparent contradiction, we might take a first look at him between the years
1640 and 1649, from his twenty-sixth to his thirty-fifth year
—a fine time for a man, and the years that Rosa remembered
as the happiest of his life.

This was his decade of residence in Florence, sandwiched
between the main stages of his professional life in Rome. At
twenty-five, Rosa could already sell anything he painted, and
at high prices. He was good-looking, witty, and a multifaceted
virtuoso, celebrated not only as a painter but as a poet (with
a special talent for satirical lampoons), an actor (with a special
talent for improvisational burlesque), and a composer of
music. Upon his arrival in Florence he bought himself an
elegant house and established his own academy there, the
Accademia de' Percossi, which became a center of intellectual
high life frequented by artists, literary figures, and the cream
of the nobility.

Rosa entertained his select and spirited circle with musi-
cals, theatricals, and banquets financed in part by members
of the academy and the considerable revenues it brought in,
and in part by the perpetual flow of income from his own
paintings. He made a great deal of money, which he spent
as easily, and as pleasurably, as he earned it. The coda to this
blissful summer song would conventionally be played on the
grasshopper-and-ant theme, with Rosa prematurely aged by
dissipation, neglected by his friends, shivering in the autumn
wind, forgotten and in rags. Unfortunately for the moral of
our story, the Florentine years were simply the spectacularly
best ones of a good life.

Salvator Rosa was born in 1615 in Arenella, near Naples,
a city always noted for extremities of poverty but also for the
ebullience of its citizenry. His teachers, who are of no other
interest, were an uncle and a brother-in-law, A. D. Greco and
F. Francanzo. The youngster might also have had some in-

struction from the Spaniard Ribera, who by that time had settled in Naples, but this possibility rests largely on a similarity between Rosa's style and Ribera's that could be either coincidental or the result of the youth's quick eye. Where his area of greatness lies, in romantic landscape, Rosa was self-taught and virtually without predecessor.

At twenty, Rosa set out to conquer Rome, arriving there in Spanish garb with a sword clanking at his side. He attracted attention immediately, as a personality and as an artist. Illness took him home briefly, but by 1639 he was back in the capital, determined to become famous. He became so. As a member of a theatrical troupe, which he formed, he was an enormous success. But he went too far in a burlesque of Bernini, the virtual dictator of Roman art, and left the city precipitously to join friends in Florence.

His successful career in Florence has been outlined. But Rome was still the art center, and in 1649 Rosa returned there, remaining until his death in 1673 at the age of fifty-eight.

Four years before his death, Rosa achieved what was in his own eyes his greatest triumph. His popularity as an artist had come from the lively attraction of his two typical products, large paintings of battle scenes and, even more, small landscapes and seascapes, theatrical in mood. But Rosa had never much respected this aspect of his talent, perhaps because he produced such pictures so easily. For all the felicity and facility of the paintings that made his reputation—and have perpetuated it—he clung to a contradictory faith in the academic tradition by which only religious and historical subjects were acceptable as significant art.

Now Rosa received an opportunity to prove himself in the grand manner with a commission for a large altarpiece to go into the Church of San Giovanni de' Fiorentini in Rome. Its subject was to be the martyrdom of Sts. Cosmas and Damian. He was elated, and it was at this time that he referred so surprisingly to the years of "shattered hopes and consistent disappointments," now at an end. Abandoning all his other talents, sometimes even forgetting to eat, he completed the picture late in October, 1669. It must be admitted that he proved, at least, the extent of his versatility by producing a painting as overblown, as full of melodramatic flatulence, hollow posturing, and turgid pictorial rhetoric as any routine concoction by the nonentities of the day.

Rosa was utterly delighted with what he had done, believing—and boasting to his friends—that he had excelled Michelangelo. (His embarrassed friends avoided comment.) To conclude your life in the belief that you have produced a masterpiece for all time is not a bad conclusion at all, and if *The Martyrdom of Sts. Cosmas and Damian* now seems only a pompous vulgarity, Rosa's reputation has been sustained by the work he thought less of.

His land- and seascapes appeal today for the reasons they appealed to his contemporaries. Filled with shattered light and threatening shadows, with the movement of wind and storm, peopled sometimes by saints but as often by soldiers, smugglers, and bandits, the scenes are wildly romantic although Rosa painted them more than a hundred and fifty years before romanticism became a formulated aesthetic. Turbulent, as showmanly as his acting must have been, and frequently seeming half improvised, they are personal eccentric expressions in a field where impersonal conformity was the rule.

Rosa became a steady force in the development of the romantic credo that he anticipated. During the eighteenth century when the romantic impulse was straining beneath the good manners and determined logic of the Age of Reason, Rosa's art was a tonic to artists and collectors who, consciously or not, were weary of polite restraint. Early in the nineteenth century, in 1824, Hazlitt called Rosa "beyond question the most romantic of landscape painters," an early use of "romantic" in such a sense. And before the century was half over, Rosa came fully into his own as an adopted colleague of the declared romantics, not only as an artist but as a personality in revolt against social conventions. (Legend has gone so far as to give him a spell of adventure as a member of a gang of mountain bandits.)

Even Ruskin, who could not forgive him an absence of moral content, and who said that Rosa "never attempts to be truthful, but only to be impressive," was attracted in spite of himself. He regretted that Rosa could not "conquer evil" by rising to "conceptions of victorious and consummated beauty" and could not even "remain in strong though melancholy war" with evil. In Ruskin's view, the human mind, "conquered by evil, infected by the dragon breath of it, and at last brought into captivity, so as to take delight in evil for ever . . . becomes the spirit of the dark but still powerful sensualistic art represented typically by that of Salvator."

Ruskin's mixture of fear and admiration of Rosa's evilness now seems an exaggerated appreciation, flattering by misdirection, of a talent that is more theatrically effective than profound. Rosa need not be taken all that seriously. If there is any evil in his work, it is in the battle scenes, which are often rather wearing in their carnage, rather than in the landscapes. As a landscapist, Rosa remains for the twentieth century one of the most attractive performers who ever stepped on stage.

But why, exactly, did he speak of "shattered hopes and consistent disappointments" and take such satisfaction in his meretricious *Martyrdom of Sts. Cosmas and Damian*? In the first place, he was probably exaggerating, in his usual theatrical way. But at the same time, he probably believed truly that he had not fulfilled himself as an artist, regarding himself not as a man with an extraordinary variety of talents, which he was, but as a genius, which he was far from being. When he set out as a youngster to conquer Rome, he wanted to conquer it totally. He was a Noel Coward who thought he should have been a Shakespeare or a Dante, a Cole Porter who thought he should have been a Beethoven. As a painter he was, simply, a Salvator Rosa who thought he should have been a Michelangelo, and he had the good fortune to end up believing that he had become one.

17

EIGHTEENTH-CENTURY ITALY: A POSTSCRIPT

To call eighteenth-century Italian painting a postscript may seem an injustice when it includes such names as Tiepolo and Francesco Guardi. But Tiepolo, even though he worked in the new century, was the artist who brought to its apogee the seventeenth-century tradition of baroque decoration, while Guardi's celebrations of a beautiful city beyond its prime seem to evoke the past. Venice as it entered its period of decay produced the finest Italian painters of a century that elsewhere on the peninsula produced little that seems of great consequence today. The center of creative force shifted north to England and France, leaving Rome a great central museum where Englishmen and Frenchmen might visit to learn from dead masters. The Italians during the eighteenth century included quantities of decorative painters whose reputations, now dim except in the history books, flourished in the re-flected effulgence of a great past.

Sebastiano Ricci was the typical Italian decorator-painter, a breed internationally acclaimed and in demand everywhere during a century when churches and palaces needed acres of paintings and Italy was still thought of as the fountainhead of the arts. He managed to live seventy-five years, nearly sixty of them as a busy professional, producing quantities of painting in Venice, Parma, Rome, Milan, Florence, Turin, Vicenza, Bergamo, and outside Italy, in London, the Netherlands, and Vienna. Detailed, his biography would read like a travelogue. There were dozens like him (if not quite as skilled as he) who were at home anywhere in Europe. Most of their paintings, and most of his, are not much more than wallpaper that tourists in coveys under the leadership of a guide look at with grudging respect. In Sebastiano Ricci's case, the historian may look with something more: he is a transitional figure between the grand rhetoric of baroque decoration—the tradition in which he was trained during the part of his life that fell within the seventeenth century—and the lighter touch that found its ideal expression in Tiepolo. Yet he remains a painter for the history books; he left little that is of anything more than historical interest.

Born in Belluno in 1659, Sebastiano Ricci was an apprentice in Venice by the age of twelve. He was a born wanderer, and the reason for the wide distribution of his work is probably that he set out for a new place knowing that he could find work there as often as he started out in response to an invitation. He once spent a relatively uninterrupted period of nearly ten years in Venice without acquiring a permanent address there.

His stay in England, where he was assisted by his nephew Marco Ricci, lasted from 1712 to 1716. He left in disgust when he lost commissions to decorate the dome of St. Paul's and some rooms in Hampton Court Palace to a local talent, James Thornhill (1676-1734). Thornhill, although English, was a somewhat desiccated follower of the Italian baroque tradition who is remembered today less as a painter than as the father-in-law of William Hogarth and the founder of a school where Hogarth studied. Altogether, Ricci was not very popular in England. There was recurrent unpleasantness when he was labeled a mere borrower of other men's styles.

To a large extent the accusation was true. Ricci's primary source was a fellow Venetian who had died some seventy years before Ricci was born—Veronese. But Ricci was always willing to learn. On his way back to Italy from England, he stopped in Paris and visited a thirty-two-year-old painter named Watteau, and copied some of his drawings. He also stopped off in Genoa, where he responded to the flair and dash of his countryman Magnasco. Ricci was an intelligent, vigorous painter whose work leaves you feeling that you should be getting more out of it than you do. What he needed for leavening was just a touch of the extravagance in which his nephew Marco indulged to excess. He died in 1734.

Only seventeen years younger than his internationally successful uncle Sebastiano, Marco Ricci (1676-1729) worked with him most of his life, which was an erratic one. Like Sebastiano, Marco was born in Belluno. One story makes him his uncle's apprentice and student from the beginning. Another brings him to Venice in his twenties in flight from a murder charge. In either case, he did work with Sebastiano in Venice, and from city to city, until 1708, when he went to England with Pellegrini to work on stage designs. The two men quarreled, and two years later Marco was back in Venice, where he picked up his uncle and returned to England in 1712.

When Sebastiano left England in a pique over the loss of commissions to James Thornhill, Marco went with him.

Despite surviving melodramatic accounts of his wildness and his eccentricity, his peccadilloes and his crimes, his life thereafter is not well documented. It is supposed to have ended in suicide. Dressed in his best, the story goes, he tried to starve himself to death, but was rescued. While recuperating he was given a prescription in which he forged a change that turned it into a lethal poison. Unless—and this possibility has also been suggested—the doctor made a mistake in the prescription and circulated the story of the forged prescription in self-defense.

What is more important is that during the last ten years of his life, Marco Ricci contributed to the development of romanticized landscape, giving his own flavor to a genre that originated with Salvator Rosa and that was also being explored by Magnasco, a contemporary of his, whose work he surely had seen. Ricci must also have seen the earliest paintings of classical ruins by Pannini. Adapting the somber theatricality and technical exhibitionism of Rosa and Magnasco to his versions of the subjects that Pannini had treated more objectively, he invested ruined architectural elements with a nostalgia, a regret for the transience of life, a sense of empires crumbling—a mood in which memories of violence past mingle with intimations of violence pending. It was a mood that became dear to the nineteenth-century romantics, although they made it more obvious and sentimental. In Ricci it sometimes has a depth and breadth that bring it close to grandeur.

Giovanni Antonio Pellegrini (1675-1741) was a pupil of Sebastiano Ricci and, like him, a peripatetic international decorator. He executed commissions in England, Germany, Flanders, Paris, Prague, Dresden, and Vienna. Increasingly appreciated nowadays as a precursor of Tiepolo, he was put in the shade during his lifetime by Sebastiano Ricci. He and Sebastiano's nephew, Marco Ricci, were taken to London by Lord Manchester, who had been in Venice on an ambassadorial mission. Pellegrini for a while was head of the school founded by Godfrey Kneller.

Giovanni Paolo Pannini (1691/92-1764/65) was at work in Rome by about 1717. His paintings of architectural monuments, both those of his own time and those of ancient Rome in ruins, are architectural records by a man less sensitive to mood than to elegancies of form, proportion, and historical style; even his synthesized arrangements look documentary. Wonderfully decorative, his renderings are cool, precise, rather detached. In his later work, a few romantic concessions appear. He also painted fetes and other assemblages with people in courtly dress, and he was tremendously popular, perhaps even more popular in France than in Italy.

Alessandro Magnasco was born in Genoa in 1667 and was established there when he died in 1749, but worked at various times in Milan and in Florence (for the last of the Medici dukes, Gian Gastone). He combined a fantastically exaggerated version of the romantic landscape of Salvator Rosa with picaresque subjects like Jacques Callot's, adding to the mixture attenuated, ecstatically tormented forms remindful of El Greco's. Since he could hardly have seen any El Grecos (although some historians are willing to believe that, somehow, he did see them), he must have developed these forms from the examples of Tintoretto and Bassano. A list of the ingredients in Magnasco's art could run on and on, with hints of a reversion to sixteenth-century mannerism included.

Magnasco's broken, dashing, explosive brushwork was all his own. It is so violent that it is prophetic not only of impressionism but, in its emotive character, of modern expressionism. The only trouble is that the restless, haunted spirit of Magnasco's paintings, shot through with supernatural stormy lights, is vitiated by the sheer bravura of his performance. He often ends by stimulating us through his showmanship rather than by touching us through the dramas that he stages with such skill. His Italian colleagues also found him stimulating. As an influence on Marco Ricci and on some aspects of the work of Francesco Guardi (his figure paintings), Magnasco was the source of a major current in eighteenth-century Italian painting.

Giovanni Battista Piazzetta's "constant study and pursuit of glory rather than gain reduced him to poverty and hastened his death," according to a petition for a pension brought to the Venetian state by his widow and her seven children. "Constant study" accords with our knowledge that Piazzetta was an extremely slow worker at a time when the quick touch of the virtuoso was becoming fashionable in painting. "Pursuit of glory" could not have referred to worldly ambition, since he is known to have been of a melancholy temperament, fond of solitude. Apparently the glory he sought was a place in the tradition that had produced the great Venetian baroque decorators, particularly Veronese. Here he was misled. In drawings, where artists tell us so much about themselves, he is tender and graceful in the best eighteenth-century manner of cultivated sensibility. In an occasional painting this same sensibility is exposed. Fortunately he was a prolific draftsman. Otherwise, the altarpieces over which he labored (to the later distress of his widow) would bear false though overwhelming testimony to his conservatism and would leave him a not very interesting artist.

Piazzetta was born in Venice in 1683 and died there in 1754. His father, Giacomo, was a sculptor. He worked for a while, when he was about twenty, in Bologna, with Giuseppe Maria Crespi, but in 1711 he was listed as a member of the Venetian painters' guild and there is no record of his ever having left Venice again. Nor is there any record of his marriage. His wife bore their first child in 1725, when he was forty-two.

Piazzetta was known beyond Venice, not only elsewhere in Italy but in England, France, and Germany as well. In Germany his patrons included the Archbishop of Cologne and Count Johann Matthias von der Schulenburg. This meant renown if not exactly the "glory" that his widow said he "pursued." But Piazzetta had cheated himself. In trying to emulate the baroque masters, he repressed a more delicate taste that could have made him a foremost rococo painter instead of the relatively minor transitional figure between Veronese and Tiepolo that he became.

Giovanni Battista Tiepolo was the culminating Italian master of the illusionistic ceiling that opens architecture into the space of an inhabited sky, the kind of ceiling that had seemed to reach its perfection in Gaulli's *Triumph of the Name of Jesus* in the Gesù before Tiepolo was born. In surpassing Gaulli, Tiepolo consummated a baroque innovation, but he leavened the melodrama of baroque operatics with a grace and an airy flourish that (even when he was decorating a vast hall) were essentially intimate in the rococo spirit of his century. He was a superb professional with absolutely no technical limitations. He was always completely the master of exactly what he wanted to produce and of exactly the means that would produce it most directly, most effectively, whether he was painting grandiose spectacles enacted by life-size figures on the ceilings of the Episcopal Palace in Würzburg, probably his masterpieces, or whether he was making notations on a scrap of paper, summarizing the stance, the mood, and the flow of the garments of a single figure in a few lines and a dash or two of wash.

Tiepolo's drawings, always avidly collected and now put on a par with his paintings of any size, are like perfect phrases or epigrams within his wonderfully facile, accomplished, and polished rhetoric, all flair, all elegance. He does not try to tell us anything about fate, life, and all that. But his art in itself is so alive, so immediate in its presence, that it is inherently a celebration of the sensuous world as poetic experience, in the Venetian tradition. Never as lyrical as Giorgione, neither as sumptuous nor as profound as Titian, Tiepolo nevertheless brought the Venetian tradition to a magnificent close with the flourish of his incomparable style.

Born in 1696, Tiepolo studied under Lazzarini and perhaps under Piazzetta, but formed his style by observation of Veronese and of an artist closer in time, Sebastiano Ricci (who was, in fact, a kind of secondhand Veronese). He was admitted to the guild at the age of twenty-one, and two years later married Cecelia Guardi, whose little brother Francesco, then only seven years old, was to become her husband's only rival for the title of greatest Italian painter of the eighteenth century.

By the time he was thirty, Tiepolo had discovered, if he had not yet perfected, the fresh, blond color scheme of the clear-skied world where his cast of well-built aristocratic actors pose as the handsomest of allegorical figures or enact, with effortless, athletic vivacity, the parts of gods, saints, and heroes historical or legendary. By the time he was fifty, his fame was international. He was in Würzburg from late 1750 until 1753. Back in Venice, he was elected the first president of the Venetian Academy. In 1762, now sixty-six years old, he went to Madrid at the invitation of Charles III, and for four years he and his sons Giovanni Domenico and Lorenzo, and the other assistants he had brought along, worked at decorating the ceilings of the Royal Palace. These decorations are not Tiepolo's most attractive work, whether because so many assistants were involved (although he customarily used many) or because he somewhat sobered his manner in deference to the extreme formality of the Spanish court.

In spite of their relative sobriety, Tiepolo's decorations were attacked as frivolous by Mengs, the prototype of the next century's neoclassical pedant and a power in Spanish painting. Mengs's adherents rigged intrigues against Tiepolo that gave him the first bitter years of his career, but he stayed on, nevertheless, to complete further commissions for Charles. This was a mistake. He died suddenly in Madrid in 1770, seventy-four years old, without seeing Venice again.

Giovanni Domenico Tiepolo (1727-1804), his son and chief assistant, was then forty-three years old, with thirty-four years before him in which to work on his own. He was not at all a bad painter, but in such a shadow ("such a light" is somehow more appropriate, in reference to the lambent art of his father) he could only suffer. There is an area where the father's lesser works and the son's better works in the father's manner are confused with one another. But there is also an area where Domenico is entirely his own man.

As an imitator of his father, Domenico Tiepolo was a somewhat heavy-handed and occasionally awkward follower of an artist remarkable for his light touch and his grace. But when his subjects were Venetian maskers, punchinellos, and other representatives of a Venice where sensual folly had replaced sensuous delight, Domenico Tiepolo could make a sardonic comment that owes nothing to the paternal tradition that dogged him. But these paintings are exceptions.

Like his father, Domenico poured out a stream of drawings. They are good drawings, and in this field Domenico has his staunch supporters, but there is a heaviness to his line that makes the flights of his angels not quite convincing.

There was a third Tiepolo, the second son of Giovanni Battista, named Lorenzo Tiepolo (1736-1776), who has survived, poor fellow, mostly as a name followed by two dates. As an artist, he occupies a position in relation to his brother that his brother occupies in relation to their father. Not much is known about him. One hopes that the forty years of his life were happier than his legacy as an artist.

Pietro Longhi, who was born in 1702 in Venice, where he lived to a ripe old age, had the good fortune to look about him, as he approached forty, and decide that the grand manner was not for him. Until then he had been an inadequate practitioner of baroque rhetoric, which in the eighteenth century demanded the dazzling airiness of a Tiepolo to keep it afloat. Even his contemporaries, who had respect for the grand manner per se, recognized Longhi as a fairly soggy member of the clan. Even so, he received some large commissions. What remains of this early work gives us no reason to regret that most of it has disappeared.

Around 1740 Longhi shifted from large to small scale, and from allegory and legend and religious subjects to the scenes of daily life that were becoming popular in England and France. But unlike his English contemporary Hogarth and the younger Frenchman Greuze, Longhi was not much concerned with moral preachment. In spite of his occasional mild satires on the clergy, he preferred to observe the somnolent patricians of the decaying Venetian Republic with a degree of irony so mild that it surely escaped the gentlefolk themselves. His interiors (like Hogarth's, but on a more intimate scale) suggest stage-sets, and he is often likened to Carlo Goldoni. But the vivacious spirit of this dramatist breaks through in Longhi only when he is treating his most festive subjects, where maskers play at their intrigues. Longhi is almost always good-humored; the bite and indignation of a Hogarth, natural to a vigorous society, could not be stimulated by the languid and static atmosphere of Venice.

Except for a period of study in Bologna, Longhi seems to have spent all his life in his native city. He was continuously busy with a variety of duties connected with the arts, and when the Venetian Academy was founded in 1756 he was among its first members. He taught in its school until 1780, when he was seventy-eight years old, and lived another five years to die at eighty-three on May 8, 1785.

Pietro Longhi had married at thirty. His son Alessandro Longhi (1733-1813) became a portrait painter of eminence with a respectable degree of perception when it came to probing the personalities of his sitters. There are even occasional hints of his father's ironic observations, *sub rosa* comments on the vanity or pretension of his sitters, who remain happily unaware of the exposure.

Three other artists named Longhi can be mentioned briefly here, in connection with the puzzle of why Pietro Longhi chose that name. His father had been a silver caster named Alessandro Falca. In changing his name to Longhi, Pietro could hardly have been inspired by the conspicuousness of that name in the arts during the sixteenth and seventeenth centuries, since that conspicuousness was of a very mixed kind. A Martino Longhi the Elder (*d.* 1591) had been a respectable papal architect who made a great deal of money, but his eldest son Onorio Longhi (*c.* 1569-1619) and Onorio's son Martino Longhi the Younger managed to make the name synonymous with fractiousness, bad language, insult, mayhem, assault, ill temper, and general troublemaking and personal unpleasantness, although Onorio was a not-bad minor artist and Martino the Younger an admirable architect. They were always in court, Onorio suing his younger brothers for what he thought was his rightful portion of his father's estate, and both Onorio and Martino the Younger appearing as defendants in suits brought by the victims of their public insult and battery. In addition to their artistic capabilities the Longhi clan had a really distinguished talent for invective, but this gift can hardly account for Pietro Falca's changing his name to adopt theirs.

Although Rosalba Carriera has secured a historical spot as an early pastellist, she has lost the international esteem that during her lifetime spread her portraits all over Europe. Every titled person who passed through Venice seems to have posed for her, and in 1720, when she was forty-five years old, she went to Paris for a year, where she met everybody who was anybody. She was always a great favorite with the electors of Saxony, and there are 157 of her works in Dresden alone.

The kind of eighteenth-century prettiness now called "Dresden doll" marks Rosalba Carriera's portrait style. If she had any perception of character, very little of it emerges from the delicate powdery faces. At her best, she exemplifies the grace, femininity, courtesy, and refinement that covered such a multitude of eighteenth-century sins of the kind that flourished in Venice. Some of these sins she reveals by indirection, in studies of young girls endowed with a pseudo-innocence that puts a candified surface on licentious sexuality.

Rosalba was born in Venice in 1675. She never married. Her chief devotion was to her younger sister Giovanna, and to her mother. Giovanna and another sister, Angela, were Rosalba's students. Angela found a more satisfactory way of life in marriage to the painter Pellegrini, but Giovanna, along with dozens of Rosalba's other students, produced works in her manner that have become inextricably confused with the teacher's.

Misfortunes struck Rosalba late in life. Giovanna died, and then their ancient mother. At seventy, Rosalba was so nearly blind that she had to stop work. She lived another twelve years. When she died in 1757 at the age of eighty-two she was totally blind, and insane.

The eighteenth century, as the first great age of Italian tourism, engendered a new form of landscape painting, the view of a specific spot rather than an idyllic invention. In Venice, which was (with Rome) the high spot of the grand tour, these views, or *vedute*, were turned out most prolifically. Where earlier painters such as Carpaccio and Gentile Bellini had used the fantastic city as a background for paintings of whatever subjects, painters now found their subjects in the canals and palaces and monuments themselves. Those who turned out these superpostcards were often hacks, which accounts for *veduta* painting's being regarded as a second-class art. Even the patriarch and archetype of the school, Giovanni Antonio Canal, called Canaletto, made three applications for membership before he was accepted in the Venetian Academy, although he was internationally famous.

Canaletto was born in 1697, the son of a theatrical scene painter, Bernardo Canal, and is recorded as working with his father and brother in Venetian theaters during his teens. About 1719, when he was in his early twenties, the family went to Rome to work on scenery for Scarlatti's operas. When they came back to Venice the following year, Canaletto was admitted to the painters' guild and was soon producing *vedute* for the English market.

These early works were free and spirited in contrast with the rigidly defined perspective drawing required for stage scenery at the time, and were influenced by the most popular *vedutista*—Lucas Carlevaris (1663-1730), who dropped to the second rank as Canaletto rose. By 1730, Canaletto had made a connection with Joseph Smith, later British consul in Venice, by which Smith virtually became his agent. Smith had his pick of everything Canaletto painted, and also arranged special commissions. Before long there was hardly a great house in England that didn't have its Canaletto or its set of Canalettos. The Duke of Bedford once purchased twenty-four at a shot.

For one reason or another, Canaletto's style changed as his popularity increased, and not for the better, it seems to us today. He reverted to the rather hard, dry manner of the perspective stage-set, detailing entire vistas in rigid, mechanical perspective, with bright color and little attention to the atmospheric effects that are so entrancing in Venice and that had so delighted him when he first began to paint. This sounds like, and probably was, a concession to the souvenir market, which wanted its record of the sights to be as complete and as obviously ornamental as possible. And the laborious business of laying out the perspective could be turned over to assistants who had no talent as painters. Thus Canaletto, who briefly seemed to anticipate impressionism, and who probably painted many of his earlier pictures on the spot, became at the height of his success a less inventive studio painter.

In 1745, when wars on the Continent interrupted international travel, Canaletto went directly to his major source of patronage—England. He had never been very popular in his own country, and except for two brief returns to Venice he was in England for the next ten years. His manner changed so much, became so very dry and tight, that he was even accused of being an impostor substituting for the real Canaletto. He prospered all the same, and if his English scenes are more prosaic than his early Venice-scapes, they are still among the most beautiful vistas ever painted to record architecture in its setting, whether an urban mélange or a countryside dominated by a palace.

Owen McSwiney, a British operatic impresario who knew Canaletto in London, speaks of his difficult temperament and the unreasonable prices he demanded for his work. The prices, however, were paid, and there was grumbling that the English had spoiled the Italian. He returned to Venice in 1755, when he was in his late fifties, but painted little, perhaps because his health was poor, and died in 1768 at the age of seventy-one. He had never had much of a feeling for England, yet he left so much work there that he sired, or grandsired, a school of English landscape that adapted his style to the expression of English moods. And his early, freely painted Venetian scenes were a point of departure for Francesco Guardi, the *vedutista* who nowadays puts him in the shade.

Bernardo Bellotto, Canaletto's nephew (he was the son of Lorenzo Belotti and Canaletto's sister, Fiorenza Canal), learned the craft of *veduta* painting under his uncle. Some of his early work has been attributed to his master. From the "de Canaletto" added to his signature he became known as Canaletto in northern Europe, and he has become "Canaletto" on the labels in many museums, with resultant confusion.

The tendency has been to regard Bellotto as a mere follower of the great Canaletto, but this is an injustice. Bellotto was a painter of great originality who, one may even dare suggest, extended the range of *veduta* painting beyond anything his uncle achieved. He brought life to the formula of decorative topographical descriptions by introducing genre incidents in the streets (where Canaletto showed everything as a staged pageant), and included in his views existing temporary structures such as hoardings and the like (whereas in Canaletto everything was always in perfect condition). Above all, he unified his vistas in natural light. All of this anticipated nineteenth-century realism. In addition, Bellotto painted *capricci*—architectural fantasies—of great charm.

Bellotto was born in 1720. In his early twenties he was beginning to be mentioned on a par with his uncle. Perhaps this brought about a friction we are often told of. Whether for this reason or another, Bellotto left Venice at the age of twenty-seven and never returned. He went first to Dresden, where, after a year, he was appointed court painter by Augustus II of Saxony. It was at about this time that he began adding "de Canaletto" to his signature, presumably to capitalize on his uncle's international fame before he himself acquired an international reputation. He visited Vienna and Munich to paint views of those cities, and on his way to Russia in 1767 paused in Warsaw. King Stanislas II invited him to remain there, and so he did, for the rest of his life, under royal patronage. He died in Warsaw in 1780, sixty years old.

Bellotto's series of views of Warsaw, now in the National Museum of that city, are so explicitly detailed that after World War II they served as documentary references for the rebuilding of the old part of the city that had been destroyed by bombing. But Bellotto was not a painter of documents. For all their historical accuracy, his paintings of old Warsaw evoke a life that the rebuilt city has not regained.

"Guardi" means first of all Francesco Guardi (1712-1793), the greatest of *veduta* painters and a great painter without reference to that or any other special category. The sound of his name brings visions of the most enchanting combinations of sky, water, architecture (bridges, palaces, piazzas, and random structures), and vivacious inhabitants who share the soft, bright, damp, and diffused light of the only city in the world that offers all this in combination— Venice. Guardi is the sort of painter whose vision of a place is so much the apotheosis of that place that he reveals rather than records it. We see the inherent loveliness of the actual Venice all the better for having seen it reflected in Guardi's painted Venice.

Francesco was only one of five Guardis who during the eighteenth century (and for a few stunted years during the early nineteenth) ran a shop in Venice where views of the city were stocked as souvenirs for visitors. The Guardi shop was not exactly a postcard stand, but neither was it a sanctum: the Guardi family represents the terminal point of the tradition of the painter as a pure craftsman, offering his wares for sale rather than his genius for patronage. Francesco Guardi's views of the city brought only half the prices fetched by Canaletto's. Perhaps to the customers, Guardi's greater technical freedom, his elimination of the sharp detail respected almost obsessively by Canaletto, seemed merely a cursory, if attractive, way of getting a canvas covered and onto the stands for sale. Today, with our reconditioned way of seeing painting, Guardi has become the imaginative artist to whom the brilliant reporter Canaletto must take second place.

The Guardi family shop was founded early in the century by Domenico Guardi. Little is known about him except that he was born in Vienna in 1678, that he worked there before coming to Venice, and that he left three sons—Francesco, who was four years old when Domenico died in 1716, Giovanni Antonio, who was seventeen, and Nicolo, who was only a year. Giovanni Antonio (1699-1769), the elder brother, was an artist of real skill if not of great consequence, who, in true craft-traditional manner, could turn his hand to any-thing. He did some genre subjects very much in the manner of Pietro Longhi, and altarpieces as well, never hesitating to borrow and adapt a successful formula. Nicolo (1715-1785) may be dismissed here, since he did not grow up to be much of an artist, although he was a faithful assistant in the shop. We may also dismiss the fifth Guardi, Francesco's son Gia-como (1764-1835), who concluded the dynasty as a rather heavy-handed imitator of his father—heavy-handedness being, surely, the least appropriate manner for imitation of Fran-cesco Guardi, the most sensitively deft of painters.

Too much can be made of Francesco's impressionistic prophecies; although technically defendable, they should not be allowed to obscure his essential character as a poet. He took the operatic tradition of Tiepolo (who was his brother-in-law) and, as if recognizing that its term was ended, scaled its vivaciousness to the intimacy of the salon. And although we habitually speak of Francesco's views of Venice, his most individual works are the caprices in which he invented his own scenes. French, Italian, and English painters in Rome during his century were rediscovering the ruins of antiquity, this time not as noble monuments but as romantic symbols of the transience of glory. In his own city Francesco made a comparable discovery independently: his invented landscapes are close to home, in time as well as in place. He was one of the first artists to romanticize the squalor of an old building in a disheveled courtyard, perhaps with laundry hanging from the windows, perhaps, too, with a ruined arcade nearby, sprouting weedy shrubs that feed on its moldings. But the water, the shimmer, the sparkle, the air of Venice, impreg-nate everything, and the closest Francesco ever comes to mournfulness (and it is not very close) is the comment that in Venice even decay is lovely.

Guardi until recently was not assigned a great place in

the painting of figures, being credited only with those fetch-
ing strollers or maskers, an inch or a few inches in height and
wonderfully described in half a dozen strokes of paint, who
people his city or ride on his lagoons. New studies, however,
have assigned to him a body of paintings dominated by figures—notably the series called *The Story of Tobias* in the
Church of San Raffaele in Venice, where he pushes his free,
suggestive brushwork to the limit just this side of dissolution.
All forms seem about to disintegrate into a last fluttering
union of air, light, color, and agitation, a pure abstract opti-
cal expression that recalls Magnasco but is somehow more
engaging in its theatricality.

Francesco Guardi's only near rival as an artist who combined topographical *vedute* with imaginative flights was a
contemporary, Giovanni Battista Piranesi—not a painter but
an architect and etcher who produced nearly a thousand cop-
perplates. His aggrandized and poeticized views of Rome,
printed and reprinted by the thousands and tens of thousands,
flooded Europe like postcards. Today, reproduced, they have
found their way everywhere not only as pictures but as
motifs for fabric designs and decorations of various kinds.
Even so, they never become too familiar to please.

Piranesi was born in 1720 and died in 1778. First trained
in Venice by his father, a stonemason, and an uncle who was
an engineer and architect, he learned etching when he went
to Rome in his early twenties and published an architectural
manual when he was only twenty-three. Except for one brief
return to Venice, he remained in Rome for the rest of his
life. Working as an architect, an artist, and a dealer in an-
tiquities, he became one of Rome's most famous citizens.

During his century and the early nineteenth, before
photography replaced paintings and prints as tourist lures,

Piranesi's views of Rome became notorious among returning travelers as having promised more than the city itself delivered. Today we see his exaggerations and idealizations not as deceptions but as means toward the end of apotheosizing the grandeur of the Eternal City, a grandeur that is present in spirit but is diminished visually by decay and by disfiguring accumulations of trivia.

As an imaginative artist, Piranesi is even more highly esteemed for an early series of fourteen etchings, the *Carceri,* designs for (nominally) prisons, with Piranesi the architect supplying the structural knowledge from which Piranesi the theatrical fantasist and Piranesi the brilliantly inventive draftsman concocted huge visions of stone and light with ink on paper. Even more, Piranesi's drawings—ragged, aggressive, and breathtaking in the speed, decision, and economy of their notation—appeal to us as fireworks that approach genius. They also anticipate twentieth-century expressionism.

Piranesi himself thought of these fantasies as relaxations, regarding his archaeological studies as his claim to immortality. He carried on excavations near Rome and drew reconstructions of ancient edifices. During the last summer of his life he measured and drew the temples at Paestum for a volume that his son Francesco completed. As a creative force, Piranesi lived on into the nineteenth century by the proxy of his *Diverse Maniere d'Adorne i Cammini,* a volume of imaginary interiors, based on classical motifs, that materialized as an ingredient of the Empire style in France.

18

EIGHTEENTH-CENTURY
FRANCE AND ENGLAND

French-English social and cultural relationships over the centuries have been marked by suspicion and antagonism so irrational that they can have been engendered only by a mutual attraction that refuses to declare itself because it does not quite understand itself. The national temperaments are, one might say, inversely identical. Privately the French insist upon a rigid code of conventions that they flout in public; the British observe public decorum while indulging in outrageous conduct in private. It is no wonder that the two nations have never got along well, and no wonder, either, that they have borrowed so freely from one another. An instance of the curious aesthetic bond between them is the kind of landscaping, identical on both sides of the Channel, that is called *"un jardin anglais"* in France and "a French garden" in England. Etymologically, the cultural exchange is symbolized by the word "redingote." When the gentleman's riding coat, a beautifully tailored affair originating in England, was adopted and feminized in Paris, its name was roughly phoneticized as *"redingote,"* after which both the garment and the name were repatriated as the English lady's redingote, a fashionable garment for street wear.

Not in hope of reconciling the two nations or the two temperaments, but because the contrasts and similarities are so provocative, six artists are paired here as an introduction to the Anglo-French eighteenth century—Watteau with Hogarth, because the Frenchness of the one and the Englishness of the other contrast so completely, Boucher with Reynolds, because both were aesthetic dictators of styles that could hardly have been further apart, and Gainsborough with Fragonard, because these two delightful men were spiritual twins. The six artists were born over a period of forty-eight years in the order just listed—Watteau in 1684, Hogarth in 1697, Boucher in 1703, Reynolds in 1723, Gainsborough in 1727, and Fragonard in 1732. By the time Fragonard died in 1806, the century had run its course not only in years but in spirit, with the French Revolution as its bloody grave.

A seventh artist, Thomas Rowlandson, seems an appropriate terminal entry in this chapter. Much younger than the rest—he was born in 1756, twenty-four years after Fragonard, and lived twenty-seven years into the nineteenth century—he was nevertheless the natural heir of Hogarth, observing a society like Gainsborough's and Fragonard's less sympathetically than they did. Also, as something of an English-French hybrid, Rowlandson can dispense with a French opposite.

Eighteenth-century France, considered either as an ideal society devoted to pleasure and aesthetic cultivation or as a less than ideal society given over to libertinage and dilettantism, had its life cut short at both ends. Beyond term and groaning not with labor pains but with boredom, it had to mark time for fifteen years after 1700, waiting for Louis XIV to die, and it lost its last decade when another society put it to the guillotine. "Do get on with it—things are so dull," the court might have said to their dying monarch; three quarters of a century later Mme du Barry cried out on the scaffold, "One moment more—life is so sweet."

Three painters neatly spaced in successive generations— Watteau, Boucher, and Fragonard—recorded the ideal promise, the surface triumph, and the lively decline of this society, without introducing so much as a hint that it was faulty and threatened by revolutionary philosophies. At the end, when the foundations were eaten away, Fragonard was still romping exuberantly about in the decayed structure as if it were perfectly sound, and although we can force things a bit to read into his art the symptoms of the fall, no world on its last legs has ever been presented more attractively by a participant who enjoyed its pleasures with less reservation.

Earlier, Mme de Pompadour had had the perception to make her sinister prophecy *"Après nous le déluge,"* but her reigning painter, Boucher, offers nothing more revealing than skillfully enameled surfaces celebrating the niceties (with an occasional lapse into the vulgarities) of established taste. Eighteenth-century France found no social critic among its artists, as did eighteenth-century England in that vigorous protestant against the evils of the day, Hogarth. But France did find an artist great enough to distill the virtues of its privileged society into an ideal expression. He appeared early, during the first decade of that society's existence, but remained an observer from outside, as if the corruption that festered beneath the ideal must affect anyone who entered the game. This outsider was Jean Antoine Watteau.

All Watteau's surviving paintings were done during the last twelve years of his life, which means the six years before the death of Louis XIV and the six after. The chronological sequence of these paintings cannot be worked out with any certainty, but Watteau's mature style, the realization of the century's ideal, was born during the middle years of the twelve from the conjunction of three circumstances: the death of the old king with its release of the new century; Watteau's adoption as protégé by the immensely rich Pierre Crozat, which placed him in a position to observe the new society intimately; and the appearance of the first strong symptoms of tuberculosis, which intensified the poignantly withdrawn nature of his spirit (and which eventually killed him at the age of thirty-six).

Surely we may assume that the dreamlike quality of Watteau's art—its quiet, half-melancholy languor, the impression it gives of having been created by a non-participant from an observation point just outside the borders of life—is connected with his frailty. He seems to understand what the passions of men and women are; yet he must reduce the tempests of physical love to a sweet, regretful tenderness. The sexual games are refined to graceful suggestions; the bacchanal becomes a stroll in a shaded park; the delights of the flesh are recognized and perhaps yearned for, but their consummations are abjured from the beginning. The murmured endearment must do for the amorous lunge, even for the caress. When a lover occasionally yields to impulse and commits an initial faux pas, he violates the truce between desire as an abstraction and love as a physical act that holds Watteau's world together so harmoniously, but so tenuously, against all the natural violences of life. It is a nostalgic world whose fragile denizens, shimmering in taffetas and satins as they wander through it, seem to look back upon the fullness of lost pleasures that, in truth, they have never experienced and never will.

It is odd to discover from comments made by his contemporaries that this greatest poet of the eighteenth century was thought of as a realist. Etienne Jeaurat (1699-1789), a genre painter who engraved some of Watteau's works, could make the closest possible translation of these visions and still call Watteau, admiringly, a painter who "marvelously imitates nature." If the comment seems inapt to us, who have seen the nineteenth century's demonstration of what the imitation of nature can mean, it does make us look at Watteau a second time from a different angle and calls our attention to an element in his art that we take for granted. In the context of his time, Watteau was not only a realist but an innovational one. It is true that Watteau's world is an invention and a lyrical dream, and it is true that the people who move within it are variants of a human race more fine-boned than birds and as exquisitely plumaged, but (and this was his innovation) he pictured that world as the impressionists pictured theirs, in its momentary, unself-conscious aspects, catching its denizens unaware, or not caring, that they are observed.

Watteau's genius for observing the casual gesture—the turn of a head, the lift of an arm, the posture of a body as it conforms to the balances of walking, sitting, or playing a musical instrument—and his sensitivity to these unstudied attitudes as revelations of mood and character, are apparent throughout his paintings. But it is in his drawings that these gestures are most wonderfully set down. He made of drawing something that it had never been before, something hardly related to his contemporaries' idea of drawing—which produced conscientious academic studies of musculature, catalogues of poses and proportions in which the body became a machine adaptable to the contrivance of compositions in the grand manner—or even to the idea of drawing as a memorandum of facts for later reference. Even genre painting, with its basic premise of echoing daily life, was a matter of setting a typical explanatory, narrative pose, which, being once-removed from the spontaneously assumed attitude, might be entirely removed from immediate perception and expression.

Watteau was so indifferent to these conventions, so alone in his use of drawing as the expression of intimate response to observed objects, that twenty-six years after Watteau's death his good friend the Comte de Caylus could still be so blind as to say, lecturing before the Académie Royale, that Watteau, "having no knowledge of anatomy and almost never having drawn from the nude," was unable to render figures properly. But no draftsman has more beautifully integrated the structure and movement of a body, clothed or unclothed. Caylus could refer to Watteau's "inadequacy in the practice of drawing" only because Watteau did not draw in the heroic manner.

No doubt it is true that if Watteau had attempted heroics he would have been lost, but nothing could be more beside the point. He is one of the few artists whose sketches, even at their most informal, can be appreciated in terms of a complete and independent art as revelatory as painting. Yet even here, in his most personal work, Watteau holds himself aloof, with an aloofness inseparable from the other qualities that made him the most sensitive of observers.

It was not only his physical frailty, it was his temperament—the record shows—that kept Watteau an outsider. He had many acquaintances, but they were persons who had to seek him out. He had no intimate friends, and he never married; if he had any serious love affair, there is no reference to it in the accounts of people who knew him and would have had no hesitation in mentioning an attachment that could hardly have escaped their attention. Solitary by nature, Watteau, during his successful years, moved in a company that included some of the most conspicuous men in France, men who were powerful, ambitious, and close to the court—hardheaded and sometimes unscrupulous. In a world of high fashion and low intrigue his paintings set a vogue in dress if not in comportment. He certainly was aware of the ferocity and cynicism that coexisted with the ideal of delicate sensibilities and exquisite refinements, and he knew as well the world of the streets, the fairs, and the hand-to-mouth existence that he shared with other starveling artists during his earliest youth.

With this top-to-bottom material at hand, an artist of different temperament might have been a French Hogarth. Watteau, however, was Hogarth's antipode. Hogarth's power was that, as a social commentator, he exposed the worms beneath the veneer. Watteau's greatness was that he redeemed society's ornamental upper crust by transposing it from the real world to the regions of poetry.

The importance of Watteau in our appreciation of the eighteenth century is greater than we generally realize. Without him we would have a record of courtly affectations in Boucher, of licentious charm in Fragonard, of costumes in portraits and popular prints. Only through Gainsborough would we get an affectionate revelation of the natural warmth that exists in good people beneath frivolity and fashion. Without Watteau, Gainsborough would remain the century's greatest painter, but, for all his poetical touch, he loses his essential character if we try to make him anything more than a single fortunate man in eighteenth-century England. Watteau alone abstracted from the froth of his century an essence that, for all the particularity of its raw ingredients, rises above time and place.

Watteau was born in the seventeenth century, on October 10, 1684, and was only nominally French by origin. His parents were Flemish, and his native city, Valenciennes, had been French for only six years at the time of his birth. But Watteau was the artist who oriented French painting, turning it quite abruptly from the seventeenth-century formalism of Poussin and Lebrun to a kind of Parisian Frenchness that, ever since, has been a steady dominant in French art. It is a Frenchness most easily recognized by most people in the art of Renoir, a Frenchness where gaiety and tenderness are perfectly matched, where casual diversions are understood as manifestations of the good things that each individual experiences, or hopes to experience, within the intimacy of his own life.

Watteau's father was a master tile and slate craftsman, possibly of unstable temperament, given to violent rages and probably an alcoholic. Tax records classify him as a bourgeois, so he must have been literate and, by the standards of his craft, prosperous enough. There is no way of reconstructing Watteau's childhood; legend makes it appropriately unhappy. The métier of painter was his own choice, and he was apprenticed at fifteen to one Jacques Albert Gérin, an obscure pedant. He was only eighteen when he found his way to Paris. This early departure suggests that things were not too happy at home.

Penniless and alone, Watteau attached himself to a group of Flemish painters who ran a workshop where souvenir paintings were turned out by the gross, like postcards, for sale to wholesalers from the provinces and peasants who came to town for the fairs. Watteau's specialty was St. Nicholas. He received virtually no pay—a few francs and a soup ration.

Slight of build, of medium height, reserved or even timid in manner, and indifferent or helpless in practical matters, Watteau was frequently underpaid or cheated, but he so inspired the protective instinct that from his late teens on he was befriended by a series of dealers, fellow artists, and collector-patrons who form in retrospect a kind of Watteau Benevolent Society. He lived in their houses or studios, coming as a welcome guest but never staying long, moving out for reasons not explained. In the reminiscences of people who held him in affection, Watteau's carelessness, his untidiness, his impatience, and his fits of misanthropy and withdrawal are accepted as corollaries to his talent, and even as part of his charm.

But Watteau was not a charmer by intention. He was a prototype of the artist, familiar today, who has replaced the hardworking supercraftsman of the Middle Ages and early Renaissance, the god-philosopher of the High Renaissance, and the practical man of affairs of the seventeenth century— the artist as a man not quite like the rest of us, whose inability to cope with the world is inherent in a talent that must be nurtured and protected. Those who discover and patronize that talent are rewarded by the satisfaction of vicariously sharing the artist's creative gift. Watteau's patrons were that special type of *amateur* peculiar to the eighteenth century— professional men, financiers, or dilettantes whose avocation was patronage and collecting, and who might enjoy the practice of an art, usually painting or engraving, as a serious hobby.

Watteau came into this circle by stages. The year after his arrival in Paris—he was now nineteen—he was befriended by a dealer and print publisher named Jean Mariette, who had a shop in the Rue Saint-Jacques. Mariette let Watteau study his stock of prints by Jacques Callot and engravings after Rubens and Titian. There were probably drawings by all three, as well. Callot's impact was immediate, in conjunction with a firsthand acquaintance with the *commedia dell' arte* that Callot had celebrated. But at this time, in a Paris that was not yet the city of public museums, Watteau must have seen very few paintings by Rubens and perhaps none by the Venetians; these had to wait until he knew the collectors. After the superb theatricality of Callot, it was Rubens's radiant color (and his glorification of the flesh) and Titian's poeticization of all sensuous experience that became the major influences in the expression of Watteau's genius.

Mariette probably brought Watteau to the attention of Claude Gillot, and Watteau worked with him from about 1704 to 1708, still at the level of apprentice and assistant. Gillot, who was Flemish, and a rebel against the academic doctrines, painted lively scenes of Parisian life and designed sets for the *commedia.* Louis XIV had banished the Italian players for their satire on the prudery of his Mme de Maintenon in a piece called "False Chastity," but the Italian tradition was carried on by French actors who became popular idols at the same fairs where Watteau's little hack paintings of St. Nicholas were sold. As a friend of Gillot's he must have met the actors and must have sketched them during rehearsals or performances, but no record of such encounters has survived. Neither, for that matter, do the bawdy high spirits of the *commedia* that delighted Callot survive in the later paintings in which Watteau echoed the theater. The *fêtes galantes,* Watteau's final and greatest works, evoke the grace and high style of the comedians, but the mood shifts to a key of dream and regret. Where the references are specific, as in *Le Mezzetin* (Metropolitan Museum) and the portrait of *Gilles* (Louvre), the models were not actors but friends of Watteau's who posed in the theatrical costumes that he kept in his studio.

When he was twenty-one, Watteau met Jean de Julienne, a young man his own age who was the manager (and later, by inheritance, the owner) of his uncle's prosperous textile factory. For the rest of Watteau's life, Julienne did his best to keep the artist's affairs in order for him. But it is important to remember that in the world represented by Julienne, Watteau was never a careerist. His gratitude to his friend-patrons accounts for the concessions he made in taking part in the social life that went on. He was drawn to the Comte de

Caylus, another near contemporary, and to the well-placed Nicolas Henin, Superintendent of the King's Buildings and Gardens, because these men shared his interests—the three met to sketch from the model—and not because they moved in the great world, or close to it. Julienne also, as an *amateur,* was a painter, engraver, and musician.

At the age of twenty-four, Watteau for the first time came into something like a position of security when he joined Claude Audran, a popular decorator, as assistant. Still trying to find his way as a painter, he competed unsuccessfully for the Prix de Rome with a picture, since lost, on an assigned subject that could hardly be less suggestive of his spirit: *David's Return After Defeating Goliath.* During these years, one feels, Watteau was waiting for self-discovery, and Paris was waiting for the court to abandon Versailles so that it could flower into a city of elegant town houses and high living. But through his connection with Audran, Watteau had discovered his true master—Rubens. Audran held the post of Keeper of the Luxembourg Palace, and through him Watteau gained access to Rubens's cycle of the *Life of Marie de Médicis* (now in the Louvre). The opulent coloring and the sensuousness of the Flemish giant, adapted to the scale of Watteau's personality and Watteau's century, became the foundation of his style.

It is not known exactly when Watteau met Pierre Crozat, but with that meeting began the realization of the Watteau we know. Crozat was not quite the richest man in France; his brother Antoine was so rich as a result of his monopoly of the Louisiana trade that he was never able to estimate his wealth. (Antoine was called Crozat le riche, and Pierre, Crozat le pauvre.) But Pierre was rich enough. He was in his fifties when he met Watteau. At forty-three he had retired from business and purchased at a steep price the office of Treasurer of France, with all the accompanying prerogatives.

His palace and gardens in Paris were on a royal scale. He staged concerts and theatricals there for his friends. His parties were famous, and although they seem to have been more sedate than the revels of the aristocracy (for instance, the routs of the Duchesse de Berry, which, as described by her contemporaries, were imposing in their debauchery), they could hardly have been given over entirely to aesthetic cultivation. Intrigues for power must have occupied the influential men who gathered in the halls of this palace. And the gardens, where the guests strolled after the concerts, were a perfect setting for the maneuvers of amorous dalliance.

Crozat probably met Watteau through the dealer Sirois, one of the most important members of the "Benevolent Society," in whose house Watteau was living at the time. In 1715 or 1716 Watteau moved out to occupy an apartment in Crozat's palace. Crozat was an avid collector (and on the side, informally, a dealer who picked up treasures for his collector friends). Among his five hundred paintings and nineteen thousand drawings there were, to give a single breath-stopping example, about twenty-five paintings and three times as many drawings by Titian alone.

While Crozat set about making him a fashionable painter, Watteau watched the gallantry of the garden parties that gave him his nominal subject matter, but it is difficult to think of him as part of the company. If he mingled, he remained psychologically removed, and after a year or so he left the palace. There was no break with Crozat; Watteau probably moved out because he wanted to get away from distractions that were a burden to him as a reluctant and increasingly ailing participant in a kind of life for which he had neither taste nor energy.

Before long he was sharing quarters with Nicolas Vleugels, a successful copyist who seems to have been as close a friend as Watteau ever allowed himself. Still unknown to the general public, Watteau had become the favorite painter of Crozat's circle, so popular that Vleugels's copies of his paintings were sold before they were finished. But he was still a bit of a wildcat artist under a system where acceptance in the Academy was not only a matter of prestige but a form of official union card in the professional hierarchy. He had been an *agréé* of the Academy for five years, meaning that he had been given permission to offer a painting to be judged for full membership. But with typical dilatoriness he had never got around to producing the large showpiece on the standard pattern that was expected. Crozat urged him to follow through with this, and no doubt also dropped a word here and there to assure a properly sympathetic reception for his protégé.

In 1717 Watteau was accepted into the Academy with *A Pilgrimage to Cythera* (now in the Louvre), his masterpiece but a most unconventional presentation piece having nothing to do with the declamatory rhetoric expected of a candidate. In a gardened landscape, gentle lovers stroll toward a gilded confection of a boat that has carried them to the realm of love where they have paid homage to Venus; others, seated on the grass, exchange a few words of tender reminiscence before they stir themselves for the return voyage. In all of Watteau's paintings of lovers, the byplay of seduction is transmuted into a nostalgic mood, most poignant in *A Pilgrimage to Cythera,* which evokes the ancient theme of the transience of life's sweetness.

Since Watteau's presentation piece fitted into none of the standard categories, the Academy had to create a special one for him: "Painter of *Fêtes Galantes*." In the war between the Poussinists and the Rubenists that divided the Academicians, Watteau's election was considered a victory for the Rubenists, and so it was, but it was more important in a way that was not noticeable at the time. A new force outside the

Academy had challenged its dictatorial powers; the regime of the private patron for the independent artist had begun. Although Watteau's election with so unconventional a painting involved no preliminary skirmish, skirmishes were to occur and grow more and more frequent until finally the Academy's defeat by the impressionists and their patrons would break its power forever.

Watteau was thirty-three when he painted *A Pilgrimage to Cythera*. Two years later he was so ill that he went to London to consult Dr. Richard Mead, the Queen's physician, and was there subjected to such treatment as the best medical knowledge could afford. He returned some months later to find that the good Julienne had managed his affairs so well that he had accumulated some money in spite of the panic caused by the collapse that year (1720) of the fabulous "Mississippi Bubble," a catastrophe connected with Antoine Crozat's speculations in the New World.

Now he moved in with his friend Gersaint, who, as the son-in-law of his old dealer, Sirois, had taken over the business. In gratitude Watteau painted for Gersaint the famous signboard (Berlin, Charlottenburg) that rivals the *Pilgrimage* as his finest work. It shows the interior of the shop as if seen from the street with the front wall removed; customers are being received, others are examining paintings, workmen are boxing a portrait for shipment. Divided between genre and poetics—or, rather, fusing the two—it is the unique example in Watteau's work that might justify for us the label of realist that seemed appropriate enough to his contemporaries.

Early in 1721 Watteau left Paris for Nogent-sur-Marne, where he hoped the air would help him. (He stayed on the estate of Philippe Le Fèvre, Master of the King's Table.) But he knew he was dying, and this knowledge seems to have caused a change in his character. His friends had noticed, upon his return from London, that he had become avaricious. With his life ebbing, he became concerned about the practical future. For the first time he complained about the prices his paintings fetched. He had never given any indication of worrying about his soul; now another future also concerned him. He painted a *Christ on the Cross* as a gift for the local curé, and destroyed a number of paintings and drawings that he feared were erotic. (Both Caylus and Gersaint, in recollections after Watteau's death, refer to a "libertine spirit" repressed beneath the purity and caution of his comportment.) He died in the arms of Gersaint on July 18, 1721, three months before his thirty-seventh birthday.

Immediately after Watteau's death, Julienne began the compilation of all his existing works—pictures, drawings, and the decorations he had painted as assistant to Audran—in the form of engravings. This was the monumental tribute and record called the *Recueil Julienne*. It was not until this work appeared that Watteau became known to anything like a large public. It also made his work an international influence on painters for the rest of the century, although only to the extent that they adapted his subjects or copied his motifs. He had achieved the ideal statement of a far from ideal society during a single decade of its existence, and though some painters—notably Pater and Lancret—imitated his manner, in spirit he found no followers.

William Hogarth (1697-1764) was born and died in London, which was his universe. During the sixty-seven years of his life he left England only once, briefly, and for a country he loathed, France, where he did not even get as far as Paris. He was a short, robust, blunt-featured man who was as aggressively insular as any cockney you could find today, a fact that would not have made him remarkable except that he was a painter in a century when English taste in painting was determined by unquestioning acceptance of Continental models. With only minor reservations, we can say that Hogarth was the first truly English painter, and he was also the last English painter of major consequence in the special way that made him English.

It is possible that he was forced to capitalize on his special kind of Englishness by the necessity of making a living by his native talents, which, with his didactic interest—a sincere interest, let there be no question about that—led him to become a kind of novelist, dramatist, and social critic in pictures instead of in words. In 1731, when he was thirty-four, he deliberately turned away from the grand manner (which had been rather uncomfortably grafted onto an English tradition ill-adapted to the assimilation of Italian gods and heroes) and from portrait painting (where he had had very little success) and painted an unprecedented series of six episodes of London life called *Harlot's Progress*.

With generous reference to figures conspicuous in the news and scandals of the day, and with accurate and multitudinous details of places, furnishings, and costumes, Hogarth followed the literary precedent of Defoe's "Moll Flanders" to tell the story of a country girl who came to the city, fell into the hands of a procuress who turned her over to a maniac ravisher named Colonel Charteris (of such evil reputation that when he died in 1732 his hearse was covered with garbage in lieu of flowers by the populace, which also threw dead dogs and cats into his grave), came into affluence as the kept woman of a rich but unattractive protector, deceived him with a fashionable pip-squeak, was thrown out, fell in with low company including a highwayman lover, was apprehended with stolen goods, was sent to prison, and finally died disease-ridden and abandoned in abominable squalor—the proper end for the protagonist of what Hogarth called a "modern moral subject."

The mawkish banality of this story line, its character of yellow journalism, is saved by the ebullience of Hogarth's narration and, more important, by the beauty of his painting. But it was the story that he counted on to make money, and when he engraved *Harlot's Progress* for popular consumption the next year, the money came in. The prints were a great success, and Hogarth followed them with another narrative sequence, this time in eight episodes, *Rake's Progress,* which took a foolish young dandy through a career of debauchery in high and low places, gambling, bankruptcy, imprisonment for debt, marriage to a hideous old woman for her money, further debauchery, and a well-earned end in a madhouse. As a "modern moral tale" *Rake's Progress* is not altogether consistent, since the innocent young girl the rake seduces suffers almost as much as he does through no fault of her own: virtue is not always rewarded, even though vice and folly are always punished. There is, running through the series, a subtheme, one not always formulated in the ABC terms of the story, but implied: that the individual is formed by society and that social ills are not natural phenomena but human failures that can be corrected.

The novelist Fielding was one of Hogarth's good friends, and the steady drip of moralizing in *Rake's Progress* is alleviated by a Tom Jones kind of cheerful vulgarity that keeps breaking through. In an episode depicting an orgy in a tavern-brothel, one of the girls spits a great stream of gin across the table into the face of another—a feat Fielding and Hogarth are supposed to have witnessed together. Although Hogarth was a solid citizen, dedicated to the bourgeois virtues that were his by right of birth, he knew his material at first hand.

Of his several other pictorial sequences, *Marriage à la Mode,* which follows the disastrous course of the arranged union between an impoverished young nobleman and a girl whose rich middle-class parents have social aspirations, is the most important and probably, of all these moral tales, the one that makes the most devastating comments on society. All the "modern moral subjects" are filled with side comments on the weaknesses of the clergy and the law as well as on all forms of vice, corruption, and stupidity. Hogarth's fire was most frequently directed against the frivolities of the upper classes, but he never hesitated to blast his fellow bourgeois or the common people. And there was nothing he was afraid to say. When his harlot goes to Bridewell, the women's prison, he shows it as the ghastly, obscene, infested, cruel, and crime-breeding place it was, and his rake's madhouse is a documentary condemnation of Bedlam (the name is a corruption of "Bethlehem" Hospital), where for an admission charge the inmates could be observed, like sideshow freaks, by any visitors seeking amusement.

Hogarth repeatedly satirized the fops and dilettantes who could have been important to him as patrons if he had abandoned the ideals of his class in order to picture the ideals of the class that bred art patrons. As a result, the aesthetes sneered at him as a non-artist. But if he was unwilling to cater to them, he was still a practical man. In a pair of satirical engravings he showed that he had no patience with the kind of poet who could sacrifice himself in a garret to write mewling verse nobody wanted to read, or with the musician so sensitive that he was enraged by street musicians, whose music Hogarth probably enjoyed as he enjoyed everything in London life that had naturalness and gusto. He would have had a wonderful time in New York today belaboring our art dealers (one of his favorite targets even then), our bohemian freaks, and the foibles of our international playtime set.

Of all diversions, Hogarth, who made it clear that he was content to be judged as a dramatist, loved the theater best. He had been more or less stage-struck since childhood, and the London stage of his lifetime offered high comedy that had all the brilliance of invention and the wit of contemporary observation that painting lacked. "The Beggar's Opera" made its great success shortly before the year Hogarth began *Harlot's Progress,* and could easily have set him off on this pictorial venture. *Harlot's Progress* itself was made into a ballad opera and was given as a pantomime at Drury Lane. Hogarth's paintings are always conceived as if the action took place on a stage; his interiors are stage-sets enclosed at back and sides, the near wall cut away for full exposure to the audience, and his characters are arranged exactly as if conforming to such directions as stage left, stage right, and so on. It is appropriate that the recent film of "Tom Jones" draws on Hogarth for its scenes in London streets.

Hogarth was the son of a schoolmaster. At fifteen he was apprenticed to an engraver of silverplate, where he learned to do coats of arms on tankards and the like. By 1720, when he was twenty-three, he had his own card as an engraver, but was soon busier with work that interested him more, illustrations for books. He was really self-educated as a painter, although at this time he enrolled in St. Martin's Academy, an art school of sorts that supplied models and taught the rudiments of painting and drawing. The establishment was run by a successful painter, Sir James Thornhill, whose work in the baroque manner was exactly the kind that Hogarth came to detest as non-English. He did not detest Sir James's daughter, however, and eloped with her. There were no hard feelings, and eventually Hogarth himself continued the operation of the academy.

Whatever the young Hogarth picked up in the academy, where he could work only in his spare time, it was not his wonderfully creamy and succulent painting, which has nothing in common with what was taught there or anywhere else in England at the time. An unexplained phenomenon in

English art, this sensuousness is paralleled in French eighteenth-century painting, but if Hogarth knew, admired, and emulated any French painter, he would never have said so. There are many foreign influences discernible in his work: the jollity of Jan Steen, the intricate compositional interlacings of French rococo (which he could have known from engravings of French paintings), the vivacity of Callot. He could even have known a series of twelve Venetian engravings of the seventeenth century on the life and death of a courtesan (called *Lo Specchio al Fin de la Putana*), and lacking that example for *A Harlot's Progress* he could have known other popular Italian prints.

But if he did, his expression was nevertheless unprecedentedly and thoroughly English, and consciously so. He was almost vehemently middle class in a family that was content to remain so. (His sisters sold clothing and haberdashery to ladies and gentlemen.) He always advised young artists not to travel in Italy, at a time when you could hardly call yourself an artist in England if you had not. And his first major engraving, when he was twenty-seven, was a volley against Raphael, Michelangelo, and Italian opera, which he hated to see on an English stage as much as he hated to see Italian paintings in the dealers' shops. He castigated "the foolish parade of the French Academy" along with all officialdom in art. Fortunately he was spared knowledge of what would have been to him (and in many ways proved to be) a calamity in English art—the formation of the Royal Academy, four years after his death, with Sir Joshua Reynolds as its Italophile first president.

Sir Joshua, who was twenty-six years younger than Hogarth, was Hogarth's antithesis in his dedication to the grand manner and his toadying cultivation of influential patrons. As a result he succeeded in the circles where Hogarth failed, and his presence as a rising star is at least a partial explanation of

Hogarth's second failure as a portrait painter when he tried again around the age of sixty. Hogarth's portraits are among the best in English painting or in any painting. They might have been popular except that it was not in him to invest the sitter with the standard air of breeding and eminent position that had been, still was, still is, and probably always will be the English formula. He had the curious idea that a portrait should be a revelation of personality. Not surprisingly, his friends and family became his best sitters, and one of his finest paintings is a group of heads representing some very real and solid people—his servants.

Hogarth certainly deserves the title of the first artist to regard art as a weapon of social criticism and to think of his art as a means of reaching a large unsophisticated audience. Other artists (including Callot) had of course used the print to obtain wide sales through mass production, but Hogarth, even with his eye on sales, also enjoyed disseminating his ideas through the nearest thing, at that time, to a mass-communication medium. Perhaps there was an element of rationalization in his enthusiasm for reaching a popular audience, since after all he had been rejected by a more select one. And he never abandoned hope that he might become a successful painter of large historical subjects. But here too he was unwilling to succeed by compromise, by the sacrifice of factual truth to idealization. This was not the way to succeed in a field where any hack could satisfy the first requisite of flattery. When Hogarth asked permission to dedicate a historical painting to George II, the King discovered that it was disturbingly factual in showing soldiers drinking and engaging in other normal pursuits, and he let it be known that he was not pleased. The rebuff contributed to Hogarth's professional decline in his last years.

In 1753, when he was fifty-six and already feeling the pinch of disfavor, Hogarth published his aesthetic theories in a book called "The Analysis of Beauty." Unfortunately it makes dull reading. Were it less dull the formal aspects of Hogarth's art that it emphasizes might not be so generally neglected for the vivacious storytelling of his pictures. "The Analysis of Beauty" shows how analytically he approached pictorial organization, and it connects his art with a style that might seem diametrically opposed in spirit, the rococo. England was not only the brawling, gusty England that comes through first in Hogarth (and in Fielding), but, as well, the highly cultivated England that produced great craftsman-designers such as Chippendale. Hogarth was a pictorial craftsman-designer as well as a narrator and social critic, and "The Analysis of Beauty" shows that his planning of pictorial composition was much more in accord with the elaborately studied effects of the rococo, with its characteristic serpentine intertwinings, than is immediately apparent. When his "stage-sets" filled with characters are studied, what looks like spontaneous naturalness is seen to be the result of the most expertly executed joining and interlocking. He was anti-aesthetic only in the sense that he was antipretension. In "The Analysis of Beauty" he reasserted his first loyalty: he dedicated the book not to a prince, not to a past or potential patron, but "to everybody."

François Boucher was born in 1703, fathered by an obscure decorator. He grew up to be a hardheaded, hardworking, extremely skillful but rather unimaginative decorative painter, who rose to the absolute top of his profession by developing a formula and sticking to it.

Boucher effected a perfect compromise between public aspiration toward classical learning and private taste for amorous stimulation, which together produced much of the hybrid character of intellectual life in the *haut monde* of

Paris during his century. Playing the middle against both ends, Boucher brought the gods into the bedroom. Venus and Diana became nubile grisettes of a seductive if synthetic pinkness, sweetly rounded, moist-lipped, golden-locked, with fresh, tiny-nippled breasts where pearls might lie as if upon a jeweler's cushion.

To put it more respectfully, Boucher rescaled the grand manner into harmony with the feminine intimacy of the eighteenth-century salon. He is an easy target for unsympathetic evaluation, especially as his work is seldom seen at its best: the effectiveness of the paintings is reduced when they are removed from the interiors for which they were done. As a superb craftsman-designer with an infallible sense of scale who did not think of paintings as independent statements but as parts of a decorative ensemble, Boucher is unsurpassed, although the frilly and ornate style of his period demanded a type of artificiality not to everyone's taste today. He was the Rubens of the boudoir, in boudoirs where Rubens would have been a bull in a china shop. He was also an excellent portraitist, expert in the presentation of decorative exteriors that betray very little of the sitter's character or personality; an excellent genre painter if one allows, again, for an excess of polishing and sweetening. In the detailed rendering of jewels, bric-a-brac, bouquets, taffetas, coiffures, and other accessories to the elegant life, he was a marvel—if only a technical one.

The middle member of the great French eighteenth-century triad, Boucher had neither the poetic genius of the older painter, Watteau, from whom, however, he learned a great deal indirectly by engraving numbers of the paintings and drawings reproduced in the *Recueil Julienne,* nor the *joie de vivre* of the younger one, Fragonard, who was his pupil. But neither Watteau nor Fragonard approached him in the variety of ends to which he put his indefatigable productive talent. Gainsborough's "Damn him, how various he is!"—said of Reynolds—could even better have been said of Boucher by many a man who was really a better artist than he. He designed objects for manufacture by the porcelain factory of Sèvres, did sets for opera and ballet—possibly his best work, for our taste—and adapted his pictorial style to the larger scale of tapestries. These, executed by the weavers of Beauvais, were repeated for monarchs all over Europe. Boucher's pupils, too, disseminated his style, so that for many years he was the most influential single painter and decorator of his generation.

But there is a coldness about this superbly calculated, impeccably crafted art—never a hint of excitement, or reflection of passion, not the tiniest grain of wit to bring life to irreproachable workmanship. Boucher's goddess-grisettes, for all their insistent nakedness, are all but sexless. They have every attribute of titillation, but with one or two rousing exceptions they have too synthetic an air to evoke the pleasures to which they are nominally dedicated. Boucher himself seems to have been a rather cold man. Although he married, and was well known for the frequency of his indulgence with the young girls who posed for him or with other quickly available female merchandise that came to hand, he seems never to have had a love affair. Perhaps he was just too busy.

Boucher was the perfect painter for Mme de Pompadour, that rather cold, ambitious, handsome woman with a sure sense of high style. He made her acquaintance before she became the King's mistress, and in multiple commissions he created for her the ambience of intellectual cultivation, feminine elegance, and amorous suggestion that she needed as a field for her skillfully calculated maneuvers. He was also named Painter to the King and became president of the Academy. In this latter function he was refreshingly non-doctrinaire. Probably because he was so successful in setting taste without trying, he had no interest in dictating an aesthetic policy. He was quite content to let the Academicians go along with their history pictures while he followed his own bent. Privately he had small use for their standards, and no use at all for their gods, Raphael and Michelangelo. He was of course a man of tremendous influence when he wanted to exert it. When the young Fragonard was wondering whether he should compete for the Prix de Rome against multiple odds, Boucher eliminated the odds by saying simply, "Compete. You are my pupil."

Boucher in his way was an admirable painter who thoroughly deserved his success because he supplied a sound product that was in demand. But he lived a little too long. The weariness of routine is apparent in his late work; the formula had been a good one, but it had worn thin with repetition. Worse, it went out of fashion, and fashion had been its reason for being.

Leading a new fashion, the philosopher Diderot, who subscribed to the doctrine that a work of art must have a moral purpose, attacked the aging Boucher bitterly, and although that doctrine was producing some frightful painting at the time, Boucher's confections were defenseless before it. "I don't know what to say about this man," Diderot wrote, and then went on to say that the degradation of taste, of color, of composition, and of the characters in Boucher's painting simply followed the artist's own depraved way of life. "What can a man have in his imagination who passes his life with the lowest kind of prostitutes?" Diderot asked, with a logic that now strikes us as a trifle simpleminded. "I dare say that this man can have no idea what grace is; I dare say that he has never known truth; I dare say that the ideas of delicacy, of honesty, of innocence, of simplicity, have become all but strangers to him."

Grace, truth, delicacy, honesty, innocence, and simplicity

make an imposing list of virtues, and indeed all of them had been foreign to Boucher from the beginning (taking "grace" as a spiritual rather than a physical quality). With the shift of taste, the virtues he did have were ignored. Boucher was sixty-two years old when Diderot wrote this almost Savonarolesque piece of pseudo-criticism in 1765. He died in 1770, lonely and discredited, and since then has never entirely regained his position with historians and critics, or public. This is a shame, for in his coldly dimpled blue-and-pink way, Boucher can be a painter of great attraction.

The career of Sir Joshua Reynolds is the most impressive success story in the history of English painting, or the most appalling, depending on how you look at it. He is an extremely difficult man to be kind to. For his contemporaries he became the embodiment of the ideal type in his century—the scholarly, talented, urbane, wise, and considerate man of the world. But in retrospect this paragon is revealed as so calculating—such a methodical climber, concealing such callousness beneath a humane manner, and such spiritual emptiness beneath idealistic rhetoric—that it becomes impossible to tell the story of his life without fulminating. And once you have done that, you have put yourself in a position where nothing will do but to bend over backward and be as kind as possible to his painting, for fear of judging it too harshly in the light of his character. The only painter Reynolds ever feared as a rival, Thomas Gainsborough, made the famous remark, "Damn him, how various he is!" And it is true that Reynolds may be granted many virtues, variety among them, but they hold only when he is judged as a first-rate second-rate artist. Judged as a truly first-rate artist he is in a shaky position, and by any measure of genius he is hardly more than an inflated mediocrity.

Joshua Reynolds was born in 1723, near Plymouth, to respectable parents of modest means, whose families were generously spotted with clergymen and educators of no distinction. It might have been better for English art if the boy had followed these examples, but when he showed an early talent for drawing he was allowed to serve an apprenticeship in portrait painting, the only branch of a hazardous and not quite respectable profession that offered some assurance of a living at that time in England. He was a good student, and in his early twenties was executing portraits for the modest fee of three pounds per head.

A visit to London showed him that he would never get anywhere much unless he could meet dilettantes and influential people on their own ground. Italy was the answer: a trip to Rome was requisite for the education of a gentleman and gave cachet to an artist. Already an artist by technical definition and determined to become a gentleman by methodical self-improvement, but without funds to go about it, Reynolds finally found his way to Italy as guest on a ship commanded by a friend. He was twenty-six, and he stayed three years.

An early response to the wonders of Italian art was a rather beefy caricature he made of Raphael's *School of Athens* in the Vatican. It is one of the few indications remaining of the sense of humor that Reynolds is said to have had but that, like other reported virtues, he successfully smothered in the process of becoming what he wanted to be. He settled down to serious study, copying the old masters and theorizing about art in terms of eclectic formula. When he returned to England he could discourse knowledgeably about the history and aesthetics of painting in the Grand Style— "Grand Style" being equally applicable to his manner of discourse and to the kind of painting his discourse endorsed.

He found immediate commissions for portraits, at first for only five pounds each. But he was able to step up his prices so rapidly that by the time he was forty he was earning something like 150,000 dollars a year, as nearly as the pound then can be translated into the dollar now. He often completed as many as four portraits a week, capturing a good likeness with minimum inconvenience to the sitter. He managed his funds well, and added to his income as a painter by dealing in old masters bought on speculation, often expertly touched up by assistants, and sold to the wealthy people who now surrounded him and took his advice as collectors. His advice was sound. Any other advice would have been injudicious. Reynolds was one of the most calculatingly judicious men who ever lived, but there is a distinction between calculated judiciousness and plain honesty.

His daily program was to work until four in the afternoon and then to spend the rest of the day and evening being amiable and prepossessing in the company of people whose impressive names he listed, like an inventory of stocks and bonds, in his diaries. He cultivated two worlds and served as middleman between them, with such figures as Dr. Johnson and Oliver Goldsmith in his intellectual coterie and every fashionable hostess in the other. He may be allowed a natural gratification over achieving such a position, but the nature of his satisfaction is unpleasantly shown when, after a visit to the Duke of Marlborough, he begins a letter to a stranger who had written only to ask his prices for a portrait, "I am just returned from Blenheim," when "I have been out of town" would have done just as well.

He had determined early to remain a bachelor, and if he was a philanderer there is no record of it in a life that can be followed almost hour by hour in his own and his biographers' chronicles. His public painting was rigorously asexual, but as a private indulgence he painted nudes of such simpering eroticism that even his staunchest defenders blush for him. At the same time, he did pictures of children that have become popular because people are stirred without knowing it by the perverse element in their coy sentimentalism.

Always discreet, he lived with discreet opulence in a great house on Leicester Square, with a carriage so fine that his servants were able to pick up an extra shilling from time to time by letting the public in to see it. A sister, and then a niece, and then another niece, Mary Palmer, managed his house and served as his hostesses. When he died in 1792, Mary Palmer received most of his fortune—100,000 pounds, perhaps up toward 3,000,000 dollars at today's value. His collection of old masters brought better than another half million. He made generous bequests to friends. Three dukes were among the ten noblemen who served as his pallbearers, and everybody who was anybody followed the casket to St. Paul's in ninety-one carriages.

Reynolds had been knighted, had received an honorary degree from Oxford, and had become the first president of the Royal Academy when it was founded in 1768. He had demonstrated that, even in England, art and artists could hold an honorable position, as honorable as the one they had held for so long in Italy and France. His personal ambition had been paralleled by a more admirable determination to raise English art to respectable international status. But here he was confused, and here lies the charge that would still have to be made against him even if he had been the most endearing of men. He recognized the special character of English genius—the gift for lyricism, for humor, for response to nature, for a wonderful combination of grace and homeliness and gaiety and reserve in everyday life—but he dismissed these qualities as symptoms of insularity. He tried to sacrifice them to the Grand Style, and although the Grand Style was too incompatible ever to catch on, Sir Joshua's ambition to substitute it for the qualities that were spontaneously English served as an inhibiting influence that has not been altogether counteracted even in this century.

As the newly knighted president of the newly instituted Royal Academy, Sir Joshua began the series of annual lectures to the students that became his "Discourses" in published form. To read them now is an exercise in ennui except as they appall and terrify when remembered for their stultifying influence. They are a conscientious work, and Wylie Sypher has called them "that most complete expression of the late-baroque frame of mind" in their effort to establish laws for an art of congruity, coherence, and consistency. They do construct an orderly system based on a hierarchy of great masters from whose work Reynolds extracted a formula for the Grand Style. Reynolds called this "the art of using other men's minds," but as he conceived it, the study of the old masters became a denial of personal imaginative invention in favor of dogma, a way of smothering talent and attempting to smother genius—which, fortunately, is unsmotherable. The "Discourses" assume that expression can be reduced to mechanics, that everyday life lacks all elements of loftiness, and that an art based on synthesis and repetition by rote can "elevate the mind to the idea of a general beauty and the contemplation of general truth."

It is always admitted that Reynolds was unable to follow his own precepts, and that the virtues his art possesses (he is given credit for a sense of character in his portraits, for a sensitive response to childhood, and for a control of color that must largely be guessed at, since so much of his work has badly darkened) are virtues that violate rather than confirm his theories. If we recognize that he was unable to assimilate his own principles, we can only guess how severely the effort to assimilate them frustrated his potential.

The final judgment on Reynolds may be that there are five great names in English painting, each of them a direct rebuttal of what Reynolds stood for. Hogarth drew from the life of England in a way that only her great novelists have equaled, inspiring even Reynolds to concede him a "mastery of familiar scenes from common life" or, as Reynolds put it less generously after Hogarth's death, an ability to depict "the various shades of passion as they are exhibited by vulgar minds." For Reynolds, the common people never existed, and he recognized the middle class from which he came only when it began to get rich enough to supply substantial patronage.

Blake, the visionary, denied every rule set down by the man he called "Sir Sloshaway," and he annotated the "Discourses" with comments that should have destroyed them forever. Constable realized the English genius for landscape in direct contradiction to Reynolds's insufferable condescension to landscape as a minor art. Turner on another scale showed that landscape could be expressive of all the grandeur that was muffed in the paintings where Reynolds attempted it. As for Gainsborough, Reynolds tried to denigrate him by calling him "the first landscape painter in Europe." The motive of this compliment being all too clear, he was immediately told that Gainsborough was the first portrait painter as well.

Reynolds was generous in his encouragement of many artists, but inevitably they were second-raters. We might take this as proof that he had a bad eye, if it were not apparent that he was simply unwilling to encourage any artist talented enough to be a potential threat to his own position. His eye was good enough to recognize Gainsborough's virtues, and his jealousy was strong enough so that he went out of his way to label these virtues faults. He was a terrible man. It is often pointed out that even in his success, after he had obtained a knighthood and the presidency of the Royal Academy, he staunchly maintained a middle-class bearing. Anything else, of course, would have been the worst kind of mistake, since even a Reynolds could not pretend to belong to the upper classes by right of birth, and any effort to identify himself wholly with the people upon whose patronage his career depended would have turned the modest genius into the insufferable arriviste. But Reynolds *was* an arriviste, and it is his duplicity that is most offensive, his cultivation of those virtues that, far from being their own reward, were imperatives in the program of self-advancement that was his life.

One might ask, of course, why a man should not advance himself by any means less than felonious. If the question is unanswerable, then Reynolds is unassailable.

Although he seemed impregnable in his success, Reynolds had a vulnerable spot, which is revealed in an unexpectedly touching way in his self-portrait as president of the Academy. Paralleling Rembrandt's *Aristotle Contemplating the Bust of Homer* (in the Metropolitan), which formerly belonged to Reynolds's intimate friend, Sir Abraham Hume, it shows Reynolds with the bust of Michelangelo. It is an admirably painted picture in Reynolds's faintly cumbersome manner, and he did not idealize his own plain, heavy, undistinguished middle-class features. But there is a pathetic air about it, as if the man were aware of the temerity of his association with Rembrandt, Aristotle, Homer, and Michelangelo, yet as if he were hoping that he just might, after all, be in appropriate company here, and that time would say so.

It was a company in which Reynolds never claimed a place, no matter what he believed and hoped. His statements about his own abilities are always becomingly modest. He said that he knew he did not have "that readiness of invention which I observed others to possess"—a full enough explanation of his dedication to synthesis through borrowing that he turned into aesthetic principle in the "Discourses."

In his old age, blind for the last three years of his life, he brooded over his limitations, and he said once that if he could begin over again he would set out on a different course.

This is sad, but it does not modify the character of the course he took.

The French, who usually forget that there is such a thing as English painting, and who are inclined to condescend a bit when they remember that there has been quite a lot of it, make an exception in the case of Thomas Gainsborough. They like to think that they have at least a partial claim to him, since Gainsborough has a light freshness of touch, a vivacious presentation, and a poetic sensibility that are combined in no other English artist, although they characterize entire schools of French painting.

Gainsborough would be a perfectly harmonious fourth in a quartet created with the great French eighteenth-century trio of Watteau, Boucher, and Fragonard. At one time, Gainsborough, who was not ordinarily a very studious person, carefully studied Watteau. Boucher had taught Gainsborough's teacher, the engraver Hubert Gravelot. As for Fragonard, he and Gainsborough would have got along together so beautifully, what with the gaiety they shared, their common indifference to the standards of the academies, the pleasure they both took in that combination of high life and low life called the demimonde—not to speak of the ebullient interest both of them felt in what Gainsborough always referred to as "petticoats"—that it is a shame they never came together for an exploration of some of those delicious spots offered by London, Bath, and Paris.

Gainsborough, however, during the sixty-one years of his life—from the time he was born in Sudbury (Suffolk) in 1727 until his death in London in 1788—never left England. He is the most English of artists in certain ways and illustrates some of the most appealing aspects of the English temperament.

Gainsborough has none of the roast-beef-and-Yorkshire-pudding heartiness and Tom Jones rowdiness that make Hogarth so English, but, on a more elegant level than Hogarth, he demonstrates the same peculiarly English gift for seeing people as part of their social milieu. The Grand Style of Reynolds with its English emphasis on dignity and control held no appeal for Gainsborough, but in a much gentler and subtler way he has an analogous reticence and detachment that, when caricatured, become the frigidity and stuffiness of the typed Englishman on the Continent. His portraits show that he had the perception of psychological nuances that has made the English such great novelists and dramatists—a perception he applied with that wholly English tact which refuses to intrude upon the privacy of the sitter. And, above all, his landscapes are filled most wonderfully with an English love for the small-scaled intimate English countryside, a response to nature that, later on, would be given its most popular expression by poets like Wordsworth with his floating clouds, his meadows, groves, and streams, and the simple people who lived among them.

But unlike Wordsworth, Gainsborough never drew morals from nature. He delighted in it with a pure, unanalytical delight. Music and nature were his twin passions, and in one of the most-quoted letters in the history of painting he wrote to his friend William Jackson, "I'm sick of Portraits and wish very much to take my viol-da-gamba and walk off to some sweet village, where I can paint landskips and enjoy the fag-end of life in quietness and ease."

Gainsborough was hardly at "the fag-end of life" when he wrote the letter in 1768. He was only forty-one, with another twenty years to live, and was a great personal and professional success in Bath, where he had moved nine years before to take advantage of the opportunities that the fashionable city afforded a portrait painter. He was to repeat the success in London—but perhaps we had better summarize his life in a more orderly chronological way.

He was born, we have said, in 1727. His father was the postmaster of Sudbury and a not very successful cloth merchant. His mother seems to have been an educated woman with a ladylike interest in the arts. There was perhaps an erratic strain in the family. Two of Gainsborough's brothers became mild eccentrics. He himself is revealed, through anecdotes told by his friends, as an altogether charming personality. But he evidently suffered from an impetuousness, an almost morbid hypersensitivity to small irritations, and a high-strung nervousness relieved through dissipations that would be identified today as symptoms of neurosis.

Gainsborough was an exceptionally mischievous schoolboy—although there need be nothing symptomatic in that—and drew with such facility that when he was thirteen his parents apprenticed him to a silversmith in London. Gravelot took him on as assistant two years later. For the next few years, Gainsborough's London education included extensive research into the city's pleasures. Much later, in a letter of warning to a young actor against excesses that might distract the young man from the pursuit of his profession, he described himself as being "deeply read in petticoats." In 1746, when he was only nineteen, he added to his personal library an exceptional item, one Margaret Burr.

All accounts, even those of people who did not like her, describe Margaret as pretty, but none reveal just who she was or where she had been before she suddenly materialized as Gainsborough's bride. To his nineteen, she was sixteen. Whoever she was, and whatever her other endowments, she was the recipient each year of generous funds from a life annuity paid through a London bank. The reasonable assumption is that she was the natural child of a wealthy man, and romantic speculations have given her any one of several noblemen as father.

Gainsborough took his bride back to Sudbury the year of the marriage, but a few years later—about 1750—they settled in Ipswich, where he was as successful as a portrait painter can become with a limited provincial clientele. When he was thirty-two they moved to Bath, and in that center of fashionable diversion he came into his own. He loved wit but loathed affectation, and must have felt about many of his patrons and sitters much as Congreve and Sheridan show they felt in their comedies of manners. But Gainsborough also found in the mixed society of Bath the actors, musicians, and free spirits generally who became his friends. He must have been a delightful talker. William Jackson, the conductor and composer, to whom Gainsborough confided his ambition to take his viola da gamba and walk off to some sweet village to paint "landskips," uses the words "sprightly" and "licentious" to describe Gainsborough's conversation. The sprightliness, at least, is reflected in Gainsborough's letters, for he was a natural writer, totally unstudied and spontaneous, whose style is unquestionably a reflection of his speech—quick, making sudden shifts from one thought to another, now bantering, now half despairing, thoughtful and impatient by turns.

During the fifteen years that he lived in Bath, Gainsborough sent pictures to London for the Academy's annual exhibitions—a normal professional measure. But he was temperamentally unsympathetic to the pretensions of the Grand Style dictated by Sir Joshua Reynolds as head of the Academy, and he was bored by the formal society that Sir Joshua cultivated so self-advantageously. When he decided to leave Bath and broaden his opportunities by moving to London, he reversed the customary procedure: he withdrew from the

Academy's exhibitions, having already quarreled with that institution the year before, and set up his own gallery at home, just as his unknown kindred spirit Fragonard did in Paris. He was not immediately successful, but in 1776 he received a commission from the royal family.

Inviolable protocol demanded that any such painting be exhibited at the Academy, and the connection with official-dom was patched up. Gainsborough became the favorite painter of the court as well as of the demimonde, and when he broke again with the Academy in 1784, he was the acknowledged rival of Sir Joshua, to Sir Joshua's ill-concealed discomfiture. Sir Joshua, that plain man who worked so hard (and successfully) at the job of ingratiating himself with the powerful, must have been as jealous of Gainsborough's easy personal attraction and independence from convention as he was of his painting.

Four years after his final break with the Academy, Gains-borough, mortally ill, wrote Sir Joshua asking if he would come to his studio to look at his paintings. Sir Joshua consented, and the men had a long discussion. "I can from a sincere Heart say that I have always admired and sincerely loved Sir Joshua Reynolds," the dying Gainsborough had said in his letter to Reynolds. But when Sir Joshua delivered Gainsborough's obituary as one of his "Discourses" before the Academy, he could not resist the temptation to get back a bit of his own. Saying that he would not enter "into a detail of what passed at this last interview," he went on to report that Gainsborough on his deathbed had said that "he now began . . . to see what his deficiencies were." Sir Joshua warned the assembled students "to remember, that no apology can be made for this deficiency in that style which this Academy teaches." The "Discourse" is an unforgivable performance—the public belittlement by a prominent man of a generous rival.

Reynolds's warning was largely superfluous. Gainsborough, who in the next century became the most influential of eighteenth-century English artists, had very little influence on his contemporaries. His isolation in this respect is easily explained. In the first place, the young painters were not adventurous enough to question the Academy, which offered the recipe for success and whose members had immediate advantages to offer in the way of assistantships. Under the influence of Gainsborough's seductive personality and with an opportunity to observe his manner of work, a group of young painters might, even so, have turned into a following. But Gainsborough did not teach. His only pupil was the deservedly obscure Gainsborough Dupont (1754-1797), a nephew of his wife's.

Nor did Gainsborough employ assistants, as all other successful eighteenth-century English portrait painters did, to help with minor passages—usually meaning backgrounds. He could hardly have done so, since in a Gainsborough there are no minor passages. The backgrounds in his portraits are integral parts of the paintings rather than incidental inventions filling the area behind the sitter. A Gainsborough is an exquisitely woven mesh of texture and color. Without ever theorizing about a relationship between pictorial and musical composition, Gainsborough liked to think of his pictures in terms of music. The directions and relative strengths of his brushstrokes are not only like warp and weft, but like theme and countertheme.

This is the technical explanation of the continuity between Gainsborough's figures and the space they occupy; in most other portraits the landscape is only an arbitrary backdrop. But beyond the technical explanation there is another: Gainsborough's love of "landskip" for itself, and his feeling for the harmonious existence of man in nature. It was probably not a sensitivity shared by many of his sitters. They were more interested in harmonizing with the drawing room, and expected a portrait to give them that air of inherited refinement that was then, and still is, the hallmark of English portraiture, to its detriment, since no distinction is made between the personality of a duke and that of a successful butcher. That Gainsborough managed to endow his sitters with an air of social elevation, and yet presented them as personalities rather than standardized effigies, is the mark of his exceptional responsiveness to psychological values. He seldom had sitters worthy of his perception; men of eminent position and achievement (if such distinction does not guarantee interesting character, at least it increases the possibility) preferred to sit for Reynolds. It was only in portraits of his friends and family, including his two daughters, that Gainsborough could make really personal and unqualified studies of his sitters.

For this reason Gainsborough has left us less than he was capable of, and yet it is difficult to ask for more even in his least interpretative portraits. How elegantly, with what natural elegance, his figures stand, "divinely doing nothing," as Ruskin put it, as if taking for granted the breeding that they might actually have been a bit short on, but that Gainsborough gives them so bountifully. How unaffectedly they wear the furbelows and ribbons and laces of an affected mode; how sweetly the satins and taffetas swathe them, as if the rich and delicate stuffs were as natural a part of man as his flesh, with neither flesh nor stuffs subject to any natural ills.

Gainsborough extended his graceful ideal beyond the world inhabited by his clients into the countryside that he liked best to paint. Without sentimentalizing them he showed its rural inhabitants as a kind of blessed race in perfect harmony with its benign setting. Here he was close to the ideas of the Encyclopedists and Rousseau that were being translated in France into the artificialities of pink milkmaids and pretty shepherd boys costumed in precious fabrics, or into the specious moralities of Greuze. But it is unlikely that Gainsborough knew the philosophical tracts that inspired these curious interpretations on the other side of the Channel. He was not much of a reader, and although the French ideas certainly cropped up in one form or another as part of the chatter he listened to in Bath and London, they probably affected him very little: his response to nature and to simple people was untheoretical and spontaneous. His expressive genius was a genius of personal response, and even Sir Joshua Reynolds was perceptive enough to note, "He had a habit of continually remarking to those who happened to be about him whatever peculiarity of countenance, whatever accidental combination of figures, or happy effects of light and shadow, occurred in prospects, in the sky, in walking the streets, or in company."

Of that last talk Sir Joshua had with Gainsborough, Sir Joshua said, "the impression of it upon my mind was that his regret at losing life was principally the regret of leaving his art." And, surely, his viola da gamba.

"Delightful" may be the adjective of minimum praise when it is used to summarize a painter's work, indicating that his achievement is something less than impressive. But in the case of Jean Honoré Fragonard we can make it "consummately delightful" to give full due to the last—and the most underrated—of the great pre-Revolutionary French artists.

Fragonard was fifty-seven years old in 1789, the year of the Revolution, and his head might not have stayed on his shoulders for another seventeen years except for Jacques Louis David, a painter whose actions as politician and art director during the years of the Terror were not always marked by charity or loyalty to old friends. Many of Fragonard's friends and patrons were condemned to the guillotine on absurd or trumped-up charges that could have applied with equal reason to Fragonard. But as a young lion-about-town he had once tossed a discarded commission to the younger David—at that time a starveling and discouraged mouse—and although David disagreed with every aesthetic principle of Fragonard's art, he intervened, in his day of power, to protect him and give him a living under a regime in which Fragonard's kind of painting had become taboo. He arranged an appointment as a member of the conservatory of the national art museum established by the Revolution. The museum, which was the genesis of the Louvre, included the confiscated collections of many people who had been Fragonard's friends in the good life.

Fragonard was born in Grasse in 1732 and was brought to Paris at the age of ten or earlier. The boy was eventually to have studied law, but his volatile, impulsive temperament put a stop to that in short order. In his teens he was accepted as assistant to Boucher, the reigning painter in the world where the court and the demimonde overlapped, after a brief apprenticeship with Chardin, who had not found him promising. Fragonard's story as he grew up became a succession of prize-winnings under official sponsorship, and by the age of twenty-four he was in Rome, the heaven where all good art students were sent. His professors sometimes complained that he had too much fire and not enough patience, but they all admired his talent and, probably, were attracted by his personality.

On his return to Paris Fragonard made a sensational success with an academic painting bearing the appropriately laborious title *The High Priest Coresus Sacrifices Himself to Save Callirrhoë,* which was purchased by the King and is now in the Louvre. But before long he abandoned the inflated official style with its pompous rhetoric to become the darling of the demimonde with the happy and luscious confections now synonymous with his name. The name was shortened to Frago among his friends, and he seems also to have been the darling of any number of fashionable kept ladies. His most spectacular conquest was the dancer Madeleine Guimard, whose supper parties and subsequent entertainments were attended by members of the court, rich financiers, artistic and literary figures, and other reigning courtesans. Fragonard was engaged in a series of decorations for La Guimard when they quarreled and separated: this was the commission he so fortunately turned over to the obscure David.

No young blade in Paris can have enjoyed the special pleasures the city offered more than Frago did, but he is not to be thought of as a mere libertine endowed with good looks and high spirits. There never was a sounder painter, no matter how many were more profound. His most important patrons were indeed *bons vivants,* but they were also that type of intellectual peculiar to the eighteenth century that the French call *amateurs,* a word not translatable into English as "amateur" or even as "art lover," and not quite as "dilettante," that designates men of great cultivation who collected art, often wrote about it, frequently engaged in painting at an unprofessional but respectable level, and demanded a high standard of performance from their protégés. Over a period of two years in Rome, and in travels around Italy, Fragonard was companion to a conspicuous *amateur,* the Abbé Jean Claude de Saint-Non, and in Paris, later, he was sponsored by Bergeret de Grancourt, an immensely wealthy man who painted on the side. On one occasion Bergeret made up a company of four—with Fragonard and his wife, and Bergeret's lady friend—to travel in two carriages for nine months in Italy, Austria, and Germany.

With the world to choose from, men like Bergeret demanded more than the amusing companionship of decorative individuals. Fragonard was amusing and decorative, but he was also a productive and versatile painter, and by the time of the international carriage tour he had somewhat settled down. In 1769, when he was thirty-seven, he had married a pretty, honest bourgeoise from his home town named Marie Anne Gérard, whose parents, rather trustingly, had sent her to Paris at the age of seventeen to study with him. Frago's quarrel with La Guimard, understandably, occurred shortly thereafter.

A daughter was born less than six months after the marriage, a son eleven years later, and the household included, in addition, Marie Anne's younger sister Marguerite. The ménage was quartered in the palace of the Louvre, where Fragonard had lived for years in one of the apartments set aside for artists under royal patronage. After she grew up, Marguerite became Fragonard's only recorded amorous defeat. She resisted the hopeless passion that led him to paint the only pictures in which he yielded in any degree to popular sentimentalism, and she managed at the same time to remain his pupil and to become a most respectable painter in her own right.

As a steadied but not chastened man, Fragonard continued to be successful, and in defiance of convention he abandoned the Academy and its exhibitions and began to sell paintings directly from his studio. If this does not sound sensational, it was historically a departure anticipating the autonomous position of the modern artist. Even in his retirement from gaiety, Frago retained the affection and support of his high-living patrons. It took the Revolution to defeat him. At sixty he was unable, although he tried, to master the incompatibly chilly new style that David had made popular and virtually mandatory. Such money as he had saved—he had earned a great deal and spent a great deal, maintaining a house in Provence among other things—evaporated in the

society of gallant caprice in which he moved with such zest. He might have done that, if he had tried, but more likely he would have broken his bootstraps. Few artists are so complete within their limits as Fragonard is within his, and it is absurd to mistake these limits for limitations on his part. An art of consummate delight, after all, can be created only within boundaries that shut out most of the world.

Thomas Rowlandson was eight years old when Hogarth died. When Rowlandson died sixty-three years later, a youngster named Daumier was serving his apprenticeship in Paris. Standing between the great English social moralist of the eighteenth century and the great French observer of the human tragicomedy of the nineteenth, Rowlandson hardly approached the power of either. But he combined, in his own way, some of the indignation that inspired Hogarth and some of the tolerance (if not quite the compassion) that made Daumier the greatest of all artists to describe the urban world. Rowlandson made his comments entirely in the form of humor, and is frequently no more than a comic artist, but to think of him as merely funny is a mistake.

He was born in 1756, the son of a tradesman whose prosperity had so far withstood the strain of a penchant for speculation and gambling. Thomas was a bright boy but not much interested in school, where he spent his time scribbling caricatures in the margins of his textbooks. Art school seemed a better place for him, and in his early teens he was enrolled as a student in the Royal Academy, where he established a legend with his high spirits and his facility as a draftsman. The facility never failed him during a long lifetime, except when it seduced him into doing what was quickest and easiest.

He was an attractive boy, and in 1771 or 1772—when he was about sixteen—a French aunt invited him to come to

Paris to study at her expense. He probably had a wonderful time there, and he certainly saw the lively and sometimes salacious prints depicting current fashions and mores that were popular during those last festive years of the old regime. Under French instruction he unfolded as a master of fresh, light, delicate but decisive line as a means of description, and he remains—to this day—the most satisfactory French-English hybrid among draftsmen. His finest drawings have all the delicacy of French rococo style without its affectations, plus an English sturdiness without the frequently attendant stodginess.

At eighteen or nineteen Rowlandson returned to England and re-entered the Royal Academy classes. In 1775, when he was nineteen, he had his first picture in the Academy's exhibition. Two years later he was settled in a studio of his own, conventionally prepared to follow the usual course of a promising young artist in England—that is, to become a fashionable portrait painter. His work was regularly accepted in the Academy exhibitions. But he was restless under these unexciting conditions. What he really enjoyed was humorous drawing and caricature. He traveled a great deal at this time, around England and again on the Continent.

He was living well and gambling a lot. His father had lost his money at about the time Thomas returned from France, but the entranced aunt continued to support her charming nephew, and when she died shortly after, she left him 7,000 pounds along with some valuable silver and other properties. Translation into current values is difficult, but the sum must have been the equivalent of between 150,000 and 200,000 dollars today. It took Rowlandson less than ten years to get rid of it—it began to give out, apparently, during his twenty-fifth year—although during this time he started to earn money by the kind of work he enjoyed doing, pictures of London high life and low life and, especially, of the world of combined sordidness and elegance where the two mingled.

He recorded a London, and its nearby resorts, filled with roistering guardsmen, rakes, sluts, duchesses who in private behave like sluts, dignitaries exposed in the most undignified circumstances, pimps, fops, seducers and flirts, honest lechers and sanctimonious clergymen with an eye out for an opulent bosom, fashion plates with fine feathers that cannot quite conceal venereal sores, filching servants, tipplers, eloping lovers, pregnant slatterns leading bawling bastards by the hand —great crowds of these people mixed in with their more fortunate and their less fortunate fellows in a steaming parade through public gardens, theater lobbies, fine houses, low houses, clubs, dens, docksides, palaces, and streets.

In his late twenties, his inheritance squandered and gambled away, Rowlandson settled down to making a living by his work. In 1784, when he was twenty-eight, he made his first important success at the Academy with *Vauxhall Gardens,* a more or less sedate version of the social brawl in which the strolling crowds are studded with recognizable celebrities. From that time on, he had no trouble selling whatever he wanted to draw, and he had a steady, profitable market for magazine and book illustrations or prints from his drawings. The Prince of Wales (George IV) was one of his patrons. About 1809 his collaboration with the publisher Rudolph Ackermann led to *The Tour of Dr. Syntax in Search of the Picturesque,* in collaboration with the writer William Combe, and then to several other narrative series.

Although Rowlandson is supposed to have married a Miss Stuart of Camberwell in 1800, when he was forty-four, she appears and then disappears immediately, and remains nothing more than a name. Biographers have speculated about Rowlandson's character and personality without much success—at least without much consistency from one speculation to the next. It is certain that he was a compulsive gambler, which is usually the symptom of some other neurosis, but it is not true that he died bankrupt. He left a small estate. After the success of *Vauxhall Gardens* until his death forty-three years later, in 1827, at the age of seventy-one, he seems to have had as much work as he wanted, although sometimes he was short of ready cash and would pay a bill by dashing off a drawing.

Rowlandson's best-known works, felicitous drawings of wonderful freshness and grace that project the social scene as one vast theatrical spectacle, leave the impression that their creator was not only an alert observer but also a lively participant who knew this world at all its levels and enjoyed it in full realization of the depravity beneath its elegance—without feeling that it required any comment beyond whatever comment anyone wanted to make for himself in the face of the pictorial description. But there was another side to Rowlandson's art that was not acceptable to his publishers. When circulated at all, it was thought of as gross caricature of (almost) the comic-valentine sort, and it is still thought of, usually, as a secondary and rather coarsened, even unworthy, aspect of Rowlandson's art.

Typical examples show man as a repulsively obese or grotesquely emaciated animal. Lechery, gluttony, and stupidity cease to be the comic attributes of stock theatrical characters and become cancers within swollen or shriveled bodies. Man is bestialized to the point where excreting and vomiting are his liveliest functions in caricatures inspired by revulsion to the spectacle that Rowlandson accepts as an entertainment in his more polite work.

Rowlandson is a fascinating artist, but he fell short of greatness. He did not recognize (as Hogarth did) that the exposure of evil is the first step toward its correction; nor did he feel (as Daumier did) that for all his foibles, man is worth saving because in spite of everything he is fundamentally good. In some aspects of his work, Rowlandson is too light-hearted to suggest that evil should be remedied; in others, he is too bitter to suggest that evil is remediable. Like most of us, he was divided between contradictory responses to the world we live in.

19

EIGHTEENTH-CENTURY FRANCE

Painting is a social document whether or not the painter intends it to be, since every work of art becomes in retrospect a record of the mores and the philosophies of its time. Painting in eighteenth-century France is no exception. The painters we have just seen—Watteau, Boucher, and Fragonard—served the privileged half of a culture that was cracking down the middle. The other half, whose champions were proclaiming the dignity of the common man and formulating the moral philosophies and social concepts that became the intellectual basis of the Revolution, received less expression because, naturally, the patrons of art were the ones who still had the money, and they were not attracted to the work of artists reflecting reactions against the kind of life that, so far as they were concerned, was right and proper.

Nevertheless, the new ideals found expression, if only indirectly and never as part of a conscious program pursued by the artists. The great Chardin certainly did not know that his still-life paintings would be thought of in the twentieth century as reflections of a social force. The silly Greuze, a prurient moralizer, followed the aristocracy in adopting the new philosophy as a sentimental vogue. Some other artists (Joseph Vernet, Hubert Robert) forecast in mild ways the romantic movement of the next century. All these artists, plus Watteau's followers, Pater and Lancret, who must have a paragraph or two of identification, are included here.

Jean Baptiste François Pater (1695-1736) was by birth Watteau's fellow townsman, by training his pupil, and by intention his second self in art. Pater copied Watteau's style as well as literally copying his paintings. It is always touching to remember that after a quarrel the two were reconciled during the last years of Watteau's life, and that apparently Watteau, regarding Pater as his aesthetic heir, taught him all he could, near the end. But Pater was often a careless painter and, by contrast with the subtle Watteau, an obvious one who reduced the poetry of the master's gallant exchanges to the level of amorous anecdote. The best Pater only makes you want a real Watteau.

Nicolas Lancret (1690-1743) who, like Watteau, was trained under Gillot, followed Watteau's manner even more closely than did Pater, and missed Watteau's spirit even more completely. He is often so explicitly an illustrator that he earns for himself Jeaurat's description of Watteau as a painter who marvelously imitated nature. "Painter after nature" became the tag attached to any French artist of the time who worked in an informal manner in opposition to the "grand manner" that still ruled the Academy.

Claude Joseph Vernet was the patriarch of a three-generation dynasty of conspicuously successful French painters whose own father was a decorative artist of less distinction. Born in 1714, he spent most of his life in Italy and became the dean of the French art colony in Rome, where he was also something of an aesthetic foster father to numerous artists. Most accounts of eighteenth-century French—and foreign—painters who made the Italian pilgrimage mention their contact with Vernet. As the man who encouraged Richard Wilson to go in for landscape, and influenced other Englishmen in the burgeoning romantic impulse, Vernet is even more important in the history of English painting than in that of his own country.

Vernet was first sent to Italy at the age of nineteen by a patron, and earned a quick reputation as the leading French landscapist (and seascapist) in a style based on that of his countryman Claude Lorrain, who, in the preceding century, had also made his career in Italy. In his early paintings, Vernet modernized the seventeenth-century classical formula, adapting it to eighteenth-century sensibility, but his greatest importance (if not all of his best work) came through his conversion to the stormy or melancholy mood that was already heaving through classical restrictions to become romanticism, and was then often called "sublime" painting. After 1750, his peaceful seascapes became turbulent and his idyllic landscapes wild and tormented, and human beings were shown as the victims of nature's violence and indifference.

Combining classical precedent with romantic action, Vernet, like Odysseus, once had himself lashed to the mast of a ship, not, however, to save himself from the sirens' call, but to observe a storm at sea at first hand. To the siren call of romanticism he yielded gladly, shifting his allegiance from Claude Lorrain to Salvator Rosa, the great progenitor of romantic landscape. In addition to scenes of stress and violence, Vernet painted moonlit nocturnes conducive to melancholy meditation for those who preferred that mood to delicious shudders.

Before he turned to "sublime" painting, Vernet produced a remarkable group of serenely poetic portraits of

French seaports during a period, beginning in 1745, when Mme de Pompadour recalled him to Paris. Commissioned by the state, fifteen of these views remain in the Louvre.

Joseph Vernet was a painter of great ability who transmitted to his son and grandson not only a degree of talent but, as well, a prestigious name that smoothed their paths to eminence in official circles. He died at the age of seventy-five, in 1789, the year of his grandson's birth. With the following notes on the two other Vernets we are violating historical sequence in the interests of keeping the family together.

The son of Joseph, Antoine Charles Horace (called Carle) Vernet (1758-1835), was a steady recipient of official honors who justified them adequately if not brilliantly. A favorite painter of the Empire, he recorded its military history in panoramic terms, but he is best remembered for his vigorous studies of horses. He was also a caricaturist with a venomous bite, and his hilarious delineations of Directoire fops and fashionable ladies, the *Incroyables* and *Merveilleuses,* have become standard items in histories of modes and manners.

The son of Carle Vernet, Emile Jean Horace Vernet (1789-1863), concluded the dynasty. Vigorous and competent, he continued his father's success as a painter of military history. He was also a man of action who accompanied armies in the field. He recorded Napoleon III's Algerian expedition and the Crimean War, and was decorated by the Emperor for service at the Barrier of Clichy, also setting down that encounter in a painting, which is now in the Louvre. He was awarded one of the ten international Grand Medals of Honor in the climactic Salon of 1855, deservedly, for he represented academic painting at its best at a time when most official painters were assiduously reducing "academic" to a term of derogation. Always busy with official assignments, he helped organize the Military Museum at Versailles.

Horace Vernet remains a better documenter than creative artist. His grandfather had been a precursor of the romantic movement; the grandson represents its conclusion in a form of history painting. A lithographer as well as a painter, he helped establish and consolidate the practice of the new graphic medium.

Hubert Robert, whose life-span coincided almost exactly with that of his friend Fragonard, was, again like Fragonard, an artist who seemed incapable of a single stroke of the crayon or the brush that was not immortally fresh. Although his reputation is firm enough, he is surprisingly taken for granted today, accepted offhandedly without sufficient thought of his really superb quality as a painter or much recognition of his imaginative creative power.

Robert is thought of primarily as a painter of architectural scenes in the classical-picturesque mode of his century, but he rose above that mode. Tremendously productive, like most of his colleagues, he was never repetitious, as most of them were in turning out recombinations of their catalogues of motifs. And he was a genuine precursor of romanticism who invested his paintings with an emotive character—sometimes happy, sometimes melancholy—that frees them from any suggestion of the well-arranged stage-set, which the standard product, no matter how ornamental, resembles.

Robert's pictures of gardens, sometimes records of existing ones like those at the Villa d'Este, sometimes inventions, are alive with his response to nature. His kind of garden shows nature as the eighteenth century liked it, disciplined and well manicured by reasonable man. But his paintings of ruins, where trees and vines consume the fallen stones, forecast the romantic concept of nature as an eternal force at work to humble man's worldly pride.

Hubert Robert was born in 1733. In 1754, when he was twenty-one, he was taken to Italy by the French ambassador. There he worked in that heaven for artists, the French Academy's Roman branch, and studied too with Pannini, the ranking and the finest, if now and then the driest, painter of Roman ruins in the stage-set manner. Robert met Fragonard at the Academy, and although he was a steadier character than the sportive Frago their friendship lasted for life. Robert also came in for attention from Frago's rather effete patron, the Abbé de Saint-Non, who took him on sketching trips to the Villa d'Este and Naples.

Robert returned to Paris the next year and, only twenty-two, became an immediate success. The fresh color and the classical references of his architectural landscapes made them perfect decorations for interiors in the new classical tone of the Louis XVI style, and their relative sobriety was in harmony with the revolt against rococo excesses. He was tagged "Robert des Ruines," and as his reputation grew he exported to foreign courts nearly as many paintings as he sold in France. Russian noblemen purchased them literally by the score, following the lead of Catherine the Great. No Russian palace could pretend to elegance without the cultural cachet of a few Roberts, and Russian museums are still full of them.

Under these conditions, Robert could have turned himself into a factory, but it is difficult to find a painting where his architectural perception and his flow of invention show any sign of haste or faltering. At the same time, he was working as a landscape architect and was eventually appointed Designer of the King's Gardens, with the opportunity to realize in solid fact schemes like those he had invented for his paintings. In addition, he enjoyed setting down pictorial chronicles of current events such as conflagrations and demolitions. (One day, he would paint the storming of the Bastille.) Combining two interests, he recorded workmen uprooting trees, planting new ones, and laying out the revisions of the gardens of Versailles, in delightful pictures where journalistic record, architectural organization, high style, and angelic painting play together as a perfect quartet.

When the Revolution put an end to this world, Robert was nearly sixty, an age when drastic change is not accepted casually. Suspect because of his association with the King, he was arrested in 1792. He spent a period of incarceration painting incessantly, and his sketches of prison life have a perhaps desperate lightheartedness. But he escaped the guillotine, just as his friend Fragonard did. In the transformed society, Fragonard shared a stroke of good fortune with Robert: as a member of the conservatory he appointed his old friend curator of the collections that had been confiscated for a new national museum.

Robert drew up plans for the modification of the Louvre as a building for public exhibitions, and at the same time painted a fantasy of the Grande Galerie as he imagined it in ruins (palace at Tsarskoe Selo, near Leningrad). Superficially this ruin-painting is an architectural tour de force, but as a fantasy it represents Robert's vision of his broken world, which his mind's eye saw ravaged like the monuments of ancient Rome. Robert's post-Revolutionary work took on an increasingly somber tone; the ruined past was no longer for him something to be treated as a picturesque spectacle: it was a fated tragedy to be evoked in romantic melancholy.

In *The Spirit of the Tomb* (Paris, Musée des Arts Décoratifs), painted in 1795, a young woman, seated on the base of a column and inspired by a winged spirit that hovers above her bearing a torch, broodingly regards an antique sarcophagus. In the background the Pyramid of Cestius bears the legend *"Vixit et ad lugendum ad huc Spiro"* ("He lived, and I breathe only to mourn him").

Chateaubriand perhaps knew this picture, which has

been compared with a passage in his "Génie du Christian-isme." But whether or not this connection exists, a more significant connection of feeling makes Hubert Robert not only a precursor but, at the end of his life, an exponent of the new romantic spirit.

Hubert Robert died in 1808, at the age of seventy-five.

Poor Greuze! Poor Jean Baptiste Greuze, born Tournus, August 21, 1725, died Paris, March 21, 1805, aged almost eighty. Hardly anyone has had a good word to say for him since his late middle age, and he retains a spot in the history of painting as an example of how badly a philosophic ideal may be degraded by an artist who, at the height of his success, seemed to epitomize it.

The ideal was a double one: in part didactic, reflecting Diderot's demand that art should teach a moral lesson; in part romantic, reflecting Rousseau's conviction that simple things and poor people are inherently noble. Of simple origins, but neither moral nor noble, Greuze assumed a stance as both, and produced some of the most affected and lecherous paintings of an age when affectation and lechery reached such proportions that their purification by wit, in the work of Fragonard, seems very nearly a manifestation of genius.

Greuze became an artist against the will of his parents, and when he was twenty he left Tournus for Lyons, where he studied for five years with a painter named Grandon. When he was twenty-five he came to Paris and worked with Charles Joseph Natoire (1700-1777), a proficient disciple of the style of Boucher. In 1755, when he was only thirty, Greuze made a sensational success in the Salon with *A Father Reading the Bible to His Children* (now in the Hermitage in Leningrad), a picture that hit at the right moment to appeal to the newly fashionable taste for a nominally high moral tone. That year, under the patronage of an abbé who was an *amateur* of art, he went to Rome, where he fell in love with a young Italian countess while giving her drawing lessons. But a common young man could not marry a countess. The affair was frustrated, and Greuze returned to Paris. If the disappointment deepened his emotional capacity, as disappointments are sometimes supposed to do, his painting never showed any signs of it, although one might force a point and argue that his view of the common man as inherently good, but seldom enjoying life, was reinforced by this firsthand experience.

In 1761—he was now thirty-six—Greuze made an even greater Salon success with *The Village Bride* (more accurately, *The Village Betrothal*) now in the Louvre, a scene staged in a lower-class interior where an aged father and mother relinquish their pretty daughter to her fiancé, while other members of the family look on with appropriate expressions of sweet sadness and one little chick of a brood gathered around a mother hen symbolically wanders off to the other side of the picture. The narrative method owes much to Hogarth, whose engravings Greuze certainly knew, but the picture has none of Hogarth's gusto.

Diderot was rapturous in his praise of *The Village Bride* and of Greuze as the great exponent of "moral painting." But Greuze was becoming more successful than the Academy really liked, and although he had been made an associate member after his first Salon success, he was barred from the Salon of 1767—he had been a regular exhibitor until then—and was told that he must get around to painting the test piece required for admission to full membership.

Greuze aimed at the top with a classical history picture radically different from his sentimental exercises and bearing a title almost as long as the letters he was fond of writing to the newspapers explaining to the public what his popular paintings were all about: *Septimius Severus Reproaching Caracalla, His Son, for Having Attempted to Assassinate Him in the Defiles of Scotland, and Saying to Him, "If You Desire My Death, Order Papinian to Deal It to Me with This Sword."*

The painting, which is now in the Louvre, was a cataclysmic failure. The Academicians, certainly with vindictive delight, admitted Greuze to membership only in the humiliating category of genre painter, thus branding him with the stamp of the second-rater and excluding him from the circles where policy was made and favors were granted. The year of this debacle, 1769, was doubly disastrous for Greuze: he also married—under duress, he later testified—a beautiful young girl, the daughter of a bookseller, who in short order proved to be a shrew, a spendthrift, and an indefatigable harlot.

Compounding his difficulties, Greuze in resentment forswore the Salon and tried, like Fragonard, to sell directly from his studio. But he did not have the friends, or the talent, that kept Fragonard going. He needed the public showing that only the Salon could give him, and although he continued to make money from his painting and from the sale of engravings from his most popular subjects, his reputation began to decline. By the middle eighties, when he was in his sixties, he had begun the twenty years of misery that concluded his life.

His wife's promiscuity had become so flagrant that he obtained a legal separation. Diderot died. But Diderot had already come to his senses, and although in his first enthusiasm he had written, "Courage, good friend Greuze—paint moral paintings and paint them always like this," he had tapered off his support, having seen in the work of a young painter, Jacques Louis David, a more significant expression of the direction moral painting could take.

Now the Revolution wiped out such capital as Greuze had accumulated and his type of painting was swept aside by a rage for a form of classicism that, ironically, Greuze had anticipated twenty years earlier with the unhappy *Septimius Severus Reproaching Caracalla, etc.* He was destitute and beyond professional rehabilitation. In 1801 he wrote to the Minister of the Interior in an effort to get a pension or any form of relief, describing himself as an old man who had "lost everything, talent as well as courage," and stating that he did not have a single picture on order.

Greuze lived for sixteen years after the Revolution, and how he lived is distressing to conjecture. But he is a hard man to feel sorry for. Except for just one thing, his wretched life provides all the material for a romanticized biography of the tragic genius—who had to overcome great odds as a boy to fulfill his burning desire to become an artist; who rose to spectacular success with pictures of high moral purpose; loved above his station and then succumbed to the wiles of a beautiful wanton; and was finally relegated to oblivion by the envy of a powerful clique. The one thing that is lacking is a great spirit.

Greuze's pseudo-nobility is sentimentalism, his morality is specious. Today, even the titles of his moral paintings suggest the nineteenth-century melodramas that are so easily burlesqued: *A Father Reading the Bible to His Children, The Village Bride, The Paralytic Cared For by His Children,* and the paired pictures, *The Father's Curse* and *The Prodigal Son.*

But if these subjects are only shallow or inflated, Greuze becomes downright offensive in another category of his pictures. His paintings of wide-eyed young girls with their garments in disarray to expose, as if all unbeknownst to them, their innocent charms, are as perversely salacious as any paintings that are exhibitable in public. The narrative content of such paintings as *The Broken Pitcher, Young Girl Weeping over Her Dead Bird, The Morning Prayer,* and *Offering to Love* is frequently combined with suggestive pictorial symbolism.

Greuze's paintings in both categories were popular not only with aristocrats (Catherine II of Russia, who esteemed Diderot, purchased them) and such demimondaines as Mme du Barry, but with the bourgeoisie, who continued to enjoy them in engravings long after Greuze's decline. Their mawkish storytelling and their salaciousness hidden under sugar frosting also endeared them to some Victorian households.

By hunting hard, three good words, with qualifications, may be found for Greuze in conclusion: he was a very good painter technically, but so were the rank and file of French painters in the eighteenth century; in his narrative paintings, the composition, sometimes reflecting Poussin's, is so clear and so nicely adjusted that if Greuze had had better stories to tell he would have been telling them well; and his portraits are so expert that if he had painted nothing else one would wonder why a man of his talent had painted so little. As it is, Greuze remains a painter who does, indeed, point a moral, but only by indirection. In its falsity, his art is an argument for truth.

Jean Baptiste Siméon Chardin came into the world just two months before the birth of his century: he was born in Paris on November 2, 1699. He lived for eighty years and one month, dying on December 6, 1779, just as France was feeling the labor pains of the decade of the Revolution. The story of French eighteenth-century art properly terminates with Chardin, since he expressed (without setting out to do so) the shift from an aristocratic to a bourgeois idealism that during his century changed the character of the civilized world. He was a wonderful painter, but the reader is warned: there is no way to make his story exciting.

Chardin was an adequately, but never spectacularly, successful painter during his long life. He was popular for reasons that seem unimportant today; he is impressive to us for reasons that were not apparent to his contemporaries. There is no indication that Chardin himself was conscious that the kind of painting he liked best to do was a significant departure from the norm. But in his quiet way he was a revolutionary artist.

He was a thoroughly unrevolutionary personality, a family man, simple in manner—in fact, the ideal bourgeois. He loved warmth and security, and was honest and straightforward in his dealings. His self-portrait in the Louvre shows the rather fleshy, very plain face of a man in late middle age who, if his eighteenth-century dressing gown and headkerchief were changed to a business suit and a bald head, and his metal spectacles to horn rims, could walk into the weekly luncheon meeting of any businessmen's club in a small American city today to join other stable, sturdy citizens of no particular distinction. Nothing we know about Chardin the man seems anything other than prosaic, although in the prosaic conduct of his life he was altogether admirable.

As the eldest son of a cabinetmaker's large family, Chardin had to earn his own living in his teens, and he did so as the dependable apprentice of various academic painters. In his twenties he was exhibiting in the annual outdoor shows held on Corpus Christi day in the Place Dauphine, the little triangular park tucked away on the Ile de la Cité just back of the law courts. (The Place Dauphine remained one of the sweetest spots in Paris for tourists who knew it until the 1960's, when the scourge of automobiles turned it into a parking lot.) The exhibitions there lasted just the one day, and although they were outdoor shows where young painters might show their work, they must not be confused with the clothesline exhibits and similar amateur events held today. Amateurism of that kind did not exist. The walls of the houses facing the Place were hung with rugs or other fabrics to become a gallery and salesroom where everything from old masters to contemporary work was offered. The show had none of the prestige of the Salon, but painters of modest reputation were not too proud to exhibit in it, and there was always the possibility of discovery.

Chardin was discovered there in 1728 when one of his paintings (*The Rayfish,* now in the Louvre) was so admired that he was encouraged to present himself to the Academy. He was accepted without delay in the minor category of painter of still life and genre. He was twenty-nine.

Chardin's professional life from that time on could be detailed here, but not to any great point. It is the story of a steady, industrious man of modest ambitions who loved to paint, and whose unsentimentalized pictures of simple people going about their simple routines in simple bourgeois interiors (mothers with their children; maidservants at work in the kitchen; children occupied with the kinds of games they must play indoors on rainy days) appealed to a habitually sentimental public that sentimentalized his tender realism. His still lifes, while less interesting then to most people, were also admired, but for their incidental virtue of verisimilitude. Chardin also painted portraits, which at the time were acceptable as dignified likenesses and are now more than acceptable as sympathetic portrayals of character.

His career was comparable to that of a merchant offering a dependable line of quality goods. Like any shopkeeper he had his good years and his less good years. He never got rich, but he maintained the respect and held the patronage of a prosperous body of customers, including a few among the nobility. His fortunes declined in his old age, but the story that he died in penury is not well founded. In his personal life he had rather more than the normal share of sorrows. His first wife and his two-year-old daughter died four years after his marriage, and in his old age he lost a son who disappeared after being captured by brigands during a trip to Italy. For the last forty of his eighty years Chardin was increasingly plagued by ill-health, and toward the end by failing eyesight. But these misfortunes are among the hazards of life. In its ups and downs from day to day, Chardin's life was never dramatic.

Nor is his art dramatic. The appeal that his domestic subjects held for his contemporaries remains valid today, even though it is an appeal that has little to do with the qualities that we regard as his great ones. His pictures of domestic interiors can still evoke for us as they evoked for his neighbors all the snugness and comfort and matter-of-fact affections of bourgeois life at its routine best. The walls of his small rooms shut out all confusions and uncertainties, and the objects in his still lifes—a housewife's well-used pots and pans, her favorite paring knife, the kitchen towel softened by many launderings, the milk pitchers and spice jars, and the fruits and vegetables from the local market—can please simply as reflections of their well-loved selves. You seldom find in a Chardin the rare bit of porcelain or crystal that served as exhibition pieces in the kind of still life popularized by the Dutch and Flemish painters who were his first models.

The critics could not understand Chardin's increasing devotion to still life, and although they always spoke well of him, they were puzzled because he refused to go in for the history subjects, the big pretentious test pieces, that made the Salon sensations. Critics like the influential Diderot would have welcomed a chance to receive Chardin as what they considered a major painter, but he insisted on remaining in a classification where by convention he could be regarded only as the best of the minor ones.

The insistent simplicity of Chardin's subject matter was exceptional, but it is not this that made him the greatest still-life painter of his century—which he was—or the forerunner of a revolution whose character would become clear a hundred years later with Cézanne. Chardin was the first of the architectonic still-life painters, the first to understand that a few objects disposed on a table could be given the logical balance of monuments, that light was not merely something to be represented illusionistically as falling on objects and creating shadows and highlights, but could be a unifying abstract force; that the simulated textures of polished copper, soft cloth, and plums with the bloom still on them could be more than a succession of technical displays—that there could be textural harmonies as well as harmonies of line and color. Above all, he knew that the representation of everyday objects could be more than a series of evocative descriptions of familiar shapes. He thought simultaneously in terms of representation and in terms of abstract interrelationships of planes and volumes. He gave dignity to simple things not only by painting them with love but by presenting them as the constituents of a well-ordered world.

The greatness of Chardin lies in the perfect concord between his technical processes and his emotional (the word is not quite right, but it must do) conception of his subjects. If he is the greatest bourgeois painter before the impressionist-bourgeois triumph, it is because the quiet monumentality of his pictorial schemes (whether in still life where it is most apparent and most original, or in his interiors where it was anticipated and surpassed by Vermeer) declares his acceptance of the simplest things as the most profound because they represent the goodness and truth upon which everything else depends. This idea was promulgated in some curiously superficial forms in Chardin's century—the silk-clad milk-maids of Boucher, the pseudo-moralizing scenes enacted by pseudo-simple people under the appalling direction of Greuze. Without knowing it, certainly without thinking of himself as a philosopher, Chardin the bourgeois was the only painter of his century to proclaim in believable form the nobility of the commonplace.

20

EIGHTEENTH-CENTURY ENGLAND AND AMERICA

Sir Joshua Reynolds, whose career we have already followed (perhaps a bit too unsympathetically), was the model and the ideal for virtually all the other English painters of his century. One of the exceptions, William Blake, loathed him with an intensity so violent that alone he does a great deal to counterbalance the general admiration. The men who disliked Sir Joshua, or who (like Gainsborough) tolerated him without emulating his standards, have become the ones whose art looks best to the twentieth century, but Reynolds's overwhelming reputation—his position as a virtual godhead —must be kept in mind in any consideration of eighteenth-century English art. The other portrait painters and the men who struggled for power in the Royal Academy are only partially understandable unless we remember that Sir Joshua, in those tiresome "Discourses" (which still have a band of residual admirers, constituting a kind of vermiform appendix in the world of art), set a standard of earnest pomposity to which his juniors aspired, but fortunately seldom attained. And he also set a formula for the practice of portrait painting that, because it had brought him complete success, was naturally accepted as the ideal one.

Holding in reserve the beautiful flowering of English landscape painting, we must now examine some of the painters in England and America whose aims and methods were directly or indirectly affected by Sir Joshua Reynolds.

AMERICANS IN LONDON

Oddly enough, the two men who after Sir Joshua Reynolds's death struggled for his position as the great man of English painting—Benjamin West and John Singleton Copley—were Americans, the first from the Philadelphia neighborhood, the second from Boston, who had returned to the mother country before 1776 and stayed on.

Benjamin West was born in Springfield, Pennsylvania—now Swarthmore—in 1738, nearly forty years before the signing of the Declaration of Independence. He died in London in 1820, more than forty years after that event, and during the eighty-two years of his life he traveled the whole road, both as a painter and as a career man, from the borders of the Colonial wilderness to St. Paul's, where he was buried. As a hybrid English-American artist he may be claimed—or rejected—by either side. He was never a really good artist, but he was a tremendously successful one, historically an influential one, and even, in spite of being self-hobbled by a belief that art is best produced by formula, an original one on occasion. He was also an extraordinary personality—surely the only man in the world who has been able to entertain the king of England, as a long-time friend, with stories of the Indian braves he had known as a boy.

Benjamin West was one of ten children born to his Quaker parents, John West—a tinsmith turned innkeeper—and Sarah Pearson West, the daughter of a friend of William Penn's. Fantastic stories are told about his precocious talent. Some of them must be taken with more than a grain of salt, having been propagated after West's death by idolatrous friends who never knew him as a boy but learned the stories from the old man when he had had time to embellish them for himself. West was always a professional American who made the most of his frontier background even while enjoying the best of London, and he probably romanticized, without intending to deceive, during autobiographical conversations.

But the facts support the claim of precocity. It may or may not be true that, never having seen a paintbrush but having heard one described, he made one from the tail of the family cat at the age of eight. He was surely aware, along with everybody else, that the Indians (a peaceable group that made annual visits to the towns) used natural earths as paints, whether or not it is true that they taught him how to manufacture his first colors. One thing, however, is certain: he was a child who, in a settlement where there may not have been a single painting, was always interested in making pictures, and who by the age of eleven was attempting to paint landscapes.

His first paints, along with a set of crude engravings for copying, were sent him by a relative named Pennington who had been impressed (we are told) by the incident of the cat's tail. The same man took him for a visit to Philadelphia, where he saw paintings for the first time—the stiff so-called American primitive portraits by migrant artists and the hardly less stiff ones by visiting Englishmen.

West was befriended and given his first lessons by William Williams (*c.* 1710-*c.* 1790), a minor English-born painter who was technically only a few cuts above the average migrant artist but whose work is marked by an unusual charm, almost a capriciousness. He was an interesting man, a sailor and wanderer who filled in the gaps between commissions not only as a tutor in the arts, but as a novelist, musician, stuccoworker, architect, and landscape gardener. He introduced West to treatises on a kind of painting that could not be seen in America, the showpiece in the grand manner. West plowed through these as a boy and was so impressed that when he died seventy years later he was still devoted to the mechanics of picturemaking that they set up as standards.

By the time West was sixteen he was painting portraits (of an extremely stiff, primitive character) in Lancaster. By the time he was eighteen he was established as a portraitist in Philadelphia, and then moved on to New York. When he was twenty-two he was suddenly thrown into a great adventure that made him conspicuous overnight in an international circle. He took an unexpected opportunity to accompany a merchant's son on a trip to Italy as traveling companion, but instead of returning with the ship he decided to get a glimpse of Rome. He went there armed with letters of introduction from his American sponsors and never went back home.

West's three years in Rome, before he went to London, were an episode of pure fantasy. He was the first American painter Rome had ever seen, and he was worth looking at—tall and slender, with a handsome, fine-boned face. If there were Englishmen in the international colony of the same British stock who were just as handsome and just as talented, they were, after all, only Englishmen, and this good-looking youth came from a country that was visualized in terms of romantic exoticism. A sophisticated and weary society cast West in the role of a frontier Candide, and he was a sensation. "Is he white or black?" the blind dilettante Cardinal Albani asked, feeling West's face as if it were a piece of sculpture.

West at first was shocked by the beggars in Rome, and briefly his Quaker asceticism rejected the ceremonial pomp and the glittering architecture of the Church, but it did not take him long to adjust. The Roman years are not well documented, and are described idealistically in the post-mortem biographies, in which West remains a Candide without the troubles. The troubles, in truth, did not arrive; he was continuously lionized, and his work was well received, whether for its merits or its associative interest. But one does not have to be very hardheaded or suspicious to guess that this very young man enjoyed the exotic role in which he was cast and responded by seeing himself somewhat as others saw him. When the Apollo Belvedere, then considered the apotheosis of classical beauty, was revealed to him in the presence of an expectant company, he is supposed to have exclaimed, "How like a Mohawk warrior!" He could not have said anything better, in his role, but if this was really his first reaction upon the sight of this rather effeminate male nude, the Mohawk warriors were of a daintiness not corroborated by other records.

But West was not a poseur. That he survived the Roman experience without becoming either a fop or a fool is proof enough that he was a levelheaded fellow. He was determined to learn all he could during this visit (which he thought of as an interlude before his return to America), and he worked hard to make himself into a painter in the current mode, a mode that he never questioned. He traveled to the great museums and copied Raphael, Titian, and Correggio. (He had not liked Raphael at first, but became an ardent convert.) But the primary influence at this time was the lamentable Mengs.

Anton Raphael Mengs (1728-1779) was a German painter who had come early to Rome to study and had settled there in 1751 after a period as court painter in Dresden. He was an excellent portraitist who became first painter to Charles III in Madrid, but in Rome he was most admired as a proponent of the new classical style based on the antibaroque ideals of purity and nobility upheld by the German classical archaeologist and historian Winckelmann. Mengs's empty, dry, and frigid application of this pseudo-classical ideal was a tremendous force in its development, and he was just the man for Benjamin West. Mengs was one of the most industrious painters who ever lived; he was famous for the long hours and rigorous discipline expended in the creation of paintings that now seem not worth the trouble. He believed in the rules, totally. And (the young American was assured) Mengs was the living master of an art that, revived from antiquity, was indisputably the summit of human expression. Under Mengs's tutelage Benjamin West, who so frequently gave signs of being a romantic at heart, strove to attain the proper degree of calcification, and was sufficiently successful. Twice during his Roman stay he exhibited history paintings that were well received—perhaps, however, too generously as the work of a fascinating exotic who was not expected to meet the standard fully.

Although West's three-year stay in Italy had been interrupted by an eleven-month illness when an infection nearly cost him a leg, he felt in 1763 that it was time to go home. But "home" for West's father was still the England he had left in his youth, and he insisted that Benjamin go there first. Benjamin did so, by way of Paris, and as an international lion was immediately taken up in the right London circles. He decided to stay, and after a couple of years decided to marry.

This was in 1765 when West was twenty-seven. His chosen bride was Elizabeth Shewell of Philadelphia, who had been biding her time these five years, and he planned to go back there to marry her. But his friends convinced him that for the sake of his career he should not leave London for so long a time (out of sight, out of mind), so Elizabeth came to London instead, accompanied by Benjamin's father and her cousin, the painter Matthew Pratt. Father John West came to London with the idea that he was returning to the land of solid English virtue that he had pined for ever since leaving it, but he was so appalled by the changes that he returned to the Colonies as soon as he could. London had become the city of vices and vanities castigated by Hogarth, and John West hated it. It was also the city of Dr. Johnson's intellectualism and of the refined sensibilities poeticized by Gainsborough, but the good Quaker was not up to understanding his native country in these terms.

Nor did Elizabeth respond favorably. She remained a good wife to Benjamin for fifty years and described him as a man without a fault, but she was so homesick that she kept trying to grow corn in her greenhouse—never with any success.

But Benjamin flourished. He was already popular as a portraitist and a distinguished practitioner of the new classicism. When the Royal Academy was organized in 1768 he was made a founding member. In 1772, when he was thirty-four, he was appointed Historical Painter to the King. He took 1776 in his stride, and remained the King's friend until both died in the same year, 1820. When Sir Joshua Reynolds died in 1792 the American, then fifty-four, succeeded him in the highest post England could offer an artist, the presidency of the Royal Academy. He made a great deal of money, established himself with Elizabeth in a fine house, and his funeral in St. Paul's was a state occasion. During his last years he had been turning out formula paintings with the aid of numerous assistants, and the younger men had grown tired of him, but he was still officially the grand old man of the arts in spite of such sentiments as Byron's merciless "Europe's worst daub, poor England's best."

West did not deserve quite so cutting an obituary, although his late work justified the damnation of a young man, John Constable, who had originally come to London to study with him. "West is only hanging on by the tail of the shirt of Carlo Maratti and the tag end of the Roman and Bolognese schools," he said, "and is only the shadow of them." It must be admitted that West's drawing was undependable, that his color was usually routine, and that his brush, if we except a handful of his many hundreds of paintings, might always have been the tail of a cat for any fluency or precision that he achieved. In the mass of his work he is a routine and sometimes absurd artist; some of his pseudo-classical paintings are hilarious to modern eyes, saved only by their persistent air of almost simpleminded innocence. And yet he was a pioneer whose example, through engravings, made a direct contribution to the triumphant neoclassical style of Jacques Louis David in France, and he was, as well, a precursor of the two other movements that dominated nineteenth-century painting—realism and romanticism—in two paintings, *The Death of General Wolfe* (Ottawa, National Gallery) and *Death on a Pale Horse* (Philadelphia, Pennsylvania Academy of the Fine Arts), neither of them expectable from a man who seemed bent on confining his originality within the straitjacket of the academic standard.

West painted *The Death of General Wolfe* in 1770, seven years after his arrival in London, when he was only thirty-two. Today it makes a first impression as an adequate composition observing the artificialities dictated by the grand manner, and filled with bombastically heroic attitudes and other theatrical complications. But it was an innovational painting for all that. General Wolfe was killed in the course of the siege of Quebec during the French and Indian Wars, and the conventional commemorative painting would have allegorized his patriotic demise in classical terms and classical garb. But West was an American who more or less knew the locale of the event. He chose to represent it in the costume of the day, and included an Indian brave, correctly rather than imaginatively costumed, among the figures who support and bewail the dying hero. (Compositionally, West was less original; the arrangement of the attendant figures is based on the formula for the Lamentation of Christ.)

In its discarding of ancient history, allegory, and religion in favor of contemporary reference, *The Death of General Wolfe* is modern in conception. Only the skeleton of the picture is traditional. Reynolds, who could be so perceptive on occasion, was among the few people who recognized the significance of West's shift of point of view. For the public the picture was only a fascinating dramatic representation of a recent event, and West made a comfortable sum by exhibiting it in his studio for an admission fee—thus supplying Jacques Louis David with a precedent that he used in 1799 to defend his similar exhibition of *The Sabines*.

In 1771, a year after *The Death of General Wolfe*, West repeated the idea of representing a historical event in the trappings and actual setting of its time and place with *Penn's Treaty with the Indians* (Philadelphia, Pennsylvania Academy of the Fine Arts), a charming painting. But in both of these pictures he was apparently capitalizing on his Americanness rather than attempting a revolution in pictorial or aesthetic standards, and thereafter his history paintings were remarkably unimaginative.

His second (and inexplicable) breakthrough as an original artist came in his sixties. From time to time—for instance, in a series of illustrations for Spenser's "Faerie Queene" and Shakespeare's plays—he had edged toward romantic expression. Then about 1787 he made the first sketch for *Death on a Pale Horse,* and in his quick notation for the apocalyptic scene—the sketch is only 11 by 22 inches—he anticipated all the tempestuousness and emotionalism of the great French romantics, Géricault and Delacroix, before either of them was born. One forgives the flimsy drawing for the rush of figures through a world in flames. By degrees, in subsequent versions, West managed to stifle the vigor of his first conception, but a version exhibited in Paris in 1802 (now in the Philadelphia Museum of Art) was still sufficiently impressive to stir excitement. In this one painting, West is comparable to the protoromantic Frenchman Antoine Jean Gros, who thought of himself as a classicist but yielded in spite of himself to the romantic surge.

It is not a bad record for a man to have been a pioneer classicist and a prophet of realism and romanticism. West's tragedy as an artist was that all his life he somehow remained a precocious provincial impressed by the academic standards of what he thought of as the great world, instead of developing the impulses that might have turned him into a truly great artist. What kind of man was he, exactly? His biographers always laud his kindness, his honesty, his simplicity, and his naturalness. And it is true that a stream of young American painters, including Charles Willson Peale, Stuart, Sully, Allston, Trumbull, and Morse, found a generous welcome in his London studio. But West remains a curious personality obscured by his legend—partly, perhaps, because his legend helped create his own idea of himself. He must have been, among other things, an adept politician, since Candide does not survive in a world of intrigue. Kindness, honesty, simplicity, and naturalness were not the ingredients for success in eighteenth-century London. In his own way, West met his scheming opponents on their own ground, and vanquished them.

John Singleton Copley (1738-1815) was one of the fine portrait painters of his century, the best American Colonial painter, and, second only to Thomas Eakins in the next century, the best portraitist America has produced. He had a double career, first as a Colonial American and then as an unreconstructed political conservative (if not quite a Tory), whose post-Revolutionary life was spent in London. Copley had twenty-one active years as a Colonial artist and about the same number of successful ones in London before the decade of personal and professional deterioration with which his life ended. He was without any question much more interesting and infinitely more his own man during his years as a somewhat provincial Colonial than when he became a converted Londoner dedicated to the ideals of the Royal Academy, although it is an exaggeration to dismiss his English work as a disaster.

Copley was probably born in Boston. By the time he was fifteen he was a professional portraitist signing his work. The death of his father before he was ten and that of his stepfather when he was thirteen may have forced his natural precocity. His father, John Copley, a tobacconist, and his mother, Mary Singleton, had emigrated from Ireland two years before his birth. When John died, Mary Copley took a second husband who had three strings to his bow, none of them of great strength. Peter Pelham taught school, gave dancing lessons, and was a mezzotint engraver. He taught John Singleton Copley the rudiments of drawing.

Copley needed very little teaching. His earliest portraits are charming examples of American primitivism, but he rapidly transformed himself into a phenomenally exact realistic draftsman. He was also a beautiful colorist. Both as draftsman and as colorist, he developed without benefit of theory. He was a practical, hardworking, cautious, and ambitious young man with a God-given talent that he perfected by assiduous application, although without much flourish or, for that matter, much imagination. But one misses neither. Copley's wonderful delineations of the faces and costumes of his sitters present the solid and prosperous Colonials of Boston, New York, and Philadelphia so convincingly that they live as personalities within any room where a Copley portrait hangs.

Beyond the introduction of an accessory clue now and then to indicate the profession or hobby of his sitter, Copley makes no comments. His painted people are so real that it is impossible to deny him a perception of character, but at the same time it is impossible to say that he revealed in a face anything not apparent to the world. He simply tells us how these people looked, and this he tells with great truth and—except for showing them posing at their best—without the flattery by which his English contemporaries reduced all sitters to the common denominator of handsome lord or beautiful lady. The common denominator of Copley's American portraits is intrinsic, not grafted on. It is the look of people in the most prosperous bracket of a society, a bracket filled with names that since then have become the aristocratic ones of America. At the time, they represented a roster of self-made men who either in professions or as merchants had become the strong men of the New World, sometimes with a father or even a grandfather born in it.

When he was twenty-eight, in 1766, Copley sent a picture, *Boy with a Squirrel* (now privately owned), to London for exhibition. It was praised by the all-powerful Joshua Reynolds. The young Colonial was elected to the Society of Artists of Great Britain, the precursor of the Royal Academy, and also acquired a helpful friend in another American who was enjoying a European triumph, Benjamin West.

Most Copley admirers are enraged when he is called a Tory. He steered a middle course in politics, which he regarded as "bad for art" and which could also be bad for business, since to be a partisan of one side or the other was to estrange one half or the other of his potential sitters. His wife, however, was a member of a prominent Tory family. (He married Susanna Clarke, the daughter of a well-to-do Boston merchant, in 1769.) By 1774 the political situation was tense, and Copley as an eminent citizen was always being urged to declare his position. It seemed a good time to leave home until the storm blew over, as Copley was convinced it would, and he took the opportunity to do something he had wanted to do for a long time—go to Italy to see the work of the old masters. He made the trip, by way of London and Paris, and the next year, in Rome, he received news of the outbreak of the war. Frantic for the safety of his wife and children, he hurried back to London, where he discovered them waiting for him. The family never returned to America. In 1776, while his countrymen were signing their Declaration of Independence, Copley's anglicization was confirmed by his election to associate membership in the Royal Academy; in 1779 he became a full member.

Copley was more interested in the gadfly politics within the Royal Academy than he had been in the conflict between the colony and the mother country, and in the power struggles that went on, his friendship with his early sponsor, Benjamin West, turned very sour. At one time Copley's and

West's factions caused so much trouble that the dispute was taken to the King, who vigorously stated that he wished the devil would take them both. Overall, Copley lost more battles than he won, and he also lost a more important struggle, the one with himself as an artist.

He had never realized that his Americanness was his strength, and in his determination to make himself over he did his utmost to become a great history painter on the academic model. He did become a superior one, perhaps as good a practitioner in this generally dreary genre as English painting offers. He was excruciatingly conscientious in his factual research on the events that he planned to illustrate, such as the death of Chatham and the siege of Gibraltar, and in his doggedly complicated pictorial constructions he seemed equally determined to incorporate every rule of composition that had ever been tested and approved during and since the Italian Renaissance. But of all these storytelling pictures, only one has the expressive quality that raises narrative to significant expression—*Watson and the Shark*.

Watson and the Shark illustrates an incident when Brook Watson, an orphan of fourteen who had gone to sea, lost part of a leg to a shark while swimming in Havana harbor. The ravening fish, the anguished naked boy, and nine fellow sailors in a dory who are trying to drive off the shark and pull the boy out of the water, are combined in a composition-by-the-rules that rises above the rules to become a protoromantic creation of such power that it has even been thought of as an unconscious allegory of the struggle between innocence and evil. The first of three versions, painted after Watson had become a prominent London merchant (he later became Sir Brook Watson and lord mayor of London), caused a sensation in the Royal Academy exhibition of 1778 and raised Copley to stardom from his position as a respected minor painter. Sir Brook later gave the picture to Christ's Hospital, a charitable school, with the conviction that it might serve as "a most usefull lesson to youth." Although he doubtless had something loftier in mind than the practical admonition not to take risks in infested waters, it is safe to say that he had no suspicion of the philosophical depths that subsequent interpreters were to uncover. The original version is now in the National Gallery in Washington, and there are variations in the Boston and Detroit museums.

Watson and the Shark is an extraordinary painting, proof that Copley had an expressive potential beyond the field of portraiture. Painted only three or four years after he had left America, it still has the special flavor of his Colonial painting—an apparent objectivity from which the artist's expressive powers emerge without his full intention or knowledge. It has the residue of provincial stiffness beneath its technical polish that distinguishes Copley as an artist not quite like any other.

Copley's personal shark was his ambition to excel by a standard more sophisticated than the one that was congenial to him by origin and education. And he lost to this shark more than a leg. He not only sidetracked his talent in the direction of history painting, but managed as well to sacrifice his birthright as an American portraitist by emulating the more fluid brushwork and the aristocratic manner of his London colleagues. He was incapable of painting a really bad portrait, and occasionally in England he painted a good flamboyant one, but his great portraits are his American ones. Fortunately there are 275 of them

ENGLISH PORTRAITS

It is sometimes difficult to decide whether portrait painting in eighteenth-century England was an art or an industry, and the scornful label "face painting" is often flattering to the lesser examples of a product that found a market apparently limited only by the birth rate. "Artist" is not often a really appropriate classification for the portraitists. "Painter" does better, since many of them were skillful brushmen even when they had nothing else to offer. But "practitioner" is the best word to describe the mass of these men who were engaged in a form of professionalism that had little to do with the creative spirit. The following painters all rise above that classification; they are presented chronologically rather than by degree of merit. Sir Thomas Lawrence, who comes at the end, spent more of his professional life in the nineteenth century than in the eighteenth, but that makes no difference. His fantastic success makes him the very type of the fashionable eighteenth-century portraitist, the last of the breed.

Allan Ramsay (1713-1784), who was ten years older than Reynolds and fourteen years older than Gainsborough, was a transitional figure between the imported court portrait painters and the native English portraitists who finally con-

quered the field. A Scot by birth and an Italian by training, he was a hardworking professional eager to make money
and successful at it. He was not particularly interested in the
personalities of his sitters, preferring to observe them as
setups of stuffs surmounted by a face that he improved somewhat when necessary. But now and then in his portraits of
women he anticipated Gainsborough's sensitivity. In 1736,
when he was twenty-three, he went to Italy, returning to
England in 1738 with a mastery of Italian methods. When he
was forty-seven (1760), George III appointed him Principal
Painter to the King, a position he held until his death twenty-
four years later while Reynolds fumed. (Reynolds, succeeding
him in the post, was by then in a position to complain about
the pay.)

Ramsay was a cultivated gentleman, a traveler whose
conversational skill was admired by the demanding Dr. Johnson, and a good businessman. Required, as Principal Painter,
to supply ninety full-length portraits of the King and Queen,
he sublet the job to Philip Reinagle (1749-1833), who copied
Ramsay's originals for a fee of fifty guineas a pair. Ramsay
then signed them and collected his fee of quadruple that
amount—which was honest enough according to the practices
of the day.

There are many interesting things about George Romney, but his paintings are too seldom among them. "Ingratiating" is the sturdiest adjective that can be applied overall to
his two thousand or so portraits; "weak and careless" are the
adjectives that apply to too many of them. Romney's life,
however, could make an excellent light novel of the type
called hammock reading if it were undertaken by the right
person, probably a sympathetic English gentlewoman of
letters.

Romney was born in 1734 at Beckside, Lancashire, and in his youth learned his father's craft of cabinetmaking, serving for ten years as assistant in the family workshop. In the meanwhile he taught himself to draw by copying (and it might be argued that even as a successful artist later on he was more a copyist than an originator). When he was twenty-one he was apprenticed to an obscure portrait painter named Steele. By 1762, when he was twenty-eight, he had acquired a wife and children as well as a small reputation in his new profession, and he deserted the former in order to increase the latter in London.

After only a year in the capital he was showing with great success in all the big exhibitions except those of the Academy, to which he was never elected because he had set himself up in opposition to its potentate, Sir Joshua Reynolds. The opposition was not aesthetic, since Romney rather shamelessly (although no more shamelessly than a host of small fry) filched Reynolds's pictorial effects, making them the basis of his own style. The opposition was financial, which for the grasping Sir Joshua was inexcusable.

In 1764, after a trip to Paris where he studied Rubens for further borrowings, Romney, only thirty, purchased a house near Sir Joshua's and before long was equaling him in the number, if not always the importance, of clients for portraits. He was recognized as a competitor of both Reynolds and Gainsborough, and even today may run as a third, if not a strong one, behind those two in the field of eighteenth-century English portraiture. He typifies the kind of portrait painter still most popular in England and in most countries with an English heritage, the dependable photographer-painter whose retouching invests the sitter with the usual requisite of ladylike grace, manly breeding, or sugary innocence, according to sex and age, in a flattering record that doubles as an expensive item of interior decoration.

This was Romney's forte. But a two-year trip to Italy, in 1773-75, was at least partially his undoing. In Rome he was seized by an ambition to excel in the more difficult area of classical and imaginative themes, either in the grand manner or, surprisingly for him, in a vein exploring the weird and supernatural. Here he was influenced by Fuseli, whom he met at this time, and he attempted a dramatic boldness in drawings on Shakespearean and Miltonic themes. Although his ambition was sincere enough—who would not enjoy the company of such great spirits?—he had neither the perseverance nor the intellectual equipment to do much more than borrow from Fuseli and, later, from Blake. Even Romney's kindest critics cannot feel that these deviations from facile charm are very fortunate.

Back in London, Romney continued to make a great deal of money. But in 1782, nearing the dangerous age of fifty, he lapsed into a condition recognizable in the context of his life as a manifestation of neurosis: he met the seventeen- or eighteen-year-old beauty Emma Hart, later Lady Hamilton, and fell in love with her. She became his obsession. Year after year after year he painted her over and over and over again, sometimes in portraits, sometimes in elaborately contrived allegories, but always in terms of a pinup sexuality that betrays the yearnings of a moonstruck adolescent in this middle-aged man. He even turned away the most profitable commissions to devote himself to these labors of delayed love.

As Romney approached his sixties, his mental confusion and the weakening of his talent became obvious. In 1789, partially paralyzed after a breakdown, he returned to the wife he had deserted twenty-seven years earlier, joining her in Kendal, where he died in 1802, hopelessly senile at the age of sixty-eight.

It is perhaps a little too easy to be hard on Romney. To

give him his due, he was an adept borrower when he chose the right sources. He had little skill of arrangement, but in his most successful paintings he often gave agreeable simplicity to the contours of a single figure, and while he was hardly equal to dealing with the complexities of what is often called color orchestration, he could touch off a portrait with a pleasant blue or plum oddment of costume in the deftest way. His paint surface suggests the richness of the best expensive candy. There was nothing wrong with Romney within his limitations, but nothing right when he tried to exceed them. His slightest sketches are charming.

Sir Henry Raeburn (1756-1823) was born and died in Edinburgh and, except for brief forays to London and Italy, spent his life there during the city's golden age. His portraits are a roster of Edinburgh's prominent men, plus their ladies and an occasional Highlander in full regalia. As Scotland's foremost portraitist, he has naturally been called the Scottish Reynolds, and he did give to his male sitters a Reynoldesque air of consequence. He could, and sometimes did, reveal or present them as men of character, just as Reynolds could.

Raeburn was trained as a jeweler and taught himself to paint by copying. His work retained a provincial uncertainty even after he was well established professionally, but after a time he developed a personal style, bold, vigorous, and spontaneous in effect (as indeed it was in fact: he painted directly on the canvas with no preliminary drawing). His hallmark, perfected about 1800, was his "square touch," a decisive, choppy brushstroke with which he reduced a face to its essential planes without blending one stroke into the next.

He had a good life. Well under way professionally by the age of twenty, he made a happy marriage with a wealthy widow at the age of twenty-four. In 1785, when he was twenty-nine, he went to Italy and on the way met Reynolds in London. Italy did not have any effect on him. Reynolds did, and in the next five years Raeburn's virtuoso style matured. He began exhibiting in London, thought of moving there in 1810 when he could have taken over Hoppner's studio upon that portraitist's death, decided against the move, and returned to Edinburgh, where he became president of the Society of Artists. He was elected to associate membership in the Royal Academy in 1812, went to London to be invested with full membership in 1815, was knighted by George IV in 1822 when the monarch was visiting Edinburgh, and died the next year at the age of sixty-seven. Appropriately, for a man so closely identified with a locale, large numbers of his portraits still hang in the halls for which he originally painted them.

In 1797, when he was twenty-eight years old, Thomas Lawrence (he was not yet Sir Thomas) exhibited his most ambitious painting, *Satan Calling His Legions,* to the unanimous disapproval of the critics. In the story of his life, this failure is the only bit of salt to bring out the flavor of fantastic success.

He was born in 1769, one of sixteen children of a minor official turned innkeeper. He seems to have issued from the womb knowing how to draw, and by the age of ten he was a professional, with such a lively market for his crayon portraits (with the inn as his studio) that he was the major support of the family.

When Thomas was thirteen, the family moved to Bath. He enlarged his technical range to include pastel—he was self-taught, insofar as he needed any teaching at all—and his portraits of the gentry of Bath, Oxford, and the surrounding country were sought after as the work not of a freak prodigy but of a proficient artist, although the fact that they were done by a boy surely lent some piquancy to his products.

When he was seventeen, and painting in oils, Lawrence wrote in a letter that he would be willing to risk comparison with any painter of heads in London but Sir Joshua Reynolds, and with this idea he went to London to take on the competition. He studied very briefly (perhaps from curiosity) at the Royal Academy school, and in 1787 (now eighteen) he exhibited in the annual Academy show. Although the Academy school offered him nothing he had not already learned for himself, he began another course of self-instruction by observing the social technique of Sir Joshua Reynolds, which he set out to emulate. Here, too, he had a natural talent. He was a born charmer, and although he made the most of it, he does not present quite the image of a callous, calculating careerist that Sir Joshua does.

At twenty, in 1789, Lawrence exhibited his first full-length portrait, a rather flashy affair, at the Academy. Queen Charlotte admired it so much that she demanded an introduction to the young artist, and forthwith commissioned him to do her portrait. This portrait (now in the National Gallery in London) is often cited as his masterpiece in its restraint—Lawrence's brush had a way of running away from him—without loss of brilliance. It was exhibited in the next Academy show along with a portrait of a popular actress, Elizabeth Farren (Metropolitan Museum), which was, appropriately, more theatrically executed. Thus, at twenty-one, Lawrence was a roaring success—with the critics and in high social circles as well.

At twenty-two he was elected an associate member of the Royal Academy. At twenty-three he succeeded Sir Joshua (who died that year—1792) in the top post of Painter to the King. But he had to wait two years for full membership in the Academy—a delay explained by his having only then attained the minimum age for election.

With thirty looming on the horizon, Lawrence decided to challenge the historical field with a "subject" picture of the kind that the leaders of the Academy—Copley, West, Reynolds—manufactured as demonstrations of a painterly and intellectual prowess beyond the requirements of portraiture. This was *Satan Calling His Legions*. Its failure got Lawrence's one misdirected ambition out of the way, and he returned to his proper course.

But his thirties seem to have been years of self-questioning all the same. His portraits between 1800 and 1810 are uneven, swinging between forced sobriety and a facile freshness that degenerates into mere carelessness. He also had financial troubles during these years, although these could never have been anything but temporary with the money pouring in as it did. He continued his tremendous success in all quarters—the amatory included. He never married, but he never lacked for love affairs, his liaisons with the daughters of Mrs. Siddons, the actress, being the best known of these.

In 1815, now settled in his forties, Lawrence was knighted. Just before he turned fifty, in 1818, he was given an assignment that enlarged his English reputation to international dimensions. The King commissioned a set of portraits of the statesmen, sovereigns, and generals who had been the leading personalities in the defeat of Napoleon. (The portraits are now in the Waterloo Chamber of Windsor Castle.) During the two years Lawrence spent on the Continent, in the company of the great assembled at Aix-la-Chapelle, Vienna, and Rome, he entranced everybody. He became a cosmopolitan lion and also did some of his finest painting. Still able to grow, he learned so much from the portraits by Titian and Velázquez in Continental collections that one wonders what might have happened to this malleable artist if he had known these painters instead of Sir Joshua as his first masters by example.

When Sir Thomas returned to London in 1820 he was elected president of the Royal Academy, and lived another ten years with no competition at all as the most eminent English artist. In this position he died in 1830 at the age of sixty-one without having exhausted his powers.

Lawrence was a man of great sensitivity who, in a standard judgment that seems to hold, was defeated by his capacity for painterly fireworks. He formed the greatest collection of drawings of his time, which was the golden age of such collecting, and this indication of fine perception endears him to connoisseurs today even when they cannot quite accept him as a first-rate painter. (The drawing collection, offered to the nation at an absurd bargain rate, was inexplicably rejected, and has been dispersed.) Even though Lawrence can still delight with the sheer theatrical brilliance of his performance and can occasionally stir in his reflection of character, he is not an artist of much range even if he is the solidest example of the successful English portrait painter who flatters his sitter while entertaining the observer with the grace and assurance of his technique and, in the process, makes a great deal of money.

Efforts have been made, lately, to rehabilitate Lawrence by interpreting as protoromantic the Byronic poses he liked to give his sitters and the emotional intensity (quite imaginary) he is supposed to have generated by flickering brushwork. But somehow Lawrence's position can never quite be maintained at the top of the heap, and contemporary critics are likely to agree with an earlier judgment by the Great Father of romantic painting. Delacroix, writing in his journal in 1855, twenty-five years after Lawrence's death, noted that Lawrence had "a kind of originality" but that a school of English portrait painting "with Lawrence first among them" was marked by "a look of artificiality that is not compensated for by virtues" that sometimes go with it. The balance, somehow, just will not shift to the side of the virtues, no matter how firmly the critical thumb is introduced on Lawrence's side of the scales.

William Etty, although he worked during the early nineteenth century (he was born in 1787 and died in 1849), is included at this point in this book partly because he was, if only briefly, a student of Thomas Lawrence's and because his art is so closely allied to eighteenth-century ideals. In his elaborate compositions he aspired to the grand manner of the Academy with Rubens and Titian as his models, and in his more intimate paintings he reflected eighteenth-century sensibility (although he hybridized it with the sentimentalism of the Victorian age, into which he lived).

Etty entered the Royal Academy's school when he was twenty, exhibited regularly after another four years, and was made a full member when he was forty-one. During his entire career he continued to paint from the nude in the Academy's life classes, and his feeling for the sensuousness of the body places him alone in his century in England and very nearly alone in all English painting. His firm position as a minor master is determined by these studies. When he labored over mythological or allegorical subjects he fell into exaggerated violence or shallow sweetness—extremes that he could combine even in a single picture—but his studio nudes are fluent, rich, and not too often overprettified. Delacroix admired Etty's painting, which may be one reason why Etty is so often called a romantic. Lawrence's tutelage is apparent in his student's fresh, caressing brush.

Etty was born and died in York, although he lived most of his life in London with frequent trips to Italy and France.

AMERICANS AT HOME

Colonial painters were subject to a circumstance that, while well known, is not kept consistently in mind: there was no first-rate (and very little second-rate) painting at hand to teach them by proxy. Those who could, like West and Copley, went to England, and after West became established there his studio was a kind of transmission center between the continents. Gradually an anglicized (and, after 1776, a more Europeanized) American school developed, replacing a kind of painting that had been an indigenous reflection of Colonial life.

The earliest American painters could not have dreamed that their provincialism, even when so extreme that it reduced their efforts to a form of folk art, might one day make them more interesting than many of the facile but routine Englishmen whom they would have yearned to emulate if only they had had the chance. American journeyman painters existed by the dozen, and frequently were nothing more than aesthetically illiterate hacks and daubers whose work can be esteemed only by a distortion of values that makes any primitive effort interesting. But there were also among them some genuine artists whose sensitivities illuminate paintings that, by Sir Joshua's standards, would have been laughable.

The eighteenth-century development of American painting can be followed here through a series of artists who might be called professionals, but no proper recognition can be given those souls who, traipsing from house to house and from town to town with their paint boxes and canvas rolls on their backs, are forever anonymous.

Although not American by birth, John Smibert (1688-1751) has as strong a claim as anyone to the title of initiator of an American portrait tradition—regrettably, for he got it off to a very dull start. For such an unimaginative artist he seems to have been a rather attractively venturesome fellow. As a youth in Edinburgh he was an apprentice house painter, but his ambitions to become a face painter led him to London, where he became a coach painter and a copyist to support himself while studying at Thornhill's academy. By 1717 he was in Florence, copying old masters, a form of hackwork that could supply a small but steady income. Three years later he was back in London to try his luck again, but apparently he did not do well (there is no indication in any of his work that he could have met the competition), and in 1729 he set sail for America with Bishop Berkeley, having accepted his invitation to join the faculty of his proposed university for Indians in Bermuda.

Smibert was now forty-one years old. He got as far as Newport, never as far as Bermuda, since the plans for the university fell through. He wound up in Boston, where he kept a shop selling frames, engravings, and art supplies, and became the city's leading portrait painter. But oh, he was dull. Basing his style on a dull painter, Kneller, he was in addition a weak draftsman, and although efforts to credit him with a certain effectively blunt realism are always made, the efforts have backfired by suggesting that Smibert's dullness reflects a dullness connected with American honesty.

To imply that Colonial Boston was dull, however, is plain calumny.

Robert Feke (*c.* 1706/10-*before* 1767) is known to have been born in Oyster Bay on Long Island and to have worked in that area, in Boston (where he appears in 1741 with *The Family of Isaac Royall,* now in the Harvard Law School), and in Newport and Philadelphia, where his presence is spottily documented until 1750. He was (it is almost certain) a sea captain, and it is said, but cannot be proved, that he died in Barbados, in the West Indies. That is just about the sum of what we know of Feke's life. But his paintings tell that he had a talent approaching genius. With only Smibert as a model, he became a master of rhythmic design, learned to render the sheen of fabrics, and in his best paintings was a truly luminous colorist. As a bridge between Smibert and Copley, he far surpassed the first and on occasion equaled the second. What with optimistic attributions, as many as fifty portraits have been identified as his including a large number in which he groped toward his final impressive work. But to stand as an extraordinary figure in American art he need have painted only his portrait of General Samuel Waldo (Bowdoin College), in which he adds revelation of character to his technical excellence. It is probable that his taste for the sea, combined with the ambiguous and precarious position of artists in Colonial America, led Feke to abandon painting or to practice it only sporadically—a great loss, since his powerful talent was only partially realized.

Gustavus Hesselius (1682-1755), a Swedish painter who came to America in 1712, was an altogether undistinguished, even inept, portrait painter. His son John (1728-1778), whom he trained but who learned more from the Englishman Wollaston, became a somewhat better than acceptable portrait painter, original to the extent that he insisted on using American backgrounds for his American subjects. He lived first

in Philadelphia and then, after 1763, when he married a
wealthy widow, near Annapolis.

Surely there has never been another man like Charles
Willson Peale. In his versatility and the range of his interests
he was a kind of corn-fed Leonardo. The qualification "corn-
fed" is intended to convey that Peale had nothing of the
subtlety and depth of Leonardo's thought, the virtuosity of
his technique, or the neurotic cast of his genius. Indeed
"genius" would be the wrong word for Charles Willson Peale,
even by stretching the definition, but no other word even
begins to describe him. He was one of a kind.

He was born in 1741 in Queen Annes County, Mary-
land, where his father, who had emigrated from England
after having been convicted on a charge of embezzlement and
forgery, condemned to death, and pardoned, was a school-
teacher. The father died when Charles Willson, the oldest of
three children, was nine years old, and the boy was apprenticed to a saddler. Saddlery gave him a respectable living
during the following years, but he was always fascinated by
any craft technique (remaining convinced to the end of his
life that painting was simply a craft that could be learned
like any other) and combined his saddlemaking with the
decoration of signs and coaches while instructing himself,
as well, in watch and clock repairing, wood carving, silver-
smithing, and brass and plaster casting. Later in life he
added taxidermy, dentistry (he invented porcelain false
teeth), soldiery, politics, and museology to a list of interests
and activities that encompassed science in general.

When he was twenty-one, Peale saw some amateur landscapes and portraits on exhibition in Norfolk and set out to
try something of the kind for himself with the aid of a
manual called "The Handmaid to the Arts" that he found in

Philadelphia. He had no intention of becoming a painter; with the curiosity of a squirrel and an energy uniquely his own, he was simply incapable of leaving alone anything that offered possibilities for exploration. He explored painting thoroughly enough so that a neighboring planter offered him ten pounds to paint his and his wife's portraits. To a young saddlemaker who had a new wife of his own (the first of three) and a baby on the way (the first of seventeen), the fee was stimulating. Peale went to the painter John Hesselius and suggested an exchange—one of the best Peale saddles for a bit of instruction in art. The exchange was accepted. Then in 1765, when Peale was twenty-four, he got a chance to learn from a finer master. In Boston that year, Copley (who was only three or four years older) let Peale stand by and watch him at work, and also lent him one of his paintings to copy.

When he was twenty-six (1767) friends collected enough money to send Peale to London, where Benjamin West, who all but ran a hostel for visiting American artists, received him helpfully. After two years of London, which happily did nothing to anglicize Peale's engagingly uncalculated American style, he returned home and set himself up in a studio in Annapolis. He did so well that when Copley left America five years later, in 1774, he also left Peale, who was then thirty-three, without any real competition as America's leading portrait painter.

When the Revolution broke out, Peale moved to Philadelphia and added patriotic stars to his crowded crown. He was a member of the Pennsylvania Assembly and one of Washington's officers, but kept so busy with his sketching apparatus during the campaigns that one of his companions made the famous and flavorsome comment, "He fit and painted, and painted and fit." The military portraits became the nucleus for a hall of fame when Peale decided to add an exhibition gallery to his studio in Philadelphia. This was in

1781. By 1784 he had forty-four likenesses of public figures in a museum that yielded a respectable gate.

Peale is an important figure in the history of museums in America. In 1786, when he was forty-five years old, he established the first museum in this country that was conceived as a serious scientific-educational venture rather than as a collection of freaks and novelties. Another indication of his forward-mindedness is that he tried to interest the government in the project—but he failed. On his own, he enlarged his art gallery so that it became a combined natural-history and art project. The art was not offered as an aesthetic experience—in truth, Peale in his direct, extroverted way always thought of art as an axillary growth from one stem or another. Art in the Peale museum served as a means of demonstration and record. The portraits of scientists were portraits first, art second, and one of Peale's most engaging pictures would never have been painted if the camera had been in existence. One of the museum's projects was the excavation of two mastodon skeletons, and he recorded the process (and added a Peale family group as spectators, for good measure) in *Exhuming the Mastodon* (Baltimore, Peale Museum).

The museum outgrew Peale's studio and in 1794 was transferred to Philosophical Hall, and then in 1802 to the upper floor of the State House—Independence Hall today. A few portraits remain there, although the collection was broken up about twenty-five years after Peale's death when its attraction for the public waned under the competition of more numerous commercial amusements of the Barnum type.

By the turn of the century, Peale, nearing sixty, was not doing a great deal of painting. He had made an informal agreement, not ironclad, to abandon the profitable field of miniature portrait painting to his brother James (one victim of Charles Willson's idea that anyone could be taught to paint) and to farm out most other portrait commissions to those of his progeny who were now old enough to take their places in the family art business. In 1795, however, when the patriarch formed the first art school in America, the Columbianum, he painted a demonstration piece for the students that is probably his masterpiece, *The Staircase Group,* now in the Philadelphia Museum of Art. The picture is a *trompe l'oeil* in which his eldest son, Raphaelle, then aged twenty-one, holding a palette and mahlstick, and his son Titian Ramsay, aged fifteen, are shown on a narrow winding staircase that, as originally exhibited, began with a real wooden step and was set into a real doorframe. George Washington—who sat seven times for Peale—is supposed to have doffed his hat and bowed to this painting. Although he was perhaps bowing only to its tour-de-force illusionism, the picture may well be the finest of eighteenth-century American portraits if we except—and perhaps even if we don't except—Copley's very best.

By the turn of the century, also, Peale had brought to a conclusion his impressive record as a sire. In 1799 his second wife, whom he had married in 1791 when he was fifty, bore him his last and seventeenth child. (A third marriage, made at the age of sixty-four, proved sterile.) The children of the first marriage (to Rachel Brewer) who survived infancy were the namesakes of a starry roster. In addition to Raphaelle and Titian Ramsay, the males in this set included Rembrandt and Rubens. Female artists (omitting those of unsavory reputation such as Artemisia Gentileschi) were more difficult to find, but there were daughters named for Angelica Kauffmann, whom Peale had met in London, Sophonisba Angusciola, and Rosalba Carriera. Rosalba lived only to the age of two, but the name was picked up again to serve a grandchild, the daughter of Rembrandt. Rembrandt also remedied an omission by naming a son Michael Angelo.

Charles Willson Peale's first child by his second wife (who was blessed with the absolutely enchanting name of Betsy de Peyster) was named Vandyke, and another son was named Titian Ramsay II after the son by the first marriage, who had died at the age of eighteen. But although eligible male old masters were still in line for Peale's form of commemoration, his increasing interest in natural history led him to shift his references, and the other two sons were named for Benjamin Franklin—as scientist rather than patriot—and Charles Linnaeus. Female scientists being unheard of, the daughters had to get along with the names Elizabeth and Sybilla.

When he was in his mid-seventies, Peale's interest in painting revived under the stimulation of the new graces that were being introduced by the younger men returning from London and Paris. It is always said that he learned from his sons at this time, but they had hardly any distinctions that he could have envied. In 1822, when he was eighty-one, he painted a most remarkable picture, *The Lamplight Portrait* (Detroit), in which his brother James sits at a table in an otherwise dark room contemplating a miniature portrait by a shaded oil lamp. His son Rembrandt had done a somewhat crude self-portrait by candlelight, but no other American had tackled a more difficult problem in representing artificial illumination, and few artists have surpassed Charles Willson Peale's careful analysis of the tonalities involved. *The Lamplight Portrait* should not be compared to seventeenth-century tenebrist painting, since it was not approached as a problem in dramatic composition. Insatiably curious and pragmatic as always, Peale set out to represent a familiar phenomenon, and found a way to do it.

Peale had limitations as an artist that should have ruled him out as anything but a fascinating character who did some painting. He had no feeling whatsoever for paint as paint, no response to its sensuous quality. It was only pigment to him, and as a colorist he could do no more than tint an area an appropriate shade. He was not a facile draftsman, and by most definitions not even a good one; the effectiveness of his representation depends to a great degree, in fact, upon an awkwardness and a naïveté that connect him with the Colonial primitive tradition. But where a painter like Smibert was always agonizingly dull in his provincial limitations, Peale conveys a homely sincerity, a genuine sense of the life of his subject, that makes up somehow for his want of technical resources and the stiffness of his manner. As a painter he combined, most exceptionally, an honest solidity with a surprising charm, a reflection, perhaps, of his character.

Charles Willson Peale was an interesting man up to the very last days of his life. He died at the age of eighty-six in 1827 when he overstrained himself carrying a heavy trunk for a mile during a trip to court a fourth wife. His awesome vitality, rather than any great talent of their own, inspired a long line of male and female Peales to adopt the profession of painter, beginning with his brother James and three of his nobly named sons—Raphaelle, Rembrandt, and Rubens. Even though the eighteenth-century American tradition came to an end—with Gilbert Stuart—as the younger Peales were reaching maturity, they are introduced here as the heirs of the Peale legacy. By dates, and also in spirit (this is particularly true of Rembrandt Peale), they belong to the early nineteenth century.

Eight years younger than his great brother Charles Willson Peale, James Peale (1749-1831) began as his brother's assistant in saddlery before either was engaged in painting, and later became living disproof of his brother's contention that painting was something anyone could learn. In fairness to Charles Willson it must be added that James did learn the mere craft of painting well enough to live by it. But James lacked all of the inspiriting qualities so liberally granted Charles Willson, and he could earn only a satellite reputation to his brother's. He specialized in miniatures until his eyesight began to fail in old age, when he did some of the first still-life paintings produced in this country. He also produced seven children, five of whom—Maria, Anna, Margaretta, Mary Jane, and Rubens II—became painters, but none of them important ones. James Peale was a patriot whose service in the Revolutionary army cost him his health. Even so, he managed to live almost as long as his brother—eighty-two years.

Raphaelle Peale (1774-1825), the eldest son of Charles Willson Peale, holds a special place in that extensive and energetic family as the one artist member who led an irregular life. It was not so very irregular, at that: he was unhappily married and drank too much. His drinking, however, can be attributed as convincingly to his convivial nature as to wife trouble. He was a man who liked people, and people liked him.

Raphaelle also had money troubles. His only period of prosperity came during the two years 1803-05 when he toured the country with a machine called the "physiognotrace" that had been a tremendous success at his father's Philadelphia museum. The "facietrace," as Raphaelle simplified the name, was a device by which a profile silhouette portrait (these were very popular at the time) could be accurately traced from the living model in a few minutes. It has been estimated that Raphaelle made about one hundred thousand of these silhouettes, which as works of art had nothing more to do with his talent than those made at the rate of around 8,900 a year by Moses Williams, a mulatto slave, who operated the gadget at the Philadelphia museum.

The silhouettes were made by the many thousands, also, in the museum established in Baltimore by Raphaelle's brother Rembrandt, in New York City by his brother Rubens, and probably in the Utica museum set up by their half brother Linnaeus (1794-1832), who, possibly safeguarded by his name, did not have any artistic ambitions.

Raphaelle made the first effort to establish a Baltimore museum with Rembrandt in 1797. It failed. But if Raphaelle was not a great success during his lifetime, he is becoming more and more highly regarded, these days, for his charming still-life painting, so much so that he takes second place only to his father among the painting Peales. Although his only precedents in still life were Dutch and Flemish, he arrived spontaneously at a more reserved style that combines bright, fresh color and very high finish with just a touch of primitive stiffness and more than a touch of the clarity, almost the austerity, of seventeenth-century Spanish still-life painting. Since he could not possibly have known these *bodegones,* he evolved the style independently through a genuinely sensitive talent.

Rembrandt Peale (1778-1860), Charles Willson's second son, was the traveler in the family. He studied with Benjamin West in London in 1802-3, was in Paris in 1808-10 painting French statesmen for his father's museum in Philadelphia, and chose to visit Europe again in 1829-30. All this traveling can be connected with his ambitions to excel in projects more grand than portraits and still lifes. But he was not really up to them. He painted some excellent, finely detailed portraits, as well as some laughably bad ones, and his intended masterpiece, *The Court of Death* (Detroit), an allegory to end all allegories, involving figures of War, Conflagration, Famine, Pestilence, Pleasure, Intemperance, Remorse, Delirium Tremens, and Suicide, is embarrassing when judged by the neoclassical standards it purports to meet. It looks a little better if one is willing to accept it as a quaint provincial expression.

Rembrandt Peale's work was not always well received. In 1812, when he was thirty-four, he was so put out by adverse criticism that he gave up painting and moved to Baltimore, where, in addition to building another Peale museum, he demonstrated the famous Peale diversity by establishing the city's first illuminating gasworks. But he returned to painting eight years later with *The Court of Death,* and this time he was sensationally successful.

Based on a poem by Bishop Porteus, an English clergyman, the picture's high-toned moralizing appealed to an early-nineteenth-century public that had become extremely susceptible to sentimental literature. The various agents of death listed above are shown rushing off on their business after having done away with a strapping young man whose body, in front of Death's throne, serves as a footrest for that awesome monarch. But an old, old man approaches the throne unafraid, because he is being tenderly supported by a beautiful young maiden named Faith. Combining languid grace with febrile heroics, the picture could not fail.

During the decade of the picture's success, Rembrandt Peale was as greatly admired in America as his namesake Rembrandt van Rijn. A portrait of Washington that he painted in 1823, twenty-four years after Washington's death, was so popular that he was able to sell eighty replicas. He settled in New York during these triumphant years, but moved back to Philadelphia in 1831, when he was fifty-three, and lived another twenty-nine years before dying at the age of eighty-two.

Rubens Peale (1784-1865), a son of Charles Willson Peale by his second marriage, wanted to be an artist but was cheated of his career by poor eyesight. He managed first the Philadelphia museum, then successively those in Baltimore and New York, selling the latter to P. T. Barnum in 1837. In retirement thereafter he did his best to paint, turning out some primitive still lifes as well as copies of pictures by the rest of the family.

Gilbert Stuart brought back from England and established on the American continent the fully anglicized portrait manner that did away with such American tradition as there was in that field. He was an excellent painter, one of the best of those generated so copiously in England under the inspiration of Reynolds and Gainsborough.

Stuart was born in Rhode Island in 1755, the son of a snuff grinder, and like West and Copley was a child prodigy. By the time he was fourteen, he was busy with portrait commissions in Newport. (Understandably, these early works have a rather quaint air.) At about this time his talent and his personal charm, which never failed him throughout his life except on one occasion, attracted Cosmo Alexander, a migrant Scottish painter who took the boy to Edinburgh to work in his studio. But in 1772—Stuart was now seventeen—Alexander died. The boy was stranded, and managed to work his way back to America as a sailor. What would have been, in the storybooks, an adventure, turned out to be an experience so unpleasant that for the rest of his life Stuart refused to talk about it. This was the one occasion when his charm, which apparently was more perceptible in polite company than among rough seamen, did him no good.

Once more in America, he was never without commissions, and worked for three years before crossing the ocean again, this time in proper style at the age of twenty, to study with West in London. By the time he was twenty-eight he was so in demand that he opened his own studio, a roaring success. His personal attraction and his grace and fluency as a painter suggested comparison with Van Dyck to a critic who was writing a bit later, but presumably about impressions of Stuart's early career.

Although he was making plenty of money, it took Stuart only four years to pile up such debts that he had to flee to Dublin to escape prosecution by his creditors, which could have landed him in debtors' prison. In Dublin he repeated himself over the same period of time, and in 1793 he returned to America to escape his Irish debts. He was thirty-eight.

After a period no longer than it took him to catch his breath, Stuart became famous in his homeland and was ever more highly regarded until his death thirty-five years later, in 1828, at the age of seventy-three. He had said that he wanted to return to America to paint Washington's portrait, and he did paint it in five versions, each of which bred multiple variations and copies by his hand and others. One type, called the *Atheneum Washington,* showing head and shoulders and done in 1796, was retained by Stuart in his studio. From it he made more than seventy copies.

Stuart's version of the appearance of the Father of his Country is the one we all know, and the fact that a portrait by Stuart became the standard image may help explain why Washington is a figure who, despite his vital historical role and the picturesqueness of legends surrounding him, is hardly ever visualized (if you stop to think of it) as a human being who participated with any degree of fervor in the events of his life. Stuart had perfected, about the time he returned to America, a formula for portraits that invested his sitters with an air of dignified removal, and he painted Washington in this way. Perhaps Washington did have this air, but it is still true that in a Stuart portrait he could have had no other. In either case, our image of Washington is disproportionately indebted to Stuart's record.

Thomas Sully (1783-1872), although a nineteenth-century painter by date, continued the eighteenth-century tradition of portraiture. He was such an engaging fellow that one keeps wishing he had been a better artist. What he lacked was the element that in Gainsborough made the difference between mere facility and greatness, and he became a second-rate Lawrence—in spite of which (or maybe because of which) he has a doting public in the United States today.

Sully was the son of actors, Matthew and Sarah Sully, who emigrated from England (where Thomas was born, at Horncastle) to Charleston, South Carolina, in 1792. The boy was nine years old. His elder brother Lawrence, a miniature painter, established himself in Richmond, Virginia, where Thomas later studied under him. He was a professional by the age of eighteen, in Norfolk, where he began to keep a record of each of his paintings, sometimes with comments. Eventually he turned out some two thousand pictures. Always systematic, he set down his directions for painting a portrait in "Hints to Young Painters," written in 1851 and published posthumously in 1872, giving directions on how to greet and observe the client and then how to go about the manufacture of a pleasing likeness without wasting time.

When Sully was twenty his brother died, and the support of the widow, Sarah Annis Sully, and her three children fell to him. He had lived with the family, and two years after his brother's death he married Sarah, who was four years his senior, and eventually added three sons and six daughters to the household. The marriage lasted sixty years and was halcyon from first to last. Sarah died in 1867 at the age of eighty-eight to Thomas's eighty-four. He lived on for another five years.

It had been a good life. Sully moved to New York in 1806, visited Boston in 1807, where he was sympathetically received by Gilbert Stuart, and then settled in Philadelphia.

There in 1809 a group of patrons collected funds to send the twenty-six-year-old charmer to England. He intended to work under that venerable expatriot, Benjamin West, but he discovered, instead, Sir Thomas Lawrence, whose fresh, graceful, and uninquisitive portraits became his model.

By 1810 Sully was back in Philadelphia. He refused official positions, including the presidency of the Pennsylvania Academy of the Fine Arts, but refused them gracefully, finding his best friends among actors, *bons vivants,* and members of the local aristocracy who shared his taste and aptitude for relaxed pleasures. The climax of his career was his commission to paint a portrait of Queen Victoria (now in the Metropolitan Museum) during another London visit in 1838. He produced a sweet, shallow, meaningless effigy, making a beauty of the nineteen-year-old girl who had come to the throne the year before.

21

ENGLISH COUNTRY
LIFE AND LANDSCAPE

Eighteenth-century English life generated one type of picture unique to the island—the scene of outdoor life featuring mainly horses but including other animals. The genre was parented by the revival of horse racing and the appearance of fox hunting as a horseman's sport rather than a trapper's job. It produced one fine artist, George Stubbs, and supplied an honorable spot for a minor one, John Wootton, as prototype of the school.

In the eighteenth century, too, the Englishman's love of his island's hills, swards, streams, trees, dells, and valleys found its first expression in painting when Richard Wilson discovered that his native countryside appealed to him more than the idyllic scenes synthesized from Italian models that were the accepted standard of landscape manners. By the end of the century, John Constable, just twenty-three years old, was on the point of bringing Wilson's innovation to fulfillment. But it seems best to place him in this book as the opening figure of the next chapter rather than as the concluding figure of this one, since, in spite of his deep roots in eighteenth-century landscape, he was part of the nineteenth century's romantic revolution. J. M. W. Turner, a year older than Constable, was also at work, but he made his great contribution after the year 1800.

This short chapter, then, deals with John Wootton as the initiator and George Stubbs as the great master among the many painters of English country life, and with Wilson and two related figures, Alexander Cozens and his son John Robert Cozens, as early landscapists.

John Wootton (*c.* 1680-1765) was a fairly skilled painter in the Dutch and Flemish tradition (he was a student of Jan Wyck) and was later influenced, after a trip to Rome, by Gaspard (not Nicolas) Poussin and Claude Lorrain. He accomplished the feat of adapting the conventions of picturesque classical landscape to the scene of English outdoor life by such means as showing a hunting party in the fields around a ruined building—a medieval English abbey replacing the standard Roman ruins—or, in another vein, substituting fox hunters for the cavalry of battle scenes. But he also fathered the tradition of the horse or dog portrait that Stubbs was to elevate from the level of a craft-profession to that of fine art.

Wootton was in great demand. One of the impressive commissions he executed was a state portrait of George II on horseback in which, however, he left the King's face to be painted by an Irish artist, Charles Jervas. When he died in 1765, John Wootton was a few years one side or the other of the age of eighty-five.

The profession of horse-portrait painter is an extremely profitable one, since the clients, usually people who own racing or hunting stables, are wealthy, and competition is not great. A good horse-portraitist has to know how horses are put together. If he thinks that one fetlock is much like another, he will get nowhere; his clients, if not his subjects, are sticklers on such fine points.

The horse-portraitist must also be a skilled technician who can properly reproduce colors and sheens. But he is not often an artist. The great exception is George Stubbs, the archmaster in the field and the supreme model for imitators in his own day and in ours. He was an authority on anatomy, a superb technician, and a very considerable artist by standards having nothing to do with his specialty. As a pure (rather than theoretical) artist, he rises above Reynolds, and in his special way he is a fit companion to an artist of very different temper, Gainsborough.

Stubbs was born in Liverpool in 1724, within the decade that also produced Gainsborough and Reynolds. The son of a prosperous currier, he had virtually no training—only a few weeks, at the age of fifteen, under Henry Winstanley, an occasional painter but primarily an engraver. By the time he was out of his teens, Stubbs was making a living painting portraits (of people) and picking up whatever other commissions came his way as an engraver. These included the illustrations for a book on midwifery by Dr. John Burton, of York, published in 1751. Stubbs, at twenty-seven, already knew enough about anatomy to give lectures to students in the hospital.

At thirty he made the usual trip to Italy, but apparently not with the usual idea of gleaning inspiration from the ruins of antiquity and from painters who practiced the Grand Style. He went, it seems, to give them a fair trial at first hand, although he was already convinced that nature was his best reference encyclopedia. "Nature was and always is superior to Art, whether Greek or Roman," he told a friend, the miniaturist Ozias Humphry—or so at least Humphry reports in a memoir based on conversations with Stubbs. The Italian experience did not change Stubbs's mind. He returned to England and continued his investigation of nature, which now included extensive dissections of horses, which he carried on in a necessarily isolated house in Horkstrow, Lincolnshire. Engraving his studies, he produced his classic "Anatomy of the Horse," published in 1766.

But by 1760, when he was thirty-six, he had already moved to London, where he lived the rest of his life. There was no end to his success; his patrons included every nobleman and member of the royal family who owned a horse. He was elected an associate member of the Academy, but never got around to painting the presentation picture that was required for full membership.

Stubbs frequently portrayed the owners of the horses, as well as the owners' favorite grooms and coachmen, in his pictures, which thus became a variety of the conversation group and even of genre. He ventured now and then into pure genre, and even into pure landscape, as well as into "portraits" of exotic animals such as zebras and tigers. His high technical polish, the serenity of his landscape backgrounds, his sensitivity to silhouette and line in the static poses of his people and animals, give his pictures an almost enchanted stillness that detaches them from the sporting world and transports them into a rational, idyllic one.

Stubbs took a sudden detour in the 1770's with a series of pictures that make him a forerunner of romantic violence. On a side trip to Ceuta (Morocco) on his return from Italy he had seen—the story goes—a lion devouring a horse it had killed. As a man who loved horses he was haunted by the experience, and in a trio of paintings, repeated many times, he exorcised the ghost, showing first a lion stalking a horse, then the horse frightened by discovery of the lion, and then the kill. The well-tended paddocks and the polite English countryside give way in these pictures to a stormy wildness, and the polished racer becomes a terrified white stallion with wildly flowing mane and tail; the peaceful contentment of a well-ordered world is shattered by a brutal conflict in which the victim-horse becomes the symbol of our vulnerability to chance and violence.

In the same mood, Stubbs painted a lion attacking a stag, and a lion and tiger fighting over the stag's carcass. (In the landscape backgrounds, he may have drawn on the services of a painter named George Barret.) But in spite of these pictures, Stubbs must not be thought of as a man who went through some kind of spiritual sea change. They are fascinating exceptions in his work, evidence of a potential that he was not much interested in developing further. His first interest remained the straightforward facts of nature rather than the emotive symbolism that could be distilled from them. Anatomy, of all natural facts, continued to be his chief concern. By 1800, when he was seventy-six, he was at work on a book of comparative anatomy ("A Comparative Anatomical Exposition of the Structure of the Human Body with that of a Tiger and Common Fowls"), and when he died in 1806, at the age of eighty-two, he had published a number of the engraved plates. The complete book appeared posthumously in 1817.

Stubbs left a natural son, George Townley Stubbs, who achieved moderate success as an engraver.

Richard Wilson is always called the father of English landscape painting, and the title is seldom questioned, but it was not a case of planned parenthood. There is some doubt whether or not Wilson would have been willing to accept his descendants as legitimate, since he was a fussy, jealous man who would not even recognize in his colleague Gainsborough a fellow revolutionary in the field. "Fried parsley," he said of Gainsborough's light, feathery technique. His own touch was more solid, his textures rich and smooth. "Creamed spinach," Gainsborough could have retorted, but was too gentle to do so.

Wilson's Englishness as a landscape painter lay in the pleasure he took in the world's natural aspects. The English countryside that he loved had little to do with the artificially idyllic landscapes of the classical school, which by the middle of the eighteenth century had lost the monumental grandeur that Poussin had given them and were being synthesized from standard sets of picturesque motifs drawn from classical ruins and the Roman campagna. Although Wilson worked with these motifs, he had a true feeling, spontaneous and original, for the countryside of England and Wales. And he understood light as a unifying element not only of pictorial composition, but of the mood of any combination of hills, streams, skies, and fields either in nature or in painting. All of this makes Wilson a precursor of Constable, who in the next century always spoke of him with enthusiasm. And Wilson anticipated, pictorially, the literary mood of the English romantic nature poets.

But Wilson's art, captivating as it usually is, was nearly always a compromise between his spontaneous response to the world and his century's idea that man's function as a rational being was denied or even debased when nature was accepted on its own terms. The function of the eighteenth-century landscape painter was not to respond to nature as a force and a spectacle, but to discipline it into order, thus demonstrating the superiority of reason over the attractive confusions of mere accident. Landscape had to be improved, not explored. A few of Wilson's small landscapes, particularly some very late ones that seem to have been done entirely for his own pleasure, are purely lyrical. Some others, done to the popular formula, are dull. Typically this compromise between two essentially incompatible points of view has attractions of the kind found in hybrids that come out well in the gene lottery.

Wilson was born in 1714, the son of a Welsh parson. After a disappointing career as a portrait painter in London, he went to Italy at the age of thirty-five, where he spent six years. There, among the hundreds of practitioners who turned out decorative landscapes for the market, he was most influenced by Joseph Vernet and Zuccarelli, both skilled in the most salable mode but many cuts above the army of hacks. At this time no English gentleman's wall was complete without a classical-picturesque landscape, and when Wilson returned to England he should have fared well in supplying the demand, since there was no question as to his technical excellence. But Englishmen preferred to buy paintings bearing the cachet of a foreign name, whether French or Italian.

Another difficulty was that Wilson did not stick closely enough to the idyllic formula to please the patrons. His secret enthusiasm was for the Dutch landscapists, whose naturalism had not yet caught on in England. There is no specific explanation why Wilson began to take interest in his native landscape, or to treat landscape sympathetically as a natural phenomenon. He seems to have indulged a predilection rather than to have applied any aesthetic or philosophical principle as to the character he thought landscape painting should assume. The romantic scenery of Wales was much admired by travelers, but Wilson was without much question the first painter to depict it.

Although he found few patrons, and managed to quarrel with the few he did find, Wilson was elected a member of the

Royal Academy upon its formation in 1768, perhaps because of his prerequisite sojourn in Italy, and was later given the post of librarian. It is reported of him that, shamefully, when he was a member of the hanging committee for the Academy exhibitions, he would put washes of dulling film over competitors' paintings that were more brightly colored than his own. His naturally difficult temperament became more so as he offended patron after patron, and he sank into oblivion. When he died in 1782, a forgotten and bitter old man, he failed to receive even a token obituary notice.

The nineteenth-century landscapists, including not only Constable but Turner as well, and the critic Ruskin for good measure, understood Wilson's originality—perhaps better than he understood it himself. And so, in a way, did Wilson's all-powerful contemporary, Sir Joshua Reynolds. Sir Joshua said that Wilson's landscapes were "in reality too near common nature to admit supernatural objects," by which he meant the gods, nymphs, satyrs, and other mythological creatures that disported themselves in the popular classical landscapes. Sir Joshua thus typically showed his combination of sensitive perception and stuffiness, recognizing Wilson's forte, but regarding it as a limitation.

Alexander Cozens, who died four years after Richard Wilson, was almost an exact contemporary of "the father of English landscape painting." And if Cozens cannot really challenge Wilson's claim to this title, he has a compensating claim as the father of romantic landscape in England. The difference may sound slight, but there is a wide gap. Wilson was specifically English in his sensitivity to the poetry inherent in landscape and discoverable within its topography. Cozens was not interested in topography. He regarded the natural look of the countryside as a limitation at least as binding as the conventions of classical landscape, for which he had no use either. His interest was in inventing landscapes to express the ambiguous moodiness, the effects of melancholy and mystery, sometimes of loneliness and emptiness, or of wildness and gustiness, of a world of moonlight and dream. This wild and yearning emotionalism and spirituality belongs to the tradition of European romanticism as opposed to the more homespun English variety. Cozens was an innovator, the first representative in England of the less cozy tradition.

The extremity of Cozens' emphasis on pure romantic invention in expressive landscape is indicated by his so-called "blot paintings." To make these, he crumpled a piece of paper, smoothed it out, and then, with sepia or ink, dashed onto the sheet a few shapes dictated largely by the motion of his hand in response to a general idea or mood, without any regard for, or thought of, natural appearances. Does this sound familiar? It should, since Cozens was anticipating by two hundred years a form of abstract expressionism now called "action painting," in which the canvas becomes an arena for the release, through the artist's brush, of emotional impulses only half recognized, or recognized in progress, by the artist. Drips, dribbles, splashes, and other accidents are accepted in action painting as legitimate, desirable expressive elements. The principle of instinctive creation is the natural romantic antithesis of the classical principle of absolute, disciplined, intellectual control.

Cozens' blot paintings, after his initial instinctive assault on the sheet, when they were covered with freely splashed shapes and liny rivulets where the ink had run into the web-like creases of the crumpled paper, must have resembled the drawings of Jackson Pollock. But at this point Cozens regarded the painting as only begun, and made the compromise that kept him from being totally Pollock two centuries ahead of time. He studied the accidental and instinctive shapes for their resemblances to landscape forms, and completed the painting by drawing over them to emphasize the resemblances and to minimize the effect of passages that remained stubbornly abstract. He described the process in a book, "A New Method of assisting the Invention in drawing original Compositions of Landscape," published in 1758.

Cozens claimed a forebear for his method in Leonardo da Vinci, who was also interested in discovering similarities to natural forms in stains on old walls. But there was a radical philosophical difference between Leonardo's interest and Cozens' that escaped the Englishman. Leonardo was convinced that the universe is governed by harmonious laws by which everything that exists can be fitted into a logical scheme, and he was fascinated by stains and moldy growths not because of accidental resemblances to other forms but because he thought these resemblances were created by universal laws operating at different levels. Thus Leonardo tried to explain away accident by referring it to a rational world order, while Cozens valued it just because it was inexplicable except as a manifestation of a romantic mystery.

Cozens could have gone as far back as the eleventh century, where he would have discovered in the writings of the Chinese painter Sung Ti a "new method of assisting the invention in drawing original compositions of landscape" by transferring to silk the impressions of a ruined wall, and then turning the prominences into mountains, the hollows into ravines, and the cracks into streams. But no list of distinguished precedents could have made Cozens' art palatable to his contemporaries, who ridiculed his "spirited sketches"— his term—as the work of "the blot-master." He failed in a bid for admission to the Royal Academy, but here the fact that he worked almost exclusively in watercolor rather than oil may have been the primary argument against him.

Cozens was born about 1717 in Russia, where his father

was one of the chief English shipbuilders to Peter the Great. (An appropriately romantic legend makes the artist the Czar's illegitimate son.) He came early to England and spent the rest of his life there except for the inevitable trip to Rome, which he made in 1746. On his way home he crossed the border into France and his representations of Alpine scenery are the first known by an English artist. He also sketched in the Rhone valley, and these drawings are romantic, hazy suggestions rather than the topographical records kept by other artists who made the grand tour.

Cozens made his living by teaching, and became drawing master at Eton. (The future George III was among his pupils.) His several books included a set of lessons on drawing the head, with tissue-paper cutouts to study the effects of different hairdos. He also published a series of cloud studies, rather more topographical than his landscapes, clearly defining clouds as to types. Constable admired these and copied them. One study showing clouds intermingled with hills and valleys has been called a precursor of Turner's cosmic landscapes.

Alexander Cozens died in 1786 at about seventy. His son John Robert Cozens (1752-1799) followed his father's romantic premises but combined them with greater interest in topography. Splitting the difference between romantic invention and the souvenir-picture point of view typical of the so-called grand-tour artists, he chose the usual famous spots for watercolor subjects but represented them without the fussy detail that made the standard product so cramped. A deft technician, he foreshadowed the next generation of English watercolorists, led by Thomas Girtin.

William Beckford, the wild man of early romanticism in England, was John Robert Cozens' close friend and traveling companion. John Robert also has the distinction of having been called by Constable "the greatest genius who ever touched landscape," a eulogy that, even though it does sound as if it must have been made in a moment of exaggerated enthusiasm, sticks to his name along with another tribute from Constable—"Cozens was pure poetry."

Whatever chance John Robert Cozens might have had to vindicate these estimates was cut off. He became hopelessly insane at the age of forty-two and, failing to confirm a romantic idea that links inspiration with mental aberration, stopped work entirely. He died five years later, in 1799.

22

BRIDGES TO THE
NINETEENTH CENTURY

The life-spans of the painters grouped in this section straddle the year 1800, but that is not why they are placed here as transitional figures. All of them were men who had deep traditional roots in the eighteenth century, but in their contrasting ways they were also revolutionaries whose originality seeded the great nineteenth-century movements and whose force (especially in the cases of Fuseli and Blake, hardly at all in the case of David) has been felt even more strongly in our own century.

The nineteenth was surely the most variegated of all centuries in the history of painting, and these five men— two Englishmen, a Swiss-German, a Frenchman, and a Spaniard—forecast its conflicts. Constable as an observer of nature was an early romantic; as a technician he was an early impressionist. Fuseli and Blake were rebels against official standards, rebels whose personal vision was not only a romantic declaration but, by post-mortem observation, a Freudian anticipation; David proved that a great art could grow within academic restrictions (an idea that died with the nineteenth century, but might be in for a revival); and Goya managed to declare almost everything at once—the importance of romantic individuality as a prerequisite for creative conception; the value of technical discipline as a prerequisite for any expression; the necessity of technical experiment to keep the disciplines alive; the richness of social consciousness as a source of nourishment for an artist within his time. Finally, as a special case, Goya's life demonstrated that personal misfortune, by isolating an artist from society, can give him a vantage point for its study.

The Englishman's affectionate response to the heaths and streams and skies and grasses of his native land, which the poetry of Wordsworth has led us to think of as native to inhabitants of the island, found difficulty in breaking through in painting. When it did break through, in the art of John Constable, it was fully recognized not by the English themselves but by the French, of all people, for whom, generally speaking, English painting hardly exists. After Constable made a sensation in the French Salon of 1824, it took the better part of a hundred years for the impact to reach England, and then it came at the tag end of a revolution, having filtered first through Delacroix, then through the Barbizon painters, and finally through the impressionists. England realized that it had produced a prophet in Constable only after the prophecy had been fulfilled three times over.

Constable was not, however, exactly a prophet without honor in his own country during his lifetime. He achieved an adequate degree of recognition, but he was not honored for those aspects of his art that were truly original and even revolutionary. He used to speak contemptuously of the "eye-salve" that he had to apply to his pictures for presentation to the Royal Academy, by which he meant the veneer of detail done with a fettered brush as a technical elaboration superimposed on paintings that would otherwise have seemed, to the academically habituated eye, unfinished.

Constable's quickest and smallest sketches, produced by the hundreds as a kind of emotional autobiography of his relationship to nature, now seem preferable to these elaborated exhibition pieces. His finest paintings are certainly those in which the spontaneous effect of a sketch is maintained—the preliminary paintings, quite complete in themselves, from which the so-called completed paintings were worked up. The final versions, by comparison, are smothered under a layer of concessions to the idea of what a completed painting should look like.

For Constable, an apparent spontaneity (a goal of the impressionists, also, even in their most studied work) was the means of expressing the sense of growth, of life, and even of movement that we feel in landscape not only when the sky and air are turbulent but when every element of the scene is quiet. This special feeling for the life inherent in nature, and his conviction that its simple aspects are as important as its more imposing ones (to him they were also more appealing; mountains, for example, bored him), placed Constable in opposition to the prevalent idea that the artist's job was to refine and idealize nature, to impose upon it an artificial order, or best of all to synthesize an ideal order in the never-never land of classical fabrications. At most the artist might be allowed a compromise between unartistic nature and unnatural art by discovering an orderliness inherent in some actual vista (as Richard Wilson did) or by poeticizing the rustic scene (as Gainsborough did).

The latter approach, the grafting of rustic elements onto

landscapes that could better have stood without them, made Constable acceptable to the Academy as an artist adept in the picturesque tradition. It took the French eye to discover the extraordinary painter beneath the salve when Constable exhibited *The Hay Wain* and *A View on the Stour near Dedham* in the Salon of 1824. (The first is in London's National Gallery, the second in the Henry E. Huntington Library, San Marino, Calif.) *The Hay Wain* was awarded a gold medal by an exceptionally adventurous jury, and with Delacroix at their head the younger artists discovered in the Englishman a painter whose romantic response opened the whole world— not just its dramatic spots, but all of it—to emotional interpretation. And Constable as a colorist impressed them even more. With exceptions here and there, shadows had been painted for centuries as murky brownish areas or as muted variations of the color of the object on which they fell. Constable painted shadowed areas with as much sparkle as any other area, introducing patches of pure color that were impressionist in all but the semiscientific application of the theories that identified light with color.

Constable was born in 1776, a date easy for Americans to remember, in the village of East Bergholt, Suffolk, and from birth he knew, and never ceased to love and paint, the pastoral scenes with gentle hills and full, quiet streams near his father's prosperous mill on the banks of the Stour. His realization that these scenes could be subjects for painting was a personal one; it was an implicit rejection of the standards of the Royal Academy, where, after a preliminary failure under mediocre instruction, he went to study in 1799, at the advanced age of twenty-three. His relatives (except for his mother) and his friends were puzzled by his adoption of a dubious profession when he had been expected to take over his father's business, and he made courageous efforts to prove himself as a portrait painter, and even as a painter in the grand manner with a pair of really deplorable altarpieces for local churches in the style of Benjamin West. But this was early in the game. By 1822 (he was forty-six), he knew quite well that "recourse to nature" was his only hope and his only interest. He wrote to his good friend, the Reverend John Fisher, "Could you but see the folly and ruin exhibited at the British Gallery, you would go mad. W. Van de Velde, and Gaspard Poussin, and Titian, are made to spawn millions of abortions. . . . It is a shocking scene of folly and venom headed by Lords, etc."

This Reverend John Fisher was Constable's closest friend, and the sentiments in the letter (including "there will be no genuine painting in England in thirty years") were confidential, for Constable was determined to attain the rank of full member of the Academy. He did so in 1829, after ten years as an associate member, but by then he took little interest in this success. The election came shortly after his wife's death, which closed the twelve happiest years of his life. The personal tragedy left him indifferent to public opinion, but partly for this reason, during the following years of withdrawal and melancholy, he produced some of his finest work.

Constable's personality is not easy to reconstruct in spite of his surviving letters and the memoirs written about him. He was absolutely dogged in his determination to succeed, but he was not ambitious in the usual way. That is, he rejected the formulas for success that demanded the cultivation of influential friends and the adherence to accepted standards of Academic production. His love affair and marriage, in their relative lateness and great intensity, are important clues in a puzzle that has never been quite clarified.

Constable had known Maria Bicknell since her childhood, and in 1811, when she was twenty-four and he was thirty-five, he first proposed to her. Whatever Maria's sentiments, her family induced her to reject the proposal: her grandfather, who was wealthy, opposed the union with a man who at that time was not too well off. But the courtship went on, with Constable insisting on meetings that had to be secret, and with secret exchanges of letters too, for five years. Maria seems to have been of two minds about the whole thing. At twenty-nine, as every reader of Jane Austen knows, she had entered the age of spinsterhood for a woman in the early nineteenth century, but she still hesitated when Constable's father died and left him a legacy that, while comfortable, was less than the one she expected from her ailing grandfather.

Constable, now forty, went to his friend, the good John Fisher, for advice. The advice was to put an end to the nonsense, and to tell Maria that on Wednesday, September 25, Fisher would be in London and would expect to perform the ceremony. "Get you to your lady, and instead of blundering out long sentences about 'the hymeneal altar,' etc., say that . . . you are ready to marry her."

Maria yielded (and in fact received her inheritance when her grandfather died three years later). Fisher not only performed the ceremony but took the not-so-young couple to stay with him for their honeymoon. Seven children were born before Maria's death in 1829. Constable wore mourning until his own death eight years later, in 1837, at the age of sixty-one.

Constable was always an articulate man. His lectures on the history of landscape painting are as sound, even as scholarly, as his informal comments in letters to friends are trenchant. Our current way of thinking of a painter in terms of his innovations has made Constable first of all the prophet of impressionism. But he is also a link in an uninterrupted history of landscape painting that runs from the classical seventeenth-century masters, whose imitators he despised, on up through impressionism and fauvism, to avant-garde landscape today. If he loathed the academic "abortions," he loathed them precisely because he understood where they missed the greatness of past masters, whose surfaces (including several coats of yellowed varnish) they imitated. He knew what Claude Lorrain was about, and Ruisdael, and Rubens, and Richard Wilson and Thomas Gainsborough.

Rubens's color and his free, rich brush; Ruisdael's clouds and cloud shadows; Claude's atmosphere, his "exhilaration and light"; Wilson's and Gainsborough's perception of the poetry in naturalistic subjects—all these Constable understood and continued. But he did not like comparisons of the kind we are making here. He might have been speaking of his own work (rather than of a Gainsborough that he rapturously admired) when he said, "No fine things will bear, and want, comparisons; every fine thing is unique."

In another letter to the same friend, C. R. Leslie, an Academician of American parentage, he wrote, in 1833, four years before his death, of "light—dews—breezes—bloom—and freshness; not one of which . . . has yet been perfected on the canvas of any painter in the world." If he could have known the work of his descendants, the impressionists, he might have felt that this perfection had been reached by the paths he had indicated, but it is just as true that in picture after picture he set a standard for this perfection that has not been excelled.

"There is little hope of poetical painting finding encouragement in England," complained John Henry Fuseli. By "poetical" he meant the kind of weird and fantastical painting that he produced. "The people are not prepared for it. Portrait with them is everything. Their tastes and feelings all go to realities."

And, "I am going to see Constable; bring me mine ombrella," he said, a jibe at the placid naturalism of Constable's showery landscapes.

Constable in turn could have said, "I am going to see Fuseli; bring me mine lightning rod." In the generally quiet scene of English painting, Fuseli is a moment of violence and morbid excitement. He is to Constable "what the incessant flashes of a tempestuous night are to daylight," a comparison that Fuseli made between the disorderly passion of Shakespeare, whom he adored, and the classical order of Sophocles, whom, along with everything else ordered and classical, he distrusted.

Fuseli's un-Englishness is not surprising. He was Swiss by birth, German by temperament as well as by intellectual conditioning, Italian by artistic training, and English only by naturalization. Until he came to the island at the age of twenty-three, he was Johann Heinrich Füssli, born in 1741 in Zurich, the son of the portrait painter and art critic Johann Caspar Füssli. He had been ordained a Zwinglian minister at the age of twenty, but, almost immediately getting into trouble, had fled to Germany, giving up the ministry and theology (he had been a brilliant student) for a career as a writer.

Fuseli's offense in Zurich had to do with preaching advanced political views, although according to one colorful story he had to leave town because he frightened a young gentlewoman out of her wits in an effort to solace her grief for a dead lover by raising his ghost from the dead. This story is consistent with some of Fuseli's paintings, so consistent indeed with one of them called *The Nightmare* (in the Goethe Museum, Frankfurt) where fiendish apparitions hover above the bed of a swooning girl, that one can't help suspecting that the painting inspired the legend.

Fuseli was regarded by some of his English contemporaries as a mild eccentric, but he was an intellectual, neither a mystic nor a believer in black magic any more than Shakespeare was when he wrote the witches' scene in "Macbeth" or the ghost scene in "Hamlet"—two of Fuseli's favorite passages. Fuseli's companion in the Zurich ghost-raising escapade, if there was such an escapade, was his close friend Johann Caspar Lavater, the Swiss theologian and mystic, exactly Fuseli's age, who wrote several books on metaphysics but is chiefly remembered for his book on physiognomy. Applying this pseudo-science of determining character from facial characteristics, Lavater decided that his friend's oversize nose "seems to be the seat of an intrepid genius." But this genius, until Fuseli turned to painting in his late twenties, was thought to be literary, with art criticism rather than art production as its province. And in truth, Fuseli's painting was always primarily literary not only in its sources, with Shakespeare and Milton leading, but in conception.

From youth Fuseli was the companion of writers and intellectuals, first those who gathered at his father's house in Zurich, then the poets and philosophers of *Sturm und Drang* in Berlin, and then the avant-garde circles of London—where Mary Wollstonecraft, the free-living author and feminist, fell passionately in love with him and made a determined but unsuccessful effort to separate him from his wife.

It is odd that Fuseli turned to painting on the advice of a man opposed to every idea of art that Fuseli came to hold— Sir Joshua Reynolds. Sir Joshua believed in plugging away according to the rules in order to achieve perfection, while Fuseli, with the romantic's love of disorder, held that "indiscriminate pursuit of perfection infallibly leads to mediocrity," pointing to Shakespeare and Rembrandt as examples of geniuses who achieved consummation by violating the rules. Sharing his friend Lavater's physiognomical ideas, and perhaps inviting reflected glory, Fuseli grew rapturous about the outsize dimensions of Rembrandt's nose as recorded in self-portraits.

But there is nothing of Rembrandt to be found in Fuseli's work. His style is a curious one, combining hobgoblin distortions that ape Michelangelesque grandeur with awkward echoes of sixteenth-century mannerist affectation. Fuseli formed this style during the 1770's in Rome, where he spent eight years following his departure from England in 1769. It is one of those contradictory styles that seem to have been conceived in three dimensions, with powerfully indicated chiaroscuro, but end up as linear. And in spite of Fuseli's anticlassical ideas, there is a strong neoclassical flavor in everything that he drew or painted.

During his Italian sojourn, Fuseli visualized a transformation of the biblical cycle of the Sistine Ceiling into a Shakespearean one. Like most painters of strong literary bent, he was always more aware of a painting's subject than he was of the formal qualities that individualize a great painter's interpretation of a subject. Apparently he saw in Michelangelo's ceiling only one more retelling of an old story.

Back in England, where he remained until he died in 1825 at the age of eighty-four, Fuseli exhibited at the Royal Academy and became a full member in 1790, when he was not quite fifty. He was appointed professor of painting at the Academy in 1799, an appointment that was later renewed for life. He was an extremely popular teacher, a breath of life in an institution that under Benjamin West had become pretty stuffy. Fuseli must have been like one of those professors familiar on campuses today, whose lively lectures and middle-aged adherence to a scorn of convention appeal to the restlessness of youth.

Fuseli needed his professorship badly. In the same year as his appointment, he bankrupted himself with his "Milton Gallery." Milton's appeal for Fuseli lay in Satan as a dramatic protagonist; when Fuseli tackled the pastoral aspects of Milton's poetry he floundered. The "Milton Gallery" was a one-man effort to repeat the success of Alderman Boydell's "Shakespeare Gallery," to which Fuseli contributed paintings interpreting scenes from the plays. The "Shakespeare Gallery," which shared a bit of the public appeal of a waxworks, had been stimulated by David Garrick's extremely popular Shakespearean productions, but there was no comparable public appeal in a Milton gallery. Most of Fuseli's forty-seven large oils for this project have disappeared, and the remaining ones do not support William Blake's later claim that the gallery's failure was a disgraceful reflection of the low state of English taste—exceeded in disgracefulness, Blake thought, only by public indifference to his own work.

Around 1810, although Fuseli, now close to seventy, continued to teach and to write, his popularity began to dwindle, and it has taken more than a century for him to make a comeback. His private fantasies have made new sense to a century that has found one of its major expressions in surrealism, and Freudianism has given psychopathological connections to paintings and drawings that seemed only bizarre to Fuseli's contemporaries. *The Nightmare* is now legible as an exposition of sexual morbidity; the girl on the bed seems to writhe in sexual torment under the gloating threat of her visionary companions, and yearns for the assault of the demonic ravishers she has invented.

With such advantages, Fuseli as an artist is more appreciated today than he was in his own century, when his personality carried a more forceful impact than his work. Among twentieth-century artists, the Englishman Francis Bacon, with his paintings of spiritual terror, is as close as Fuseli has ever come to finding a follower in a major painter. Blake admired Fuseli, and so did the American nineteenth-century romantic Washington Allston, even at a time when Fuseli was generally laughed at, but it was Fuseli's theory, and his criticism, that these artists most respected.

Fuseli's ranging, inventive, and independent mind is well summed up in his published volume of aphorisms, even though they share the rather uneven quality of his achievement as a painter. "Fashion is the bastard of vanity dressed by art" is as good now as when Fuseli said it. And in a time when commercialism dictates so many innovations, Americans could give a thought to Fuseli's "Art among a religious race produces reliques; among a military one, trophies; among a commercial one, articles of trade."

William Blake was born in London on November 28, 1757, and died there on August 12, 1827, three months short of his seventieth birthday. This means that he was trained as an artist in the eighteenth century, that he grew to maturity in its ambience, and that he was forty-three years old by the time the bells rang out for the year 1800. But he was never a part of the eighteenth century. He loathed Reynolds, the century's spokesman in English art, and reviled him at every opportunity, or without waiting for an opportunity, declaring, "This Man was Hired to Depress Art." He abominated the grand manner, which was the official yardstick for measuring excellence in painting, and contrarily found beauties in Gothic sculpture, which was thought of as a souvenir of the past that could have a degree of historical value but was inadmissible aesthetically. He was terrified by the system of patronage by which eighteenth-century artists lived best, although he could be seduced into its coils when it was disguised. Such were the symptoms of Blake's displacement; the essential problem was that, born in the Age of Reason, he was a man who believed in unreason. He was not the first artist or writer to recognize the validity of intuition as a flowing spring of creative genius, but he was the first artist (and writer) to make his life one long broadside against rational and systematic approaches to the creation of art—in other words, to defend what comes naturally. "All Pictures that's Painted with Sense & with Thought / Are Painted by Madmen as sure as a Groat," he wrote, taking off from a Reynolds self-portrait to turn the tables on the sensible and thoughtful people who called him, Blake, in his flouting of convention and his visionary fervor, mad.

He was probably a little mad, at that. In 1809, a writer in The Examiner, who may have been Leigh Hunt, described Blake as "an unfortunate lunatic whose personal inoffensiveness secures him from confinement." Blake was fifty-two years old at this time, and on many occasions his "personal inoffensiveness" had been relative: he could be a quarrelsome, belligerent iconoclast to the point (by retrospective diagnosis) of paranoia when he was not being a mild-mannered innocent singing with childish wisdom in a wicked world. At the age of four he had been favored by God, who appeared to him as a head at the window, and at the age of seven he had surprised the prophet Ezekiel in the fields accompanied by angels in the trees, "their bright wings bespangling the boughs like stars." These two incidents were recounted much later by Blake's wife, who of course must have learned of the supernatural hobnobbing from her husband, rather than from God, His prophet, or His angels. Blake was never secretive about his impressive connections: "I am not ashamed, afraid, or averse to tell you what Ought to be told: That I am under the direction of Messengers from Heaven, Daily and Nightly."

Blake's conviction that he was under direct heavenly supervision must have grown in him as a child under the influence of his father (little is known about his mother), a hosier by trade and, by religion, a dissenter who read Swedenborg, the Swedish scientist, religious teacher, and mystic. Swedenborg claimed that he had direct insight into the celestial realm, that "heaven was opened" to him in 1745, and that the Lord himself appeared to him in order to clarify the doctrines of the Church while he, Swedenborg, was studying the Divine Word. Swedenborg believed that the second coming of the Lord had already taken place—that it had taken place in 1757. Seventeen fifty-seven was also the year of Blake's birth, and although Blake did not go so far as to believe that he was the Messiah, we may at least conjecture that the coincidence of date was suggestive to him or to his Swedenborgian father, and affected his recollection of the childhood visions of God in the window and Ezekiel in the fields gamboling with angels.

Blake was such a nervous child and so sensitive to punishment that he was never sent to school. When he was ten years old, he went to drawing classes, however—at Pars' drawing school in the Strand—and he showed such talent that his parents bought him casts from the antique to draw from at home, and gave him pocket money to buy prints of the old masters to copy. Blake never went to Italy—during his long life he hardly left London at all—and had no access to the great houses of Londoners who had collections. His familiarity with Renaissance art came through reproductions, probably not very good ones, and it can be argued that his own drawing always reflected a second-rate version of the art he most admired—Raphael's, Michelangelo's, and Dürer's. It is possible—though to Blake devotees the suggestion is heresy—that his linearization of the styles of Raphael and Michelangelo was at least partially the result of his never having seen the originals. The engraved reproductions through which he knew the Italians usually offered only hard-bitten, exaggeratedly outlined approximations that tended to flatten into silhouettes the noble volumes of the masters.

When Blake was fourteen and it was time for him to begin learning how to make a living, he was apprenticed to an engraver, James Basire. He worked for him for seven years. Basire had a commission to publish a series of prints on mortuary monuments of England, and Blake was assigned to draw the Gothic tombs in Westminster Abbey. Although the figures ornamenting these tombs are not among the noblest examples of Gothic sculpture, they are the best in England and their linear pattern affected Blake's drawing for the rest of his life. (It is paradoxical that this contact with a three-dimensional art should have so strongly affected Blake as an unrelentingly two-dimensional designer.) Basire also engraved Raphael and Guercino, thus no doubt widening Blake's acquaintance with them at a flattened second hand.

In 1778, when he was twenty-one, Blake studied at the Royal Academy school. He did not fit in very well there and soon left, but between 1780 and 1808, a period of nearly thirty years, he had watercolors accepted with some regularity in the Royal Academy exhibitions. The stories of Blake's obscurity are exaggerated, although it is true that he lived a hand-to-mouth existence, that the general public was indifferent to his work, and that in the light of current appreciation for his work he was neglected.

When Blake was only twenty-one he was supporting himself by making engravings for booksellers. In 1782, three months before his twenty-fifth birthday, he married a twenty-year-old girl named Catherine Boucher or Butcher, the illiterate daughter of a market gardener. (She signed the marriage register with a mark, although during her years with Blake she made some progress in reading and writing.) Catherine Blake has come down in history as a woman of simpleminded devotion to her eccentric husband. The most touching picture of her that we have we owe to Thomas Butts, Blake's most generous patron. He called at the house one day and found Blake and Catherine naked in the summer house of their garden, playing at Adam and Eve while Blake read "Paradise Lost" aloud. The idyllic picture is marred by the fact that the couple were in their forties at the time, and neither had ever been famous as a beauty.

Thomas Butts's association with Blake began in 1799 when the artist was forty-two. Blake had not been doing too well in the world, which is not surprising in a man who could say, "Imagination is My World; this world of Dross is beneath my notice," even though he complained bitterly when the world of Dross failed to turn the other cheek and supply him with a livelihood. Not that he didn't have friends who often did their best to be helpful. Among his intimates he counted not only Fuseli but the very successful (and very conventional) John Flaxman (1755-1826), Blake's contemporary to almost the exact years of birth and death. Flaxman is thought of first as the man who set the classical pattern for Wedgwood; as a sculptor, he had much to do with the affected and rather frigid purity of the neoclassical ideal. But he was also a student of Renaissance art—even of baroque art, which he seems to have understood while disapproving of it—and he shared Blake's interest in Gothic monuments.

Flaxman introduced Blake—and his bride—to a circle of dilettantes that surrounded a Reverend Henry Matthew and his wife, an ardent bluestocking. The simple Catherine and the iconoclastic Blake must have seemed odd birds in this company. In 1783 the Matthews supplied money for the printing of Blake's "Poetical Sketches," but Blake quarreled with them—he resented Matthew's condescending reference, in the preface, to his poems as "the products of untutored youth"—and later satirized them cruelly. He seemed never able to abide for long the idea that he could be an acceptable and accepting member of a conventional society: acceptance in the polite world was for him a form of degradation or, perhaps, a mortal danger. He was one of those people who feel that their integrity is threatened whenever their way of life slips over into the norm.

Reconciling himself to making a living as an engraver and printseller, since he could not live by his poetry and his art, Blake set up a partnership with a James Parker in 1784. It lasted three years, its dissolution coinciding with the death of Blake's youngest and favorite brother, Robert. He changed his mind and decided to devote all his time to original creative work. In 1788 he began developing his technique of "illuminated printing," an elaborate process that combined a form of engraving with hand tinting and allowed him to fuse his poetry and his art in a manner that would do justice to both. He published his "Songs of Innocence" in this way in 1789, and "Songs of Experience" in 1794. He thought of these books as continuations of the medieval tradition of manuscript illumination. (As indeed they are.)

Blake, who was not as much of a recluse as he has been made out, was in contact at this time with a circle of political radicals and freethinkers, friends of Fuseli, who was always loyal to him and, miraculously, managed never to forfeit Blake's esteem. (Whenever Blake found something in Reynolds's "Discourses" that he agreed with, he decided that Reynolds had stolen it from Fuseli.) Fuseli's circle included Thomas Paine, who, back in London from America to exhibit the model of an iron bridge that he had planned for the Schuylkill River, was at work on "The Rights of Man"; Joseph Priestley, the scientist and theologian, whose "History of the Corruption of Christianity" still existed as a disquieting scent in the English air after its official burning in 1785; William Godwin, the philosopher, who was developing his theory that men, being guidable by reason, could live without laws and institutions; and Mary Wollstonecraft, the vigorous feminist, who, having set her cap for Fuseli (among others) and failed to catch him, married Godwin in 1797, the year of her death.

The sympathies that these intellectuals held for the French Revolution led Blake for a while to sport a red freedom cap. They might have had something to do, also, with his horror at the idea of becoming tutor in drawing to the royal family. He had been eking out his income by giving drawing lessons in people's houses, and in 1795 an enthusiastic pupil had managed to procure for him an offer of the post. Blake not only refused the offer but, feeling the world of Dross breathing too temptingly down his neck, gave up all his other pupils also.

At this time it began to look as though his luck might be changing. He received the commission to illustrate a deluxe edition of Edward Young's "Night Thoughts," which would sell by subscription at the price of five guineas (several times that much in modern money). This long didactic poem ("The Complaint and the Consolation, or Night Thoughts on Life, Death and Immortality") had first been published in 1742-45, and was still enormously popular thirty years after Young's death. The commission by reasonable expectations should have been a very good thing for Blake, but the venture did not catch on, and he completed only 43 of the projected 537 colored designs. He wrote a friend, "I am laid by in a corner as if I did not exist."

He was in this sad state when Thomas Butts appeared in 1799. Blake was forty-two. Next to Fuseli (whom Blake called "The only Man that e'er I knew / Who did not make me almost spue"), Butts was the man who most patiently understood Blake. He became a patron in disguise, giving Blake a guinea each week for a picture or drawing without making restrictions or suggestions concerning the work. Blake did his first "frescoes," as he called them, for Butts. These were small paintings in a form of tempera that has deteriorated so badly that the best-preserved are flaked, discolored, and ghostly, while those that have suffered most are hardly decipherable. Time has made them a contradiction of Blake's principle that the most unreal subjects be given the sharpest definition. His way of putting it was, "A spirit and a vision are not . . . a cloudy vapour or a nothing; they are organised and minutely articulated beyond all that the mortal and perishable nature can produce," a principle adopted by the surrealists in the twentieth century.

The year after he met Butts (that is, in 1800), Blake found another patron in the poet and man of letters William Hayley, one of Flaxman's well-to-do friends. Hayley not only commissioned some illustrations from Blake but invited him and Catherine to settle in as his guests in Felpham, Sussex—which they did, for three years, Blake's first and last prolonged absence from London during his long life. Hayley found local commissions for Blake and also teaching appointments. What with these and Butts's guineas, it was a period of financial ease. But the seaside cottage that had been turned over to Blake and Catherine was damp and dreary. They took sick, and when Blake was offered a commission to decorate some screens for a local lady's evening party, he fled. The stay ended with a bit of incidental unpleasantness. Blake had had an altercation with a dragoon named Scofield and during its course had uttered "seditious and treasonable words," according to the charge on which he was tried in January, 1804, in Chichester. He was acquitted, and further assuaged his resentment in a composition, *Vala, Hyle, and Skofield*.

In 1805 he began work on a set of illustrations for Blair's "The Grave" for the publisher Cromek, who announced in a prospectus that Blake would both design and engrave the pictures. But Blake refused to work in the stipple technique that had become popular, and the translation of the drawings into engravings was turned over to a Louis Schiavonetti, with a consequent softening of Blake's manner. ("A petty sneaking knave I knew / Oh! Mr. Cromek how do ye do?")

These were hard times for Blake. Butts remained loyal, but his house by then was rather crowded with pictures. The official exhibitions rejected Blake's entries. In his depression, Blake was a trial to his friends: he quarreled with Flaxman, although Flaxman, for his part, continued to do what he could to get Blake work as an engraver. In 1809, now fifty-two, Blake decided to hold his own exhibition, with the special purpose of calling attention to his "fresco" technique. The show was installed at his brother James's house in Broad Street and was advertised with the motto "Fit audience find tho' few." The entrance fee covered a copy of the descriptive catalogue, whose subtitle was: "Poetical and Historical Inventions, Painted by William Blake in Water Colours, being the Ancient Method of Fresco Painting Restored: and Drawings, for Public Inspection, and for Sale by Private Contract."

The Examiner critic who was perhaps Leigh Hunt made the personal comment on Blake already quoted, called the pictures wretched, and described the catalogue as "a farrago of nonsense, unintelligibility, and egregious vanity, the wild effusions of a distempered brain." The description is exaggerated rather than false: we tend to forgive Blake everything today, but the catalogue is bothersome reading—pugnacious, confused, and repetitious. Of the sixteen paintings, Butts bought two, but the exhibition failed and Blake exhibited only once more during the remaining eighteen years of his life, with the Associated Artists in Water Colour in 1812.

At the age of sixty, Blake was obscure and solitary, even though he had produced a considerable body of work and had been intermittently the acquaintance if not the close friend of some fairly conspicuous people. But the last years of his life were brightened by a young artist named John Linnell (1792-1882), whom he met in 1818. During the ninety years of Linnell's life—he lived through the Pre-Raphaelite

movement and reflected it, not at its best, in his late work—
his encouragement of Blake remained the only sign of benev-
olence that people could find in him. He was not trusted in
his dealings (Constable is said to have helped spread the word
of Linnell's sharp practices). His work—portraits, miniatures,
pastoral landscapes, and Bible illustrations—was consistently
rejected when he submitted it to the Royal Academy exhibitions.

Thirty-five years younger than Blake, Linnell was only
twenty-six when the two met, and thirty-five when Blake
died. He was attracted to Blake much as Butts had been, by
his work as an artist and by his curious simplicity as a person.
He flattered Blake, strengthening his morale by the indirect
assurance that his eccentricities were manifestations of wisdom, not of madness, and he collected a circle of other young
artists and literary men around Blake as a revered master.
They called themselves "The Ancients," and included Linnell, Samuel Palmer, George Richmond, Edward Calvert, and
Frederick Tatham, who became Blake's executor and first
biographer.

John Linnell's teacher had been John Varley (1778-1842),
a watercolorist who doubled as an astrologer. In 1819-20,
Blake drew for Varley a series called *Visionary Heads*, depicting personages (for instance, *The Pharaoh Who Built the
Pyramids*) who, Varley firmly believed, obligingly materialized from the spirit world for Blake upon request, following
suggestions by Varley. Some of the portraits were used to
make points in Varley's engagingly titled "Treatise on Zodia-
cal Physiognomy," of 1828. (Linnell engraved Blake's pictures
for the book.) It was at Varley's house that Blake had the
vision he turned into one of his most arresting pictures, *The
Ghost of a Flea* (London, Tate Gallery)—a combination of
wild humor and metaphysical inference that could be (and
probably has been) assigned to Paul Klee's ancestral line.

Although Blake was the kind of man who could say

casually, "After dinner, I asked Isaiah . . . ," he seems to have been pulling Varley's overcredulous leg a bit on the subject of his visions. "There he comes!" he once cried out, announcing a materialization of the Flea, "his tongue whisking out of his mouth, a cup in his hand to hold blood, and covered with a scaly skin of gold and green." According to Varley's reports, the Flea and Blake enjoyed an obliging give-and-take kind of friendship. On one appearance, the Flea assured Blake that "all fleas are inhabited by the souls of such men as were bloodthirsty to excess," and among the spirits who appeared as heads, the Flea further obliged, in order to satisfy Blake's curiosity, by making one appearance offering "a view of his whole figure."

John Linnell commissioned Blake's illustrations for the Book of Job, executed between 1821 and 1826, and Dante's "Divine Comedy," begun in 1824 and unfinished when Blake died in 1827. These series are probably Blake's finest work. Even his most obdurate admirers admit that he was an artist who could touch abysmal lows, but they maintain that the high points are of such elevation that the failures ought, in fairness, to be overlooked. There are, however, many admirers of his poetry who feel that his drawings, paintings, and engravings seldom rise above mannered imitation of Raphael and Michelangelo, in spite of the originality of their rhythmic linear organization, and that his general tenor of expression is both sentimental and pretentious.

But even from behind a blind spot one may see Blake as a precursor of modern art in his aesthetic convictions. His "No Man of Sense can think that an Imitation of the Objects of Nature is the Art of Painting or that such Imitation . . . is worthy of Notice" forecasts modern art's rejection of the visible world as subject matter for the artist. His rigidly geometric compositional patterns, and his emphasis on line and color as primary means of expression, are technical alliances with abstraction pushed somewhat further than similar alliances in many dozens of pre-nineteenth-century artists. As a personality he represents both the visionary and the naïve artist in revolt against the art of the schools.

Blake's denial of nature—of what he called the "vegetable" universe—if accepted at full face value would rule out the legitimacy of the entire nineteenth-century school of realism including impressionism, but he was always a prophet who limited himself to statements so flat and so pugnacious that they belied his sensibilities. Confronted by one of Constable's drawings of the "vegetable" and visible world, Blake said, "Why this is not drawing but inspiration!"

"I meant it for drawing," Constable answered.

Jacques Louis David emerges from most biographies as one of the least sympathetic personalities in the history of art, an impression not mitigated, for most people, by his painting, which they find as hard and as chilly as the man. Such a judgment—on both the man and his art—is superficial. But even if it were accurate, his life simply as a factual record would stand as an extraordinary combination of adventure tale and success story.

For anyone who can get through the layer of iciness, David is an endlessly fascinating painter. Nominally a classicist, and traditionally the archexemplar of the classicist as a painter who reduces antiquity to a kind of sterile purity, David is really a pseudo-classicist, whose variation of the formula is dominated by a combination of staggering realism and true romanticism. In his most frigid paintings an obsessive sensuality is just beneath the surface. His nudes are at once adaptations of the idealized bodies of antique sculpture, carefully analyzed anatomical studies, and declarations of the allure of human nakedness that on occasion can amount to revelations of concupiscence. David must have been a lustful man beneath his aesthetic puritanism, but he never thought of his idealized forms as a transmutation of sensual experience, as the original forms were with the Greeks. Only in an occasional portrait does he allow himself so much as a hint of tenderness, when he paints a member of his family or a very close friend. But his portraits are brilliant renderings of surface that become by second nature revelations of personality.

David's immaculate surface, the often enamel-like finish of his paintings, conceals preliminary stages that were as fresh and sensitive as the best rococo painting that he abominated. There are portions of unfinished works that might have been struck in by Gainsborough in his most delightful mood. David's last painting, *Mars Disarmed by Venus and the Graces* (Brussels), a love scene painted by an old man, is closer in spirit to his first master, Boucher, than to the rationalism into which he forced himself. And one portrait of Napoleon, on horseback, *Napoleon Crossing the St. Bernard Pass* (Versailles), is so full of wind and storm, with flying draperies and a rearing wild-eyed steed, that it has become accepted as a protoromantic conception. During the century that followed David's death, three forces struggled for dominance in French art—classicism, romanticism, and realism. But their initial struggle took place in the art of a single painter, Jacques Louis David.

David began his career as a protégé of the state under the *ancien régime,* continued it as a powerful figure in the Revolutionary government, went on from there to become a favorite of Napoleon's and the grand old man of French painting—and in the process redirected the course of French painting at just the time when Paris was emerging as the art center of Europe. His single faux pas during his career as a political chameleon—his enemies prefer the word turncoat—

cost him the support of the Bourbons after the fall of Napoleon, but even so he holds the record for adaptive longevity under hazardous circumstances.

David was born in 1748. As if to make his success story perfect, his origins were simple if not quite humble, and his early years a struggle against a series of defeats that very nearly cost him his life by suicide. His father was a Parisian tradesman, but he was brought up by two uncles, one a builder and the other an architect. It must have been in his boyhood that a tumor began to grow at one side of his mouth just above the upper lip. A self-portrait (Louvre) painted in 1794 shows it grown large enough to twist his face. It also impeded his speech. Little attention is paid to this disfigurement by David's biographers, which perhaps is just as well. It could easily be interpreted as the kind of harassing physical inferiority that helps breed dictators, and David did become a dictator with a record that can be read to his disadvantage.

David enrolled in the Académie Royale as a student in 1766 when he was eighteen and (we are told) was immediately attracted to the antique revival that was beginning to chasten the dainty flourishes of the rococo style. When he became eligible to compete for the Prix de Rome he did so, and failed. He continued to compete, and to fail, year after year.

The Prix de Rome was (and remains) a fellowship awarded annually to a student of the Academy who had demonstrated, in the eyes of his teachers, exceptional talent. A test picture on an assigned subject was required as the nominal basis for the award, but the prize went regularly to the student who had not only demonstrated an acceptable talent but had been respectful to the standards of his teachers and had made himself personally engaging. At the Ecole des Beaux-Arts in Paris—the current school of the Academy—the Prix de Rome pictures, hanging together in a large room, are a history of the taste dominating the Academy from year to year. Some of the winners are forgotten; some of the pictures are important early—almost juvenile—efforts by names that became great ones in the history of painting. The Prix de Rome winner had every chance to succeed. He was immediately starred with the cachet of official approval. The only requirement during his stay in Rome was that he send back pictures at regular intervals for inspection (and to prove that he was working). If he was obedient and industrious he returned to Paris an established artist who had no trouble obtaining commissions from the state and private patrons.

David had few of the requirements for a Prix de Rome other than talent, but he was absolutely determined to win it. He hung on through successive failures that in themselves were an informal blackball, managing to support himself with any work he could pick up. One godsend came through Fragonard, the reigning favorite of Paris's café society, who had begun the decorations for the Hôtel Guimard but abandoned them early and turned the job over to David. To David's credit, he remembered this kindness after the Revolution when he in his turn was up and Fragonard in his turn was down, and repaid the favor by granting the old painter a sinecure with the state. Fragonard's help had come in 1773, just when it was most needed. This was the year of David's fourth failure to win the Prix, and the low point of his life. He had attempted suicide by means appropriate to a painter who was to establish a new stoic style, locking himself in his room to starve to death. When he did not appear for several days his fellow students broke in and rescued him. He competed again the next year and won, and in 1775, at the age of twenty-seven, he was in Rome at last. It was as if he had been reborn.

The Academy maintained a Roman branch under the supervision of a resident head (an appointment nearly as coveted by established Academicians as the Prix was by students) who acted as a kind of housemaster. For the typical Prix winner, the stay in Rome was a rounding off of his student days, a semiholiday earned for good behavior. Most of the winners, when they returned to Paris to begin their professional careers in earnest, were much younger than David was when he finally set out for Rome. David was ready to dismiss the Academy altogether except for such help as it, alone, could give him. His failures to win the Prix had embittered him so deeply that he regarded his winning it at last as a victory over an enemy. A mature and independent personality rather than a tag-end student, he plunged into Rome determined to exhaust all it could offer him before his time there ran out.

He stayed three years, and began by gobbling up everything. The first paintings he sent back to Paris puzzled and disappointed his sponsors: they seemed dark and heavy, inspired by the Bolognese painters, whose work he had discovered. It was a brief pause in his development, but can be read as significant in its repudiation of the airiness and freshness of the rococo style, a first declaration of independence from the society that had rejected him for so long.

His sketchbooks from his first year are filled with notations of all kinds, from studies made after details of baroque paintings to on-the-spot sketches of classical monuments. And it was classical Rome that fascinated him. His rejection of rococo artifice inspired him to a vision of the heroic grandeur of ancient Rome, not the opulent Rome of the Empire but republican Rome, whose severe moral code and virility stood in sharpest contrast to the taste for frills and laces of prerevolutionary France. Even the classical revival that was under way there, with the style now called Louis XVI but for which a more appropriate name would be Marie Antoinette, was a style of extreme delicacy in which the classical motifs were adapted to the ideals of the boudoir and the drawing room.

When David returned to Paris he was accepted as a Prix de Rome man usually was and had no trouble exhibiting in the Salon. He had not yet achieved the style of heroic severity that was to set him apart in opposition to the Academy's standards. His classicism was relatable to that of Poussin, officially an Academy god, and he was also a supreme draftsman in the Academy's tradition of the studio nude. Further, his celebrations of the virtues of the ancient world appealed to the didactic philosophers of the Age of Reason. There was no indication that the Academy was harboring a murderous rebel, and in his personal life David was also following a course proper for a steady, ambitious young man.

In 1782 he married well, a bit above his station. Marguerite Charlotte Pécoul was the daughter of a contractor who was the royal superintendent of construction in the Louvre, a position that had made him wealthy and carried with it a degree of entree likely to be helpful to a son-in-law. Marguerite was seventeen when David married her and was perhaps a bit of an ugly duckling who, by the evidence of a portrait (Washington, National Gallery) he did of her in 1813, never grew into much of a swan, even when decked out in the finest feathers that money could buy. But over the years she proved herself to be both spirited and faithful—spirited, once, when she left David for what she considered a morally reprehensible action on his part; faithful, when she returned to him because he was in trouble.

By 1784 David was well set. He had a rich wife and a brilliant success in the Salon with a picture called *Andromache by the Body of Hector* (Paris, Ecole des Beaux-Arts) that brought him election to the Academy. In the same year he received a commission from the Comte d'Angiviller (whose position as general supervisor of all building under the King suggests a connection with Marguerite's father) for the painting that was to raise him from the position of successful artist to sensational innovator.

D'Angiviller wanted a painting based on a Corneillian subject, and David's *Oath of the Horatii* (Louvre), like Corneille's "Horace," dramatizes the patriotic zeal of the legendary Roman heroes, the Horatii. It shows three young Romans taking a solemn vow before their father, who offers them their swords, that they will return victorious for Rome or dead upon their shields. David began the painting in Paris (where he had a studio in the Louvre—not yet a museum) but decided that he could get into the spirit of it only in Rome. His father-in-law provided the money for the trip, and David returned to that inspiring city, this time not as an aging student but as an established painter accompanied by his family, his studio assistants, and his servants. He came back to Paris as the leader of a revolution in painting and was adopted in some quarters as the prophet of a revolution in government.

Whether or not the atmosphere of Rome contributed to its conception, *The Oath of the Horatii* fulfilled David's classical ideal. He exhibited it first in his studio in Rome: it was a sensation. The elements of the picture had been stripped down to the minimum; every furbelow had been eliminated; the brush was kept under rigid control, there was not a flourish, not a squiggle of paint, to mar the icy impersonality of its execution. The drawing was as hard as stone. All fluidity, all spontaneity, all feminine elegance, had given way to a stoical masculinity. The grieving women, who see their men pledging themselves to almost certain death, are subordinated to the tableau of males dedicated to the honor of country.

It was the style of the painting that created the sensation in Rome. In its contrast with the sweet graces of the current fashion it was as revolutionary as cubism was in the twentieth century. But in Paris the sensation was doubled. *The Oath of the Horatii* was exhibited in the Salon of 1785 and was interpreted not as a mere retelling of Corneille's theme but as an allegorical exhortation to civic virtue. It was time (the picture said, although there is no reason to think that David had any such interpretation in mind) that France save herself from the degeneracy of the old regime by returning to the ideals of firm republicanism, whatever sacrifices might be entailed. The picture had been given an unfavorable position in the Salon, no doubt because it challenged the accepted style of the Academy, but the furor was such that it was rehung as the star of the show—and the King, for whom it had been commissioned in the first place, accepted it. David was now thirty-seven years old and the Revolution was only four years off.

When the Revolution finally broke in 1789, David was exhibiting another picture illustrating a classical history subject. This picture, which is now in the Louvre (and whose full title is its description) shows *Brutus, First Consul, home once more after having condemned his two sons who had joined the Tarquins to conspire against Roman liberty. Lictors bring the corpses in order that he may give them burial.* The revolutionaries saw Brutus as the symbol of all Frenchmen who would make any personal sacrifice to protect French liberty, and David was again credited with a disguised political purpose—denunciation of the émigrés who, with as much of their property as possible, had fled France in the crisis.

Early in the Revolution David supported Robespierre and the Jacobins, and for the next five years he was not only the artist of the Revolution but a political figure as well. He began a tremendously elaborate painting (whose structural skeleton, however, can be connected with the severe simplicity of *The Oath of the Horatii*): the propagandistic *Oath of the Tennis Court* (Louvre), commemorating the occasion when the deputies of the third estate, on June 20, 1789, swore not to disband until they had given France a constitution. David's intention was to include portraits of every one of the deputies in re-creating the scene, but the picture (begun in 1791) never got beyond the stage of a sketch and a mass of preliminary drawings, since too many of the personages involved had become suspect in the period of confusion and violence that followed.

During this time David rode very high. In 1792 he was elected a deputy in the Convention and a member of the art commission. Becoming the virtual art dictator of France, he made drastic reforms. After a petition from a group of artists to abolish the Academy (with its hated name, Académie Royale), he prepared a report and succeeded in doing away with the Academy along with all the secondary organizations that had been training craftsmen throughout the provinces. Whatever else the Academy had done, it had preserved technical traditions and standards, and this mass abolition was a blow to French craftsmanship from which it never recovered.

But Frenchmen could hardly conceive of art without government sponsorship, and the Academy was replaced by a Commune of the Arts, a body of three hundred members. Private patronage in the new society was supposed to vanish (one thinks of the Russian reforms): the Commune of the Arts would replace it. The function of art would be to glorify the new ideals of the state and to record its triumphs (again, Russia today), and the state would purchase these patriotic pictures from open competitions.

The Commune of the Arts lasted not quite two months. It took only that long for it to fall under the accusations of favoritism and dictatorship that had been leveled against the Academy. It was replaced by a smaller replica of itself called the Popular and Republican Society of the Arts, consisting of fifty members—appointed by David. (Eventually—in 1795— this body gave way to the Academy of Fine Arts, which was established as one of the five branches of the Institute of France. It was the old Royal Academy with a slightly altered name, except that it displayed an even more active antagonism to any artist who did not conform to its standards.)

Under David the government founded a National Museum of the Arts, the genesis of the Louvre, to inventory and preserve the confiscated works of art from churches, the royal palaces, and the houses of émigrés. It was in this museum that, thanks to David, Fragonard became a member of the conservatory. The government also set aside money to purchase works of art at private sales in order to keep them in the country, and David saved numbers of pictures in this way, including some by Rubens and Rembrandt.

He was a busy man. In addition to these administrative functions, he had others: he was in charge of commemorative monuments, state funerals, and popular celebrations, which could be elaborate affairs involving, by some of David's plans, virtually the entire population of the city. And meanwhile he was still the state painter. There were plenty of martyrs, and something had to be done about them. *The Death of Marat* (Brussels), possibly David's masterpiece, commemorated that colleague's assassination.

During all this time, the atmosphere was increasingly hysterical. When David is judged, this hysteria must be remembered. He made no effort to save certain of his friends from the guillotine, but the reason could have been that he was convinced that they deserved their fate, not that he was afraid to risk his own neck. His ruthlessness toward the Academy, which after all had treated him well over more years than it had, in his opinion, treated him badly, is easily explained as a personal vendetta but just as easily attributed to a conviction on his part that its system was inhibiting to art, especially an art that he sincerely believed must serve new purposes. But it is difficult to forgive him (and his colleagues) for the execution of the ineffectual creature who had been king and whose protégé—even though once removed, through officialdom—David had been. David voted for the death of Louis XVI, and it was on this occasion that his wife left him.

In the next year David's triumphant progress suffered a check that threatened to be permanent. His friend Robespierre fell from power and went to the scaffold where he had sent so many others. David had once said that if necessary he would share a cup of hemlock with Robespierre, a form of classical suicide that he had celebrated in his painting *The Death of Socrates* (Metropolitan Museum), but the guillotine was another matter. David came to trial, and is reported to have conducted himself without dignity on the stand, mumbling and sweating in his defense. But neither the mumble nor the sweat can really be held against a man whose speech was impaired and whose life was in danger.

David was imprisoned for four months, released, and then in 1795 rearrested and imprisoned for another three months. The Luxembourg Palace had been turned into a temporary prison for political offenders, and here, with a pleasant view of the gardens, which he recorded in his only landscape (now in the Louvre)—a delightfully fresh, vernal scene—David spent his time planning a new picture as the start of a new career. His friends supplied him with materials for his work, and his wife forgave him. From his window he could see her or a nursemaid with his children, playing in the park. It was not too bad.

The new picture was *The Sabines* (Louvre), too often referred to with careless inaccuracy as *The Rape of the Sabine Women*. David chose not the episode of the women's abduction by the Romans, but the subsequent one when, having been taken to wife and begun their families with their Roman husbands, the Sabine women intervened between their husbands and their brothers and fathers who had come to rescue them. The Sabine woman Hersilia is shown at the center of a huge canvas with one arm stretched in appeal toward her husband, the Roman Romulus, and the other toward her father, the Sabine Tatius, who pause at the moment of conflict, while other figures are disposed in an exceptionally orderly delineation of climactic confusion.

David now made every effort to minimize the importance of his Revolutionary paintings and decided to devote himself to pure art, the Revolution having failed of the nobility of the Roman republic. But his painting was again interpreted as political allegory. *The Sabines* became a symbol of the new conciliatory mood in France, an appeal to the warring factions to let go of one another's throats for the good of the nation. David exhibited the picture in his studio for a fee, publishing a long defense of this unconventional practice (which in the old days would have resulted in his expulsion from the Academy) and defending, also, the nudity of his warriors, which he imagined to be in the Greek tradition. Greek glory, and grace, as it was then envisioned, now preoccupied him at the cost of Roman grandeur, and although *The Sabines* is a chilly picture it is a sensuous one in comparison with *The Oath of the Horatii*.

The admission fees while *The Sabines* was on exhibition brought David a small fortune, with which he bought a farm-estate, but the painting did more than secure him a new place in popular favor. It greatly impressed Napoleon, who, though his private taste in art ran to a more sentimental style, preferably with lascivious overtones, recognized in David the artist who could present him, in accordance with the image he was cultivating, as a modern counterpart of the great empire builders of ancient Rome. He never gave David the dictatorial powers he had had during the Revolution, but he showered him with honors and David became again, in effect, the head of a school of official art.

Although his paintings had become more graceful, with an increased emphasis on such gentle subjects as love, David was still interested in the re-creation of the ancient world as he imagined it. His influence on fashion and decoration can hardly be overestimated. The Directoire and Empire styles are virtually his invention. Women imitated the gauzy costume of Hersilia in *The Sabines* even to the extent of exposing their breasts. The pieces of furniture he had had constructed from his designs, for use in his pictures and incidental use in his studio, became the models for fashionable rooms everywhere.

By the time Napoleon declared himself emperor in 1804, David was fifty-six years old and quite content with his renunciation of politics. He was indefatigably industrious as a portrait painter, and in his execution of the paintings commissioned by Napoleon he employed enough assistants to amount to a school. Between 1805 and 1808 he painted the largest of his Napoleonic tributes, a mass group portrait 30 feet long and 20 feet high of the coronation, in which Napoleon, already wreathed in the style of a Roman emperor, is about to place a crown on the head of Josephine. The painting is an efficiently executed bore that may be found in any French history textbook or seen in the Louvre, where it is surrounded by crowds every Sunday.

When Napoleon fell and the Bourbons were restored to power, David sent all his compromising pictures to his house in the country and was left as undisturbed as if he had never been a right-hand man of the Emperor. But when Napoleon re-entered Paris for his ephemeral reign during the Hundred Days, he saw David and in an incautious moment the painter signed the "Acte Additionnel." As a result of this pledge of loyalty he was exiled in 1816, and spent the remaining nine years of his life in Brussels, where he died in 1825, seventy-seven years old.

David was a contented old man during these years, even if he did miss Paris. He was still highly regarded there, and in Brussels he received pilgrimage visits from his admirers. He continued to paint to the end—usually in a rather desiccated way—and concluded his career with the previously mentioned *Mars Disarmed by Venus and the Graces*. It shows an incredibly, almost mawkishly, handsome nude Mars disposed upon a draped couch against the background of a classical frieze and, except for clouds beneath his feet that identify the scene as Olympus, he might be in the house of the most beautiful of all Greek courtesans, the Venus who seductively leans toward him with one hand on his thigh.

In the tradition by which David's other paintings were given allegorical interpretations, this one could be interpreted as his ultimate conclusion that war and violence (Mars) must inevitably yield to the charms of love and the arts. And one must admit that David's life, if hardly a typical one, was at least a unique proof of that thesis.

Of all the great masters of the past who have been claimed as ancestors by modern artists, Goya is the favorite by an easy margin and across the widest field. Romantics have been nourished by his violence. Realists point out that in a time of artificialities he found his point of departure not in formulas but in response to the streets and the people in them. The social rebels and the commentators on social ills feel themselves descendants of Goya the liberal thinker, who drew and painted his indictments instead of writing them down. Fantasists recognize a kinship with this artist who was a master of nightmare. And even artists who renounce the pictorial image, or at least one large school of these, can consider themselves Goya's heirs because there are passages in his late work to seize upon as approximations or prophecies of the abstract-expressionist aesthetic.

And yet Goya is also the antithesis of all these modernisms. He was a first-rate eighteenth-century rococo decorator, or, to go even further back, he is in many portraits the natural continuator of Velázquez's baroque tradition. It is never safe to stand in front of a Goya and explain its beauties, its power, and its expressive significance in terms of any standard preconception of what Goya's art is all about. He was an artist of multiple aspects who during his eighty-two years covered a great deal of the ground of the two centuries that his own lifetime straddled.

Goya's life was split in two near its midpoint by an illness that very nearly killed him when he was forty-six years old. If he had died, he would have left a large body of work establishing him as one of Spain's finest artists and her only great representative of eighteenth-century style. But he lived, and the traumatic experience released powers that had hitherto not been fully expressed. During the latter half of his life, Goya became the genius we think of him as having been from the first. In this late blooming he is exceptional among painters, who usually demonstrate their genius very early even though its expression may grow richer in maturity.

Francisco José de Goya y Lucientes was born in Fuendetodos, near Saragossa, in 1746, the son of a gilder. By the time he was fourteen he was apprenticed to a painter named José Luzán, who followed the Neapolitan baroque formulas. Luzán was not much of a painter, and it would probably be forcing a point to suggest that as the first influence on Goya he instilled much that lasted. But the black-shadowed Neapolitan manner, whether through Luzán or from later direct acquaintance with the work of Neapolitan masters, can be traced as a persistent and eventually triumphant factor in Goya's stylistic development.

In his teens Goya was executing small commissions in the churches of Saragossa. Legend has created a sympathetic picture of the young Goya as a fine, vigorous, full-blooded, free-loving, joyfully battling son of the Spanish earth—the perfect foil for the conventional degenerate aristocrat. His letters show that he loved bullfights and street festivals. But an occasional biographer rejects the ideal honest-and-earthy picture for one of a quarrelsome, undisciplined, and uneducated youth at the mercy of his emotions. His reason for leaving town in 1763 may or may not have had to do with what legend tells us was an emergency created by complications (on the order of knifings) in connection with some amorous adventures. Ambition would have supplied as reasonable a stimulus for leaving Saragossa for Madrid, since Goya had a fantastic capacity for work—a really compulsive need to keep at it—and a great respect for money.

For either reason, Goya left Saragossa and, not quite eighteen years old, competed for a scholarship in the Royal Academy, which he failed to win. He entered the studio of Francisco Bayeu (1734-1795), who, like Goya, had come from Fuendetodos where he had studied under Luzán. Bayeu, twelve years Goya's senior, was a hardworking, efficient, and uninspired artist whose perseverance finally won him the directorship both of the Royal Academy and of the Royal Tapestry Factory of Santa Bárbara. When Goya arrived in Madrid, his fellow townsman was well established as a decorator and follower of Raphael Mengs, but apparently not well enough to be of help to Goya when he tried for the Royal Academy scholarship a second time. Failing again, Goya went to Italy, partly covering his expenses by traveling with a company of bullfighters. He visited Rome and Parma, where he won a competition with a painting now lost, but praised at the time.

Probably discouraged by his reception in Madrid, he went back to Saragossa. Tax returns show that he did quite well there, but he could not have felt anything but restless and cramped in the provincial city. At any rate he left again. He was twenty-seven years old when he made a trip to Madrid in 1773 to marry Bayeu's sister Josefa, and in short order he was back in Madrid to stay. Bayeu recommended him (along with his, Bayeu's, brother Ramón and another artist) as a designer to the Royal Tapestry Factory of Santa Bárbara. Goya and Josefa began their life in Madrid in Bayeu's house, and their first son was born there at the end of 1775. During the thirty-nine years of their marriage, before Josefa died in 1812, she bore perhaps as many as twenty children, of whom few—perhaps only one—survived.

For ten years or so, Goya's cartoons—completed paintings—for tapestries were his major work, although he also did engraving and began his career as a portraitist. His successful assault of Madrid, beginning when he was turning thirty, took place in a desert. There had not been a Spanish painter of consequence for a hundred years, hardly even a first-rate follower of the foreign artists, mostly French, who were imported by the Spanish court. A conservative eclectic atmosphere prevailed, with Raphael Mengs,* and such of his followers as Bayeu, setting the academic standard with a slickly sterilized version of the century's taste for graceful neoclassicisms. But there had been one sparkling exception: the great Tiepolo had come to Spain in 1762 and had worked at court for the last eight years of his life. His tradition, which was carried on, even though reduced in force, by his son Lorenzo, was Goya's point of departure for the tapestries.

It was the late-rococo tradition of lightness and gaiety but minus the allegorical pegs that ordinarily supported its

---

* The ubiquitous Mengs has already been mentioned in connection with Benjamin West. Mengs was in Spain as court painter, decorating royal palaces, from 1761 to 1771, and again from 1773 to 1777.

fancies. Goya brought to it a new emphasis on the informal, even the bohemian, life of Madrid that had a literary counterpart in popular farces and satires, and a precedent, for that matter, in Bayeu's tapestry designs, which show an interest in genre subjects. But Goya intruded a sinister note now and then. A cloaked figure, easily linked traditionally to the Venetian maskers at play, changes character inexplicably and becomes a threatening presence at the revel or the picnic.

Goya quarreled with Bayeu during this period over a division of authority in a dual commission for the Cathedral of Saragossa, and lost the argument. Leaving some work in progress unfinished, he went back to Madrid, his professional and personal relationship with Bayeu violently ruptured. But in the meanwhile Goya had found a new teacher. With access to the royal collections, he discovered Velázquez, who became, in effect, his first master in portraiture.

The quarrel with Bayeu was patched up a few years later, but now Goya, who was beginning to outrun his first sponsor, was probably relieved to be rid of him for a while. In favor at court, he was doing well at countering the intrigues that, naturally, began to rise against him. So much is made of Goya's humanity, his liberal aesthetic and social vigor and conscience, his independence and his fearlessness, that we forget how many years he had to spend winning a position where these virtues could be indulged.

He had to cope with the nagging fear of insecurity left over from his experience of poverty, and in coping with it he could be irascible, envious, and merciless in winning a small point over an opponent. Impatient by nature, often rude by impulse, he worked hard at curbing his temper before influential patrons whom he held in contempt personally. Degree by degree, Madrid fell to him. In 1780, when state economies cut down his commissions at the tapestry factory, he was elected to the Royal Academy in compensation. In 1785 he was given the position, not an important one, of the Academy's Deputy Director of Painting. The next year he was named Painter to the King—a title enjoyed by a generous number—and then, in 1789, he became Painter of the Household to Charles IV. There were other honors and titles to be won, but it was already apparent that Goya was the leading Spanish painter no matter how many functionaries among his colleagues might nominally outrank him. And as an unrivaled portraitist he was making money.

This was the situation in 1792 when his illness (which has never been satisfactorily identified) struck him. For more than a year he could not paint, but by January, 1793, he had gone to Andalusia to recuperate, and by July he was back in Madrid. The illness had left him stone-deaf, but this isolating misfortune crystallized or released powers that had been checked by a fuller contact with the world, and birthed Goya the genius—Goya the humane and bitter social observer, the scourging and despairing delineator of vice and cruelty, the fantasist whose pictured nightmares were explorations of the most desperate realities.

At the Spanish court, Goya was advantageously placed to observe the extremes of weakness and vice. When he became Painter of the Household to Charles IV in 1789, this guileless but ineffective monarch had just replaced his elder imbecile brother on the throne. Charles himself, if not an imbecile, was a simpleton. His queen was the monstrous Maria Luisa of Parma, a dissolute and unsightly woman whose bed was occasionally shared by well-muscled stableboys but whose official lover was an ambitious army officer named Manuel de Godoy. Fifteen years her junior, Godoy was well paid for his services: Charles relinquished not only his wife but virtually the government to Godoy, appointing him chief minister in 1792. Between them, combining stupidity with corruption, Maria Luisa and Godoy managed to involve

Spain in a series of debacles that ultimately led to the Franco-Spanish defeat at Trafalgar.

Goya observed these repellent creatures as individuals rather than as the disastrous social and political forces that they were, and his portraits of them seem so revealing of their grotesqueness that it is difficult to understand how the subjects could have tolerated them. Actually, the portraits are less interpretative than realistic, in spite of what seem to us their flagrantly satirical overtones. Blinded by vanity, these freaks were probably flattered by Goya's accurate reflection of the images they were familiar with in the mirror.

But if he saw vice, corruption, and foolishness in high places, Goya was unaffected by the reaction that led his century (in France and England) to discover a compensatory nobility in the common man. His first great etchings, the set of eighty called *Los Caprichos,* are fantastic visions of universal greed, vanity, superstition, and cruelty—forms of stupidity that were the Four Horsemen of Goya's own Apocalypse. Goya's friends in Madrid were the intellectuals who represented the Enlightenment, the triumph of reason. But he seldom shows Reason or Truth in anything but a beleaguered position at best. Vice and Folly are the victors in a war that they do not even bother to wage, since the forces pitted against them in human nature are negligible.

In the *Caprichos* Goya continued to find motifs in the life of the city, but the sinister hints that he had introduced earlier in such subjects now became the main theme. The modernity of the *Caprichos,* in the eyes of the twentieth century, is of a kind not even half formulated until a hundred years after Goya's death. His nightmares anticipate a conception of society as a precarious structure held together by conventions that are only a thin skin ready to burst at any time from the inner pressures of the irrationalities that motivate us without our knowledge—a considerable extension of the first inkling, won by such eighteenth-century occultists as Swedenborg, Martínez Pasqualis, Mesmer, and others, that the world of dream can reveal truths that the world we have built around ourselves conceals from us.

The *Caprichos* were created between 1796 and 1798, and were put on sale as a book the following year. Their gestation had begun soon after Goya's recovery from his illness, in the form of sketchbooks, particularly one called *The Madrid Sketchbook*. In the silent, sequestered world that Goya now inhabited, his observations of city life shifted from genre, satire, or burlesque to an appalled and bitter commentary on the nature of society. Whether or not this new tone accounted for the poor reception given the *Caprichos*—they could easily have puzzled, even if they did not shock, a public that had never seen anything like them before—only twenty-seven sets were sold in fifteen days, and then the prints were withdrawn from the market.

The Inquisition, perhaps, insisted on the withdrawal, or it might have been made as a matter of precaution in anticipation of such a demand. The *Caprichos* included monks and priests among the devilish and folly-ridden assembly, and Goya was denounced by the authorities of the Church. But with his talent for skirting the edge of disaster without going over it, he turned the incident to his advantage. He made a gift of the plates to the King—who returned the favor in the form of a yearly pension granted to Goya's son, Francisco Xavier.

At about the same time that he began work on the *Caprichos,* Goya also began his famous but somewhat ambiguous affair with the Duchess of Alba, probably the most vivid figure that her society produced. In 1795 (Goya was just a year short of that sobering birthday, his fiftieth) she visited his studio, as we know from a coarse reference he made to the incident in a letter. The Duke died the following year, and whether or not the affair had begun during her husband's lifetime, it continued until the Duchess's death in 1802.

The Duchess of Alba was a spirited and capricious beauty, that much is certain, and in combination with Goya she opens the field for romantic speculations in any direction. A sophisticate who had every handsome young buck in Madrid at her feet, she chose as her lover a stocky, coarse-featured man of the people nearly fifty years old and deaf. In spite of his association with aristocrats and intellectuals, Goya had never taken on much polish. His letters are crudely written. His manner of expression, while cogent, remained that of a countryman. He seems to have had no elegance, no subtlety. But he had force. Whatever the details and the satisfactions—physical, emotional, or intellectual—of their relationship, Goya and the Duchess of Alba were lovers, and when they could they left Madrid for her estate in Andalusia.

Goya made an ambiguous comment on the affair in the form of a portrait of the Duchess wearing two large rings, one of them bearing Goya's name and the other her husband's (New York, Hispanic Society). But while she looks the observer straight in the face, she points at an inscription scratched in the earth at her feet. *"Solo Goya,"* it says—"Goya only," perhaps referring thus to the death of the Duke, which left Goya the only man in her life. The inscription was revealed by a recent cleaning. Whether it was part of the original scheme, and when and why it was painted out, are questions that have yet to be answered. In odd ways, Goya and his Duchess have maintained for posterity a remarkable privacy concerning their liaison. We know for certain hardly anything more than that, in one form or another, it existed.

In his sixties, Goya's personal isolation from the world where he seemed to move so freely was increased by another factor than his deafness. In the final stage of her dissolution as a great power, Spain was in a state of political and social chaos. The libertarian idealists made temporarily effective forays against the regime and were repeatedly and mercilessly repressed. Some of Goya's friends were imprisoned or exiled. Goya had not yet made any directly political statements in his art, and was in a divided position: his libertarian sympathies conflicted with his professional standing as the first artist to the King. As a painter at court, working first of all as a portraitist, he was perfectly safe because he was not required to turn his art into an instrument of support or propaganda. But as a draftsman and printmaker observing man as a member of society, he could comment only in opposition to the ideals (if they could be called that) of his royal patrons. As a result, Goya, except as a portraitist, began to work, if not quite secretly, then at least only for himself and his friends.

The Napoleonic invasion of Spain in 1808 with its guerrilla violences supplied Goya with the most appallingly direct evidence of man's capacity to degrade himself through butchery of his fellows. Between the year of the invasion and about 1814, he created a second series of etchings with aquatint, *The Disasters of War,* scenes of this butchery punctuated occasionally with political allegories. Their publication during French occupation or Spanish alliance with the French was of course impossible, and the plates were not printed until 1863. Even then, half a century after their creation, they were without precedent in their treatment of war for what it is, without any overtones of the picturesque or the ideally heroic.

Goya's single direct declaration of his liberal political sympathies was not a belligerent statement in the face of authority but the result of a commission for two paintings, in 1814, from the brief-lived liberal government that was to be suppressed in a matter of weeks by the reactionary Ferdi-

nand VII. In *The Second of May, 1808* (Prado), Goya commemorated (six years after the event) an uprising in the
streets of Madrid, when citizens armed only with sticks,
stones, and knives attacked the Egyptian cavalry that Napoleon had sent into Spain to support his puppet brother Joseph
Bonaparte's usurpation of the Spanish throne. The picture is
a turbulent melee of forms and colors devoid of any hints of
the classical tradition of history painting, a romantic fan-
faronade that is more immediately recognizable as an exciting battle scene than as a patriotic tribute. But the companion picture, *The Third of May, 1808* (Prado), is another
matter.

The uprising was immediately quelled, and on the following day batches of suspects were rounded up more or less
indiscriminately, taken to the outskirts of the city, and shot.
Goya shows a group of half a dozen victims standing among
the bloody corpses of their fellows, while files of other citizens, awaiting execution, cover their faces in horror. We are
at the moment of firing. One of the men about to be shot
hides his face; another, a monk, prays; two others in spite
of their terror glare at the riflemen. The group—and the
picture—comes to its climax in the figure of a young man
who in a final gesture flings both arms upward in defiance,
a gesture that says with furious vehemence that while one
man is easy to kill, the human spirit in its battle for freedom
is unquenchable.

Like all great historical and philosophical themes, that
of the Third of May is extremely vulnerable to trite interpretation. The fervor of Goya's version is sustained from
passage to passage, but its originality is in his reduction of
the executioners to robots. Where they might expectably have
been represented as villains or fiends, they are anonymous,
inhuman forms; thus by contrast the men who in a moment
will fall to the bullets are all the more intensely alive.

Just how the reactionary authorities rationalized these pictures as anything but what they are, is hard to understand. Most likely, Goya's eminence and his reversion to tactful political reticence account for his remaining unmolested in his position as Spain's first painter. Even so, when he finally went into exile, *The Second of May* and *The Third of May* must have been resting uneasily on his mind.

Between 1815 and 1816 Goya completed his third series of prints, the *Tauromachia,* relating the history of bullfighting in thirty-three plates, to which he added another eleven later. Since 1813 he had been at work on another series that extended the nightmares of *Los Caprichos.* By 1818 or 1819 he had completed the twenty-two plates now known, and probably some others now lost. He called the series *Disparates,* or "Follies," but they are usually given the name *Proverbios,* which became attached to them when the Academy published a set of eighteen in 1864. The exact subjects are seldom identifiable; some seem, indeed, to be illustrations of Spanish proverbs, but there are others that are uninterpretable except as personal visions of evil as the indomitable source of universal energy.

The utter blackness of this view, however, is not exactly despairing. It is characteristic of Goya that while he offers no hope for the triumph of good, and while he refuses to recognize evil as anything but evil, he pictures it not with despair but with unrelenting vigor and passion. He is never admiring of witches and devils, but he is always fascinated. He never consents as a partner, yet he never rebels as one of the universal victims. The question is why we do not find this ambivalent attitude a symptom of moral flaccidity in Goya. Somehow we never ask why a man whose friends in maturity were among the most enlightened thinkers and the most devoted moralists of the Age of Reason—a man who, we keep telling ourselves, shared their convictions—gives so little indication, in his powerful art, that reasonable convictions can be translated into effective action or even that there is a moral obligation to make an effort in that direction.

The answer to the contradiction may be inherent in Goya's last, perhaps greatest, and certainly most personal paintings, done for himself alone as murals in his house near Madrid, the Quinta del Sordo (Deaf Man's House). He bought the villa in 1819 when he was seventy-three years old, and during the next three years covered its walls with his famous "black" paintings. (They were detached from the walls in 1873 and are now in the Prado.) Black in color, relieved only by grays and gray-ochers, and relentlessly black in spirit, the murals represent a congress of witches, skeletons, crones, violent gods, hysterics, monsters, and lunatics that—howling, struggling, dancing, devouring one another—suggest at once the genesis of evil out of primordial chaos and its ultimate triumphant universality.

These demons were the old man's chosen companions during his last years in Spain. They had also been, if not the companions, at least the ever-present spirits of his childhood. In the part of Spain where Goya was born, the fear of witches was still alive in the early twentieth century. It would be too much to say that, in spite of his association with humanistic intellectuals, he continued to believe in them; yet an emotional response to nonsense or fantasies or superstitions can endure even after, intellectually, one has put aside childish things. Goya painted the evil spirits of the black pictures with total conviction. In essence, he did believe in them. Nothing of all that he had seen of the world had managed to rout the idea that whatever is good in it exists only so long as the forces of evil suffer it to exist.

Goya lived in his Quinta del Sordo for only a scant four years. In 1823—he was seventy-seven—he gave the house to a grandson, and the next year he received permission to leave

Spain for France. He still held his position as first painter to the court, although he had gone into hiding as Ferdinand's despotism grew more and more oppressive.

Goya saw Spain once more, briefly, in 1825 or 1826, but he ended his life as a voluntary exile, joining the Spanish colony in Bordeaux. In his last years he mellowed a bit. He discovered the newly invented medium of lithography and employed it in 1825 to create a series of five bullfight scenes, *The Bulls of Bordeaux,* of orgiastic vitality. His painting was as fresh, as sparkling, as the happiest painting of his youth, and as rich as the best painting of his maturity. He visited Paris, and was glimpsed in his round of the studios by the young Delacroix.

Delacroix became his first true heir. Goya found no followers during his lifetime, but by the middle of the nineteenth century he was a god of the romantics—not only of the painters, but of such literary figures as Victor Hugo. He has been adopted on one ground or another as the foster father of successive generations of innovational painters. But, all historical considerations aside, the last question, the crucial question, in the case of Goya is an uneasy one: what has he told us about ourselves?

He has told us that we are vain, cruel, superstitious, and easily deluded, that at our best, when we rise to any affirmation of our potential nobility, we are most likely to be annihilated as individuals. But he believed in one thing: his work says again and again that in spite of the suffering and the folly, to have been alive has been worth while. He believed in a perpetual fact called life, the only fact in human experience that is constant and self-justifying. He knew that life is as wonderful as it is terrible, and that the only thing more terrible than life is its alternative, nothingness.

He died in 1828 shortly after his eighty-second birthday, in Bordeaux.